THE FUNNIEST COMEDY ICONS OF THE 20TH CENTURY: VOL 1

The Funniest Comedy Icons of the 20th Century Volume 1
by John Stanley
© 2016, ALL RIGHTS RESERVED
No part of this book may be reproduced in any form or by any means, electronic, mechanical, digital, photocopying, or recording, except for inclusion of a review, without permission in writing from the publisher or John Stanley.

Published in the USA by:
BearManor Media
P O Box 71426
Albany, Georgia 31708
www.bearmanormedia.com

ISBN: 978-1-59393-908-3

BearManor Media, Albany, Georgia
Printed in the United States of America
Book design by Robbie Adkins, www.adkinsconsult.com

JOHN STANLEY

THE FUNNIEST COMEDY ICONS OF THE 20TH CENTURY

Volume 1

By John Stanley

Erica Stanley

Russ with his daughters Shelby (left) and Jordyn

DEDICATION

To Erica Stanley, my wife for fifty-three years, who had the pleasure of attending many of the interviews in this book, and who impressed so many comedy stars that they often autographed photographs to her instead of to me.

To Russ Stanley, our son, who has worked for the past twenty-five years for the San Francisco Giants and was responsible for helping to establish computerized ticketing in the world of baseball when the Giants moved to its new ballpark along the Embarcadero in 2000. Recently, he was promoted to Senior Vice President of Ticket Sales & Services for the Giants, even though I am the real senior in the family, having this year reached the age of seventy-five. He's fifty—still a young kid!

TABLE OF CONTENTS

DEDICATION...v
INTRODUCTION viii
SID CAESAR/IMOGENE COCA..2
BOB HOPE..22
BING CROSBY 39
KATHRYN GRANT CROSBY 49
GEORGE BURNS...56
LUCILLE BALL 68
ART CARNEY 74
JACKIE GLEASON 83
AUDREY MEADOWS..93
MILTON BERLE...102
JACK BENNY 117
DENNIS DAY 131
SHELDON LEONARD...136
MEL BLANC..142
HILLIARD MARKS 150
RODNEY DANGERFIELD..156
JOAN RIVERS...164
WOODY ALLEN.. 174
DONALD O'CONNOR.. 181
MAE WEST...195
JIMMY DURANTE...210
LIBERACE..220
PETER SELLERS...225
HENRY MANCINI 233
MOE HOWARD (THE THREE STOOGES)..................... 240

WALLY COX	252
GREG GARRISON (DEAN MARTIN'S PRODUCER)	260
FRANK GORSHIN	268
RICH LITTLE	286
ELLIOTT GOULD *(M*A*S*H)*	290
DONALD SUTHERLAND *(M*A*S*H)*	292
ALAN ALDA *(M*A*S*H)*	300
LORETTA SWIT *(M*A*S*H)*	304
HARRY MORGAN/ MIKE FARRELL *(M*A*S*H)*	308
LARRY LINVILLE *(M*A*S*H)*	314
SALLY KELLERMAN *(M*A*S*H)*	318
FUNNY MOMENTS	325
OTHER BOOKS BY THE AUTHOR	332

INTRODUCTION
A Journey Into the World of Comedy And You Are There–Eyewitness To the Comic Geniuses of Yesteryear

Almost all of the encounters in this book are exclusive, one-on-one interviews with celebrities from the world of entertainment. A majority of them would be ranked as comedians or comediennes, men and women who designed their careers with an emphasis on stand-up comedy, movie satire, cartoon-character creation, voice impressions—anything that can be labeled funny. Some were the top iconic talents of their time, and memories of them live on within us after they have passed away. Others were performers that moved in and out of TV situation comedies or motion pictures, though almost always with a sense of humor that had become part of their on-camera personas. Some we might remember more than others, but they all made their impact on us at one time.

From the time I was fourteen, I had wanted to work at an American newspaper as a writer. It came about after watching a 1954-1955 TV situation comedy, *Dear Phoebe*, which was set in the newsroom of an American newspaper. During my later high school years, I wrote many articles for the Napa High School and Napa Junior College newspapers, and even for a while had a recurring column that reviewed then-current TV programs. I also worked at a downtown Napa weekly, where I did the police reports and occasional feature articles.

The stories in this collection date as far back as 1961, the year I started writing for the *San Francisco Chronicle*, following a short career as a copy boy. When I had started at the paper in the summer of 1960, I was told that I would not be promoted from copy boy to cub reporter, that it was a "dead end job." However, by writing sample book, movie reviews, and news stories for major editors I became friendly with, within ten months I had a part-time summer-long writing job, and that turned into a full-time position in just four more months. Meanwhile, I earned a Bachelor of Arts Degree at San Francisco State College while working full time. I continued at the *San Francisco Chronicle* as an interviewer of the stars of films and TV for thirty-three years, the job I coveted most of all.

That's me in front of the San Francisco Chronicle *building at Fifth and Mission Streets in downtown San Francisco. We would remain inseparable for thirty-three years.*

At first, my stories were limited to the city's nightclubs in North Beach, the Venetian Room of the grand Fairmont Hotel, and Bimbo's 365 Club, where old and new entertainers were constantly popping up. Due to a friendship with the paper's leading nightclub editor, Vic Befera, I was soon covering icons in the showrooms of casinos-hotels at Lake Tahoe and Reno, Nevada.

I wrote for what was called *The Sunday Datebook*, or "*The Pinkie*," given that it was printed on pink paper so readers could quickly find it, pull it out from the other sections, and preserve it for the week. *The Pinkie* contained a Sunday-through-Saturday

TV listing plus what was currently playing in movie theaters, on stages, in music halls, and in nightclubs, not to mention the numerous stories each week that focused on the most breathtaking and popular of the stars.

Gradually, as I made more contacts with San Francisco's affiliate TV stations and publicity directors at the three major TV networks and motion picture studios of Hollywood, my phone began ringing more frequently. I even made contact with Los Angeles public relations firms that handled superstars. As long as those superstars were available, I would have the chance to question them and take back to my readers what I could.

Suddenly, I was meeting some of the most memorable comedy icons of the twentieth century, although I must admit that, at the time, I never dreamed a book like this one might be the result. On occasion, personalities dropped into San Francisco and I met them at a local restaurant, usually near the *San Francisco Chronicle*, located just a block from the world-famous cable car turnaround at Powell and Market Streets.

That's me with a group of other newspaper writers, during a 1966 trip to Hollywood. At left is Howard Duff, one-time Sam Spade of the radio days, who was then starring in a new TV crime series, Felony Squad, as Detective Sergeant Sam Stone.

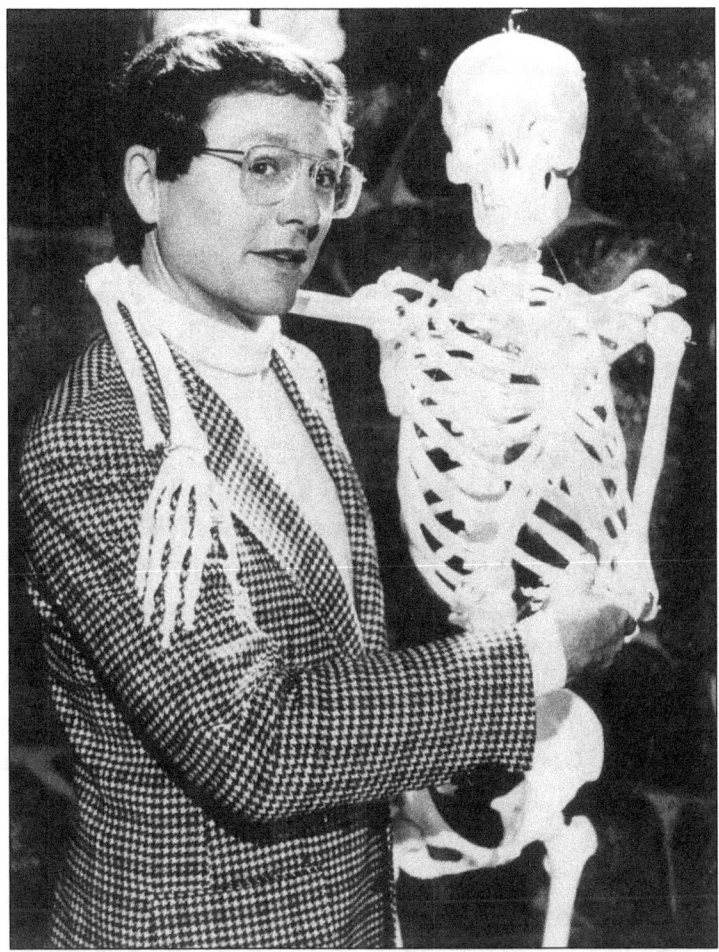

One of my early publicity stills as host of Creature Features.

Eventually, I began making frequent trips to Los Angeles, where I would interview major stars in their homes (Bob Hope, Jack Benny, Lucille Ball) or in major restaurants, such as the Hollywood Brown Derby, Musso & Frank's Grill on Hollywood Boulevard, or Romanoff's in Beverly Hills, where Humphrey Bogart had once shared drinks with Peter Lorre.

I also ventured to the very studios where they were making movies and/or TV series. I was able to walk the streets of Warner Bros., 20th Century Fox, Paramount, Desilu, Metro Goldwyn Mayer (MGM), and Universal. Then came "the movie junket" after *Jaws* became a box-office hit in 1975. Now, instead of the celebrities coming to my city to meet the media, I was going to a faraway city for a major movie preview, attended by directors, producers, writers, and stars. Usually, these were in Los Angeles, although a few were also held in Chicago and New York City.

My career suddenly, unexpectedly went off in another direction, even when I was still writing for the *San Francisco Chronicle*. I became the host of the TV series, *Creature Features*, on Channel 2, KTVU, an independent station in Jack London Square, Oakland. I followed in the footprints of Bob Wilkins, who had first introduced the series in early 1971 and built it into one of the most watched horror-host shows in America, not to mention the San Francisco-Bay Area. After Bob retired in 1979, every Saturday night I introduced a sci-fi, horror, or fantasy film, and then in periodic segments presented iconic guests, such as Christopher Lee, Ray Bradbury, Robert Bloch, Leonard Nimoy, William Shatner, Vincent Price, and countless others. Those contacts in Hollywood were really paying off. I had it timed so the Walt Disney publicists would schedule a personality to be in town on Friday, my taping day, to discuss a movie opening the next week. Then, that evening, I would don my reporter's cap and meet the Disney celebrity at a San Francisco restaurant. Two of my favorites from that time were impressionist Frank Gorshin, who was performing at the Fairmont Hotel, and Cloris Leachman, who was starring in a new *Herbie* movie (Cloris will be featured in Volume 2).

As a result of my experience as a horror host, I began seeing fantasy films almost daily and tried to see as many as seven a week, writing each review immediately. What resulted were six editions in *The Creature Features Movie Guide* series (from 1981 through 2000) with literally thousands of reviews. I also wrote *I Was a TV Horror Host*, a kind of "autobiography" of my years at KTVU along with a collection of interviews I had done with all those wonderful icons of the time. Finally, in the summer of 1984, with cable television taking over the industry, *Creature Features* was cancelled and I now focused entirely on celebrity interviews for the *San Francisco Chronicle*.

This book really came into being because of another career I pursued after leaving the *San Francisco Chronicle* in 1993. I joined

The motto for Creature Features *for thirteen years was written on a sign posted on the wall of the program's set: "Watch Horror Films, Keep America Strong."*

the ranks of Bay Area Classic Learning, a franchise of what was then called Elderhostel, a Boston-based business that arranged for senior citizens to visit cities all over America and be newly educated by special instructors. (Today the organization is called Road Scholar.) The old-timers would stay for five nights in a Bay Area hotel and be visited during the week by three of us "teachers," who would each give three presentations on whatever topics had been chosen.

In my case, I became an entertainment world specialist for the franchise holders, David and Pat Kleinberg. I had worked with David for thirteen years when he was chief editor of the *Sunday Datebook*, and we had forged a strong friendship. We had both left the *Chronicle* around the same time, and he asked me what I was planning to do now that I was unemployed. I had no idea. He suggested I might fit into the new Elderhostel he and his wife were planning.

I had no idea what an Elderhostel was, but soon learned that it mainly attracted the men and women of the World War II Generation. They came as couples, as singles, and some even came in wheelchairs. Eventually, Bay Area Classic Learning became the most heavily attended Elderhostel in America, with as many as a hundred elders showing up per week.

David chose me to be his entertainment-world expert, and over a period of seventeen years, I presented dozens of different topics. Among them: *The Golden Classics of the Silver Screen*; the stars and programming of early television; jazz music as it was used in motion pictures; women in cinema; the careers of Frank Sinatra, Louis Armstrong, Bob Hope, and Bing Crosby; major film composers such as Max Steiner, Miklos Rozsa, and Alfred Newman; the history of Walt Disney; and on and on. It was a grand time and I thrived on the joy of describing all the things I loved about entertainment.

Of all my courses, one would stand out as the most popular, and it started with a phone call from Kleinberg.

"John," David said, "a large percentage of our attendees are Jewish. And I've decided we should do some classes with Jewish themes. And I'd like you to do a course on Jewish comedy."

"But, Dave," I said, "I don't know anything about Jewish comedy."

"That's what you think," David replied. "Don't you remember that I was always assigning you to interview Jewish comedians?"

"Jewish comedians? What're you talking about, Dave?"

"Sid Caesar, remember?"

"Yeah, but I never thought of him as being Jewish."

"Shelley Berman, Jack Benny, Rodney Dangerfield, Joan Rivers. And that comic you did on your own. It was your idea. Remember Milton Berle?"

"Gees, I never thought of them collectively as Jewish. To me they were funny guys and gals. Comics, period."

"Great comics. The best. Stars of their time. And you can take all those personal interviews you did and retell them to the groups."

And that's what I did for seventeen years. *The Jewish Contribution to Comedy* became my most popular and oft-repeated class. I learned the importance of personalizing each of my interviews so it would make the senior feel as if he or she was reliving the moment with me. One thing I noticed was that not everything these comedians told me was funny. Some of their stories (such as Sid Caesar's or Shelley Berman's) had grim moments or negative pieces of history, so not everything you are going to learn about these men and women is necessarily amusing. But those elements were part of their lives, part of what had made them into the stars they had become. In a way, they become even more real in how they overcame the down sides of life.

Thanks to Elderhostel, I realized I had the makings of an unusual glimpse at comedy, and wanted to make this book a reality. I hope that's how you will feel as I knock on a door, walk into a strange front room, restaurant, or movie set, and meet a comedy personality. I want it to be as personal for you as possible. I want you to see and hear the individual under examination, and I want you to feel as if you are seated or standing at my side.

All you have to do now is turn the page. Unwind, take a deep breath, and leap into the action with me as we meet the men and women I consider among the funniest!

        –John Stanley, Pacifica, CA, August 2015

SID CAESAR / IMOGENE COCA
A Sid-Istic Side to Comedy

Sid Caesar and Imogene Coca as they looked in 1988, when she received a Life Achievement Award in Comedy and they were occasionally performing as a comedy duo in various cities across America.

There is nothing funny about how my story of one of America's funniest comedians begins. The year is 1977, and Sid Caesar and Imogene Coca have reunited to appear together for the first time since costarring on *Your Show of Shows* (1951-1954) on the NBC network. The setting for the team's revival is set to be the Venetian Room in San Francisco's Fairmont Hotel. The underlying concept: to revive some of their comedy routines from the well-remembered TV series and give them renewed spirit and life.

But, on the night of their debut, there is something totally dark and foreboding about the way Caesar looks and behaves. A vacant stare fills his eyes and an ominous cloud seems to hang over his manner—all in sharp contrast to the happy memory of Caesar most of the older spectators have brought with them to the opulent Nob Hill hotel's famed showroom.

Ironically, I think at the time, *Your Show of Shows* still remains one of the most popular shows from the 1950s, wherein Caesar displayed a brilliant technique on his feet, creating great ad libs and vibrant, fresh zaniness in the days when TV was live and still a spontaneous, immediate experience. (*Your Show of Shows* would win three Emmys as most outstanding variety series and Caesar would win two Emmys out of eleven nominations.)

So why, that night, does Sid Caesar seem to be such a gloomy, unfriendly, distant man, and why does his timing and presence now seem a mere shadow of his former talents?

It will take five years to get most of the answers, and those answers are not going to be pretty. It is all presented in a revelation-filled autobiography, *Where Have I Been?*, written in collaboration with a longtime journalist friend, Bill Davidson. Although it reprints some of Caesar's best comedy sketches and tells anecdotal stories, most of *Where Have I Been?* is not exactly a barrel

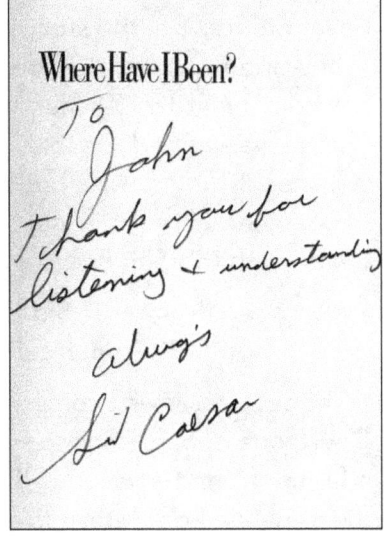

This is the slipcase cover of Sid Caesar's 1982 hardback autobiography, released by Crown Publishers. That hat on his head tells us he is dressed as Professor Ludwig Von Knowitall, one of his unforgettable recurring characters from his TV era. And (right) is the title page which Sid autographed with a short note of thanks.

of laughs. Nor is anything in his life deemed sanctimonious, as Caesar, page by page, admits to having been a pill (aka drug) addict, an alcoholic, and a depressed, insecure entertainment star, whose dissipations ultimately brought him to the brink of mental and physical ruin.

On the other hand, the book is also the detailed account of how Caesar went cold-turkey and rehabilitated himself so that now, in the closing pages of his "expose," he can declare himself "a new man," who has conquered all of his past ailments and downfalls.

The first I hear about the book is from David Kleinberg, the editor of the *San Francisco Chronicle's Sunday Datebook*.

"Sid Caesar," Kleinberg tells me, "has written a new book about his life that's supposed to be controversial, and he's scheduled to be in town on a promotion tour. Get a copy, read it, and set up an interview. This is one story we've got to have. I grew up watching Caesar, and this book could be a real revelation. Carl Reiner read it and said he cried. That he suddenly realized there was a Sid Caesar he'd never known before. And now he admires him like never before. Get the story behind all that."

"Me and my folks," I told David, "we watched the show every Saturday night too. Reiner, he was a major part of the comedy. That's amazing he'd say that."

Reiner, it turns out, is but a tip of the iceberg. I read the book front to back. I set up a meeting with Caesar. What happens next begins with this *San Francisco Chronicle* headline:

Sid Caesar: Back From the Pills and the Booze

The Sid Caesar who comes to the door of his suite at the Stanford Court, one of San Francisco's finer hotels, does indeed seem new, a far cry from the vacuous Sid Caesar I had seen stumble across the Venetian Room stage five years earlier. His eyes are clear and sparkling, his stance is starch-stiff straight, his attitude is jovial and relaxed. He no longer looks bloated and pudgy. No dark clouds hanging overhead, no moodiness. And, as if he wanted his dress to make a statement, he is casually clad in blue jeans and a Lacoste polo shirt, with his neck adorned with a sparkling gold chain.

This is exactly how Sid Caesar looked on the day we met, as this was snapped shortly before the book's publication.

The new Sid Caesar, so he says, has just finished exercising: 300 leg-ups, 100 push-ups with his feet on the bed, 50 knee bends, 35 chin-ups. Considerable physical effort for a man sixty years of age, who openly admits that until four years earlier he never did anything more strenuous than lift a whiskey glass off a bar top or screw off the cap of a bottle of questionable pills. It is all part of what Caesar calls "the repair of the mind."

"Where did it all start?" Caesar asks the opening question himself as he sits on a sofa, telling me to take a seat across from him as he crosses his legs and beats a tempo on the heel of his boot with his hand. "Where did my life go wrong? I guess with the insecurity of becoming so famous so fast. I was never able to accept my success; I felt I hadn't really earned the right to be a TV star. If you've never known failure, how can you know success? Better to fall on your face first, then you can appreciate a good thing. My excuse for drinking was always 'the enormous pressures' of doing a live show every week. Ninety minutes at that. In those days there was no room for error; you went out and had one shot at it, period. Retakes didn't exist."

Caesar swears he never drank on the days he was preparing the show, Monday through Friday. Only after Saturday night's 90-minute ordeal was over, then would he and his co-stars Carl Reiner and Hal Morris and maybe some of the staff writers (brothers Neil and Danny Simon, Mel Brooks, Mel Tolkin, depending on the year) pile into a row of idling limousines and head for Manhattan's best eating/drinking joints. Toots Shor's, here they come!

Food and drink, indeed, were plentiful. In Caesar's case, the booze was always too much. "I would frequently drink myself unconscious, or maybe I'd just vomit in public. Sometimes they'd find me passed out in the men's room. Or I might be in the corridor leading to the men's room, depending on how good my timing was."

One night, he ordered a New York steak as he downed drink after drink. No sooner had a waiter placed the steak in front of him than Caesar passed out, his face falling into the plate of food. (This very scene would be reenacted in Neil Simon's 2001 TV movie *Laughter on the 23rd Floor*, a drama inspired by Caesar's hardships.)

What was really embarrassing about that moment? Caesar asks me, then answers himself. "My cronies at the table kept on talking and eating after my face hit the plate, as if nothing had happened, as if I was merely rehearsing a comedy sketch." But those surrounding him knew of his voluminous drinking, and tried to ignore the collapse. There were those, he adds, "who grew to dislike me."

Out of this period of history-making TV shows developed "a different Sid Caesar. I turned into a lousy, aggressive drunk. I was angry, I was violent, I was belligerent. I was paranoid and not pleasant to be around. My wife [Florence, married to Caesar since 1943] always stayed at my side and cleaned up my messes, but my family life was nowhere. I hardly knew my three children.

I would scream at taxi drivers and I'd pick fights for the dumbest of reasons. Even with the people I liked the most."

One night at the Palmer House in Chicago, something happened that almost changed Caesar's life and career forever. He and Mel Brooks (at that time a staff writer) were in the same room together as Caesar got drunker and drunker. Brooks, a major contributor to *Caesar's Hour*, the follow-up to *Your Show of Shows*, kept telling Caesar, "Come on, let's go out. I wanna get some food."

As Caesar remembers it: "He said, 'Let's go out' so many times, I finally replied, 'You wanna go out? Okay, you're going out!' I grabbed Brooks by the throat and carried him over to the nearest window and shoved him against the glass. Fortunately, there were others in the room who stopped me. Did I mention we were staying on the 18th floor? I was so out of it, I was so drunk, I didn't have a clue what I was doing. I could've killed Mel."

A doctor would give him a sleeping tranquilizer, chloral hydrate, to help him get off the booze, but he "faithfully" always washed down the pills with a glass of booze. Eventually he graduated to Seconal and finally to Valium. "But, I had this incredible iron constitution and I'd wake up the next morning, if not afternoon, without a hangover. My mind would be sharp and ready to create new comedy sketches all over again. And my routine kept going."

It was a pattern that went on, he says, for nearly thirty years. Eventually, in the late 1970s, the prescribed drugs and never-ending booze flow began to wear down his faculties. Life turned into "a Valium blur." Caesar began to forget his lines and would often black out for long periods, remembering nothing in the wake of soberness. "Here's an example of what was happening to me. I was in Australia in 1975 to make the film *Barnaby and Me*, a comedy with Juliet Mills. Apparently, I was so drunk day after day that, two years later, when I finally saw the finished film, I couldn't remember making any of it. I couldn't recall a single moment on the set. It was like watching a stranger up there on the screen.

"In 1978," said Caesar, "I reached my suicidal period. I was fat with giant jowls. I didn't leave the house for three months. I sat around, I slept a lot, trying to read and contemplating suicide. Finally, I accepted a role in a stage comedy in Canada. On opening night, I couldn't remember my lines and I was missing cues. I barely got through the first act and went backstage to lie down. When I got up, I looked into a mirror and asked myself, 'Do you want to live or die?' I knew I needed help and for the first time in my life I cried out for just that."

Because he wanted to be cured, he admitted himself to Regina General Hospital in Saskatchewan and began a regimen to end his booze and drug addictions. "I knew I could get the drugs if I wanted them," says Caesar, "but I didn't want them." His weight dropped from 240 to 175. Detoxified, Caesar began exercising for the first time since 1948.

"I learned that you never tempt fate. I was at home that Thanksgiving, having dinner with my family, thinking I was a new man, when I decided to have a glass of wine. Just one lousy glass of wine. Well, my body had grown so unaccustomed to alcohol that after several glasses of wine I turned into my old monster. We had a terrible scene, fighting each other, me and the monster. When I sobered up it hit me like a ton of bricks, and I realized I couldn't slip, ever again. Now just the smell of alcohol makes me ill. To go near a glass of booze is to step toward death."

In 1979, Caesar took another major step in his self-rehabilitation, though it came about by accident. He had gone to Paris to co-star with Peter Sellers and Helen Mirren in *The Fiendish Plot of Dr. Fu Manchu*, and he took a tape recorder along "so I could talk into it to describe the museums and places I wanted to visit." Instead, he began to talk to himself, addressing his alter ego as Sidney. (Unknown to Caesar then, he was employing a Jungian technique of therapy, where the personality is split into two—the father and the wayward child.) Now he does this double-talking each morning. This, he says, rising to his feet, is the conversation he had just before I arrived at his hotel room:

"Well, Sidney, your book tour has started. It's working. Be positive about it because your attitude is important. Talk to yourself. You have nothing to be ashamed of. Verbalize your feelings and hear it back. Listen for the swings in your mood . . . ." (At this point, Caesar becomes two different characters, using different voices.)

"Hey, Sidney, you want a drink?"

"Sure, I want a drink...."

"Become a little happy. You really enjoy that. Or do you? Sidney, you're an oaf and a drunk and an idiot. Have a drink."

"No, no drink. A drink ... stinks."

Exchange over, Sidney vanishes and Caesar sits back down, sighing. "I went through several failed therapies. Analyses, three or four times. It never worked. But being my own analyst, that does work. Dr. Sid Caesar says it straight: There are no more lies to myself."

During our interview, Caesar occasionally leaps to his feet to act out a scene. He seems to have regained all of his comedic sharpness and deftness in creating character attitudes and situations. When I ask him about his attitude toward comedy, he says: "Comedy is based on truth or near truth. People must believe you. If they don't believe you, they'll laugh at you, not with you. They must relate and feel it. A guy in trouble is a funny guy. If he's in a dingy and a yacht comes sailing by, washing him with waves, he's the funny one, not the guy sailing the yacht."

Caesar says he has watched new generations of comedians grow up behind him, boats floating in the wake he has helped to create, but he feels his generation had the best advantage, given the availability of movies, television and live performances. I ask him to explain what he means by "best advantage," and learn some fascinating Caesar history.

He was born Isaac Sidney Caesar on September 8, 1922, in the factory town of Yonkers, New York. According to Sid, his father Max and mother Ida had come to America from Poland decades earlier. Max was passing through Ellis Island's immigration procedure when an official couldn't pronounce his real surname, Ziser.

Suddenly, the official pounded on the table to get the attention of those nearby and exclaimed, "Everyone! Hail Caesar!" Thus was his father given a new surname, which he was to pass on to Sid. "Here's the facts," says Caesar. "I was a make-up child. Mom and dad got mad at each other, then made up. I was the result.

"My father ran the St. Clair Luncheonette, a one-arm joint, as they were called in those days. You've been to a greasy spoon? It was there I worked as a kid bussing tables, later waiting on tables.

Caesar served in the U.S. Coast Guard during World War II, helping to form a military band in which he played his instrument of choice, the saxophone. He would continue to play the sax off and on over the years.

Even 'bouncing' out those who caused disturbances. Dad's place was in an industrial area where the workmen were of many nationalities, Italian, Russian, Polish, to name a few. I'd listen to their different dialects, and years later I'd put those dialects to use as foreign double-talk in my parodies and comedy sketches. And to this day, I love to order a meal in four languages. The flavors mix beautifully.

"In my day, we had the Catskill Mountains resorts in upper New York state. Huge, popular hotels, full of Burlesque and Vaudeville routines. The Jewish Alps, the Borscht Belt. It was a great training ground for comedians, musicians, entertainers all around." When he was all of fourteen, he made his first appearance in "The

Jewish Alps" as a saxophone player, but no way was he given the chance to do comedy. That would come in 1939 when he returned to play sax and do his routines at the Vacationland Hotel, having finished high school and now wandering on his own. In late 1942, he began active service with the Coast Guard and helped to form an official Coast Guard 65-piece band as its sax player. He became acquainted with Broadway composer Vernon Duke (also serving with the Coast Guard as coxswain). Sid's deep-rooted desire to become a comedian still motivated him and he created routines in his spare time.

Once in a while, when the Coast Guard band was setting up its instruments, he would leap up in front of the group and deliver a comedy routine, just to see what the reaction might be. Duke, impressed by what he saw, was able to create a musical revue, *Six On, Twelve Off*, which toured various Coast Guard camps. By the time he was a lieutenant, Duke introduced Sid to Austrian-born producer Max Liebman. Years earlier, while running the Tamiment Playhouse in the Pocono Mountains of Pennsylvania, Liebman had discovered Danny Kaye and Imogene Coca and taken them to Broadway in 1939 to star in *The Straw Hat Revue*.

Now, as he watched Caesar's comedy routine about American fighter pilots battling Nazi warplanes, a parody of a World War II motion picture, Liebman realized a major talent was standing before him. Before Caesar knew it, he had been hired by Liebman to perform in a new revue destined to play at military bases, *Tars and Spars*. As a "Coast Guardsman comedian," he repeated the fighter-plane comedy piece, "Wings Over Boomerschnitzel," receiving more applause than the musical portions of the show. It was so successful, the revue went to the Strand Theater on Broadway.

In 1946, Caesar and his wife Florence moved to Hollywood to make a film version of *Tars and Spars*, duplicating his fighter-pilots routine. The Columbia-produced film was in its final stages of editing when Caesar received word that his father Max was dying—and had only a short time left to live. Caesar urged the producers to get a print made as swiftly as possible so he could screen it for his father. An initial copy was finalized and immediately shipped to Yonkers. Sid and his father saw the movie together in a local theater–and almost instantly after that, Max died.

Back in Hollywood, Caesar had a cameo in a 1947 Film Noir, *The Guilt of Janet Ames*. When nothing he was doing in movieland seemed to help his career, he returned to the East Coast. Suddenly, things began to come together. He did comedy at the Copacabana nightclub and rejoined ranks with Max Liebman, who put him into the 1948 Broadway revue, *Make Mine Manhattan*.

One of his most popular routines was "The Five-Dollar Date," in which he whimsically described the difference between what it cost to take your girl on a date in the late 1930s and in 1949, with the emphasis on not only higher prices but the sarcastic attitudes of cab drivers, restaurant waiters, and theater ushers. He portrayed all these characters with those satirical dialect voices he had learned working in his father's luncheonette.

In 1949, Liebman cast Sid as a regular on *The Admiral Broadway Revue*, a TV series he shared with Imogene Coca, but which lasted only one season. Nevertheless, the networks liked elements of the show, and as a result, Liebman and Caesar joined forces in 1950 to create the ultimate comedy-variety format for Caesar and Coca, *Your Show of Shows*.

Coca and producer Liebman left the series at the end of the 1954 season. She had chosen to star in her own Liebman-produced half-hour comedy series, *The Imogene Coca Show*, but it quickly became a complete disaster and was cancelled after only one season). Meanwhile, NBC changed the title of *Your Show of Shows* to *Caesar's Hour* and the 90-minute format was condensed to one hour. It was the end for Liebman and a new beginning for Caesar. At least for a while, with Nanette Fabray taking over the Coca role. At least for a while, until . . . .

In 1957, NBC canceled *Caesar's Hour*. "I was finally losing my coordination and timing, and NBC could see it," Caesar confesses. "I would never regain the network popularity I had enjoyed. And during the twenty-year decline that followed, I really believed that the cancellation was a form of punishment for having achieved too much too soon."

In addition to signing my copy of Where Have I Been?, *Sid pulled out this publicity photo being used to promote his autobiography and signed it, as well.*

In the beginning, after the cancellation, "I had a bitter taste in my mouth. Today that's become a sweet taste. I've swept aside all that ego stuff and now I consider a little attention—even from you—to be marvelous. Thank you for coming today, John. I feel happy and relaxed, and if new career things happen, that's fine, that's wonderful. But these new things don't have to happen. I have my self-esteem back no matter what else happens."

About comedy and its future, Caesar is optimistic. "Comedy is coming back. We need it, desperately. It's as essential as a piece of bread–and I'd like to be a couple of pieces, even if it's only crust."

THE END

But wait! It isn't to be the end. For there will be another meeting with Sid Caesar. Nine years later he will return to San Francisco. Only this time he will have Imogene Coca at his side. And unlike their show in 1977, this one will recapture the full comedic essence of their working together.

The time will be February 1992, almost a decade after that Stanford Court interview with Sid Caesar. Imogene Coca had deeply fallen into a state of depression two years earlier and Caesar, informed of her deteriorating state of mind, had called her on the phone to tell her to pack her bags because they were going to go on the road and re-create some of their classic TV material, as they had first done back in 1977. This was Sid's way of hoping to bolster her spirits and personality and give her new hope. What he would call "new purpose, new energy, new everything!"

Her depression had begun as far back as 1987 following the death of her husband-actor King Donovan, to whom she had been happily married for almost twenty-seven years. (Donovan is perhaps best remembered for his role in the 1956 version of *Invasion of the Body Snatchers* and for his role as the bookstore clerk on the half-hour TV comedy series starring George Burns and Gracie Allen.) At first, Imogene hesitated. But Caesar kept working on her. One thing that got her moving was winning an American Comedy Award for Lifetime Achievement in Comedy in 1988. And after that, they were a team again on the move, displaying two wacky styles of physical comedy side by side. Their reunion could have been a newspaper headline, "Your Team of Teams, Once Separated, But . . .

Caesar And Coca Are Together Again."

When last he saw me, Sid Caesar had said, "Comedy is coming back . . . It's as essential as a piece of bread, and it's coming back . . . and I'd like to be a couple of pieces, even if it's only crust."

Since then, Caesar has done better than break off crust, or even crumbs. He has sliced off a part of his dead past and toasted it

Imogene Coca had a way of looking that made you feel she was staring into your soul. Those bulging eyes gave life to her comedy characters and set her apart from other comediennes.

back to life, and "no longer feels like a heel." Two years ago, he and Imogene Coca started going on the road again, presenting their most popular comedy routines in an anthology show, Together Again. It is scheduled for the Helen Hayes Theater on Broadway later this year, but first the team will perform for an entire month in San Francisco's Marines Memorial Theater.

What's amazing is that the two stars—forty-two years since they first met and began working together on *The Admiral Broadway Revue* (forerunner to *Your Show of Shows*)—are still able to perform their sketches with nary a change in dialogue or attitude. Even the ages of the characters have not been altered, with Coca still portraying the stripteaser Miss Jet Lag and doing "her breast" take-off of Sophia Loren in a *Bicycle Thief* movie parody.

Although Coca is now eighty-two, and Caesar will be seventy in September, they bring the same vitality and compatibility to their comedy as they did as "youngsters." While the material is venerable, originally written with the help of Neil Simon, Larry Gelbart, Woody Allen, and Mel Brooks, Coca and Caesar have remained just as ageless.

In February 1992, theirs is an evening of physical and intellectual comedy made up of delightful dialects, mime, monologues, and sketches. Satires of situations we have all experienced or can relate to. They have always dealt with the familiar, touching on what they call "the truth in comedy."

There is the famous Hickenloopers' marital-spat sketch, set to the music of Beethoven's *Fifth*, and the "At the Movies" sketch in which they portray strangers who meet in a theater and fall instantly in love, even though Coca's boyfriend is seated with her.

When we meet, Coca speaks with the enthusiasm of one who has just discovered an old school chum. "Sid and I've been together so long. We never have to fight about billing or who gets the best lines. We've always taken the attitude that if something works for the other, then that's fine. It's the act that counts. I think that's why the duo has worked for so long. We are for eternity."

But, she is forced to add, "I don't understand why we get along so well. It doesn't make any sense. I mean, we're quite different. When we're not working, we don't see much of each other. It's not that we go out of our way to avoid each other, we just go our separate ways. Each of us has a different set of friends. And, Sid lives on the West Coast, while I live in the East."

Does something magically "click" when they get together on a stage? "In a way," replies Coca. "We really know what the other is thinking. I'm always ready for Sid, even if he changes a line or throws out an ad lib." She describes her co-star as "very quiet, very intellectual. Such a sharp mind. He's not shy, but he's reticent. He has a brilliant sense of comedy. His dialects are incredible. Without him, I'd never get dinner ordered."

Why do their sketches, created in the early 1950s, still work so well? She laughs heartily. "As long as the situation is set in reality, everyone can relate. Such as a husband and wife arguing because she's just wrecked the car. Once you've established a believable premise, you can fly off into fantasy or absurdity or utter slapstick all you want. You can soar into outer space if it pleases you."

What Coca has found amazing is that "the show is not just attracting our old audience from the TV days. All different ages are coming. It's not all about nostalgia. Something bigger than that is at work."

That same afternoon, I drop into the Pan-Pacific Hotel to see Sid Caesar all over again. Having just finished his daily 300 sit-ups and 100 chin-ups, he greets me at the door dressed as young as he looks—in tight-fitting blue pants, a bright reddish-pink shirt, and glistening brown boots. A silver belt buckle gleams at me from his slender waist.

"I haven't changed since the last time we met, back when I was selling that book," he says, as one taking a vow. "No pills, no booze. I swear. That positive attitude I told you about? Still there. I take nothing for granted."

In *Together Again*, Caesar reprises his famous Professor Ludwig Von Knowitall; portrays a gumball machine; a young boy at a dance trying to get up the courage to ask a girl to dance with him; a six-month-old baby eager for feeding time; and a pianist having a bad night at the concert hall.

"Our show is not about today. It's in a timeless place somewhere. It's a kind of art form that isn't done much anymore. I can't define comedy. All I know is, it's something that makes us laugh, and it can verge on tragedy. Because laughter and crying are almost the same emotion. Laugh too hard and you cry. Cry too hard and you laugh."

Caesar agrees with Coca that "comedy has to be about the truth. We don't tell jokes. We deal in characters, in people caught up in situations you've been in. Such as a man about to get married, who's thinking about all his doubts as he walks down the aisle? How many of us have been through that?" As for parody sketches, which he did constantly on *Your Show of Shows*, "You can't parody the mundane, only the classical, that which is known to an audience, which is understood by both men and women."

Asked about the "click" that occurs when he and Coca appear on stage, he laughs and shakes his head. "No click, no light bulbs going on. Performing beside Imogene has become a natural part of life. Like breathing. I swear, she can read my mind. And I guess I can read hers. That's why we're doing this show. You find a partner that works and you stick with it . . . she says we never fight? That's true. The main concern should be 'Does it get a laugh?' That's all that counts. Whatever is good for the show."

In what ways do they differ? "Ah, I'm the gruff one. She's the gentle one. If we were The Odd Couple, I'd be the sloppy one." (Ironically, it was Caesar's staff writer, Neil Simon, who created the play/movie/TV sitcom *The Odd Couple*.)

Reminded of Coca's age, Caesar shakes his head again disbelievingly. "What an amazing woman. Nominated six times for an Emmy, and she won in '52. And she's still going strong. This incredible transformation occurs when Imogene walks onto a stage. She becomes those characters. The Bag Lady. Mrs. Hoopenlooper. The ballet dancer bouncing through the air. What characters she created. I believe those characters. The audience believes those characters. They're wonderfully goofy and adorable."

For *Together Again*, Caesar does three dialect sketches, so he begins doing sample voices for me in French, Italian, Spanish, and German. At no time is he really saying anything, yet it's gibberish that sounds true to the languages. "It's what I call the language of song. I just ordered a meal in four languages."

Each day, as he had done that day back in 1982, Caesar still talks into a tape recorder. It is now an ongoing dialogue he has been doing for more than ten years, remember? Sid talks to Sidney. Sidney talks to Sid. "It's my way of straightening out whatever is mentally bothering me. It's a way of discovering myself. Freud made it all a mystery, didn't he? But the clouds don't have to open nor does the Earth have to split open. You simply verbalize the problem, and you can make friends with yourself."

"Too many of us hate ourselves," he continues. "We have forms of punishment that we love to self-inflict, such as eating foods we shouldn't eat, or promising to start a diet tomorrow while we stuff ourselves today. Do what I do next time you feel like a chocolate mousse. Take one spoonful and roll it around in your mouth. Taste it and taste it and taste it. That's the best it's ever going to taste. It isn't going to get any better. Now, push the dessert away. You don't need it anymore. You've satisfied yourself without stuffing yourself."

Caesar seems to bristle when I ask if he intends to have his show taped for television. "No," he responds quickly. "Once it's taped then everyone can see it. I want to keep going and going around the country with Imogene, performing the show wherever

One of the last things Sid Caesar did the night of our dinner together was to sign this photo for my son Russ. It's a photo of him furiously smoking in his 1976 feature film Silent Movie.

it's wanted. This is a live event. Live is beautiful. When you're alive you have nothing to fall back on but your own resourcefulness. Your own talents. For me and Imogene, that is the great challenge of comedy. This is the great challenge of our careers together."

As our interview comes to a close, I feel that Sid Caesar has given me not one but two unforgettable interviews. I figure this is it. My wife and I will see the Caesar-Coca show and that will be the end of our relationship. But it's not the end. There is to be one final incident, one final moment that will surprise the hell out of us.

A few nights after my final interview with Caesar, *Together Again* proves to be a very funny evening at the Marines Memorial. Afterward, Erica and I are invited to go backstage, much to our surprise. We all shake hands and Sid invites my wife and I to join him for dinner on Sunday evening at a restaurant in San Francisco's North Beach.

Sunday turns out to be a gloomy, rainy day and traffic is slow as molasses on the main avenues into North Beach, which is being heavily drenched in the downpour. Finally, despite the deluge, I'm able to get the car parked. But looking at my watch, I realize we are about fifteen minutes late. We hurry but we are an additional five minutes late by the time we approach the restaurant's main entrance.

I can see a figure standing in the doorway, illuminated by streaks of light coming from inside the half-open door. As we step up to that door, I realize there's a man standing there with a very worried look on his face. I blink, realizing the man is . . . .

Sid Caesar!

He breaks into a broad grin. "Thank God, John! We thought something might've happened to you!"

He throws his arms around me and hugs me as if I were a long-lost son. Then he hugs Erica. My wife and I are, to say the least, stunned. To think . . . Sid Caesar had stood at the door waiting for us, so concerned about our whereabouts, our safety.

"Come on. Dinner's waiting." We follow Sid inside, feeling a combination of guilt (for being late) and ego (for being cared about by a major comedy star). It is a wonderful dinner, a wonderful memory. This night will be the last time we see Caesar, but it will be a night my wife and I still remember vividly and talk about once in a while when he reflect on all the wonderful people whom we had the opportunity to meet. And of all of those people, Sid Caesar had been one of the most serious . . . and yet, one of the funniest!

Imogene Coca died on June 2, 2001, at the age of ninety-two. Sid passed through a decade when it was generally known he was in failing health, yet he was always making public appearances. He died of cancer on Feb. 12, 2015, at the age of ninety-one. Many gave him praise after his death, but I was especially moved by the words of Billy Crystal: "What kind of comedy would I be doing if I hadn't seen Sid Caesar? Would I be a comedian at all?"

Sid was more than pleased to sign another photo to me on the last night we met.

BOB HOPE
A Moment of Hilarious
And Hope-Filled Revelation!

By the mid-1980s, word is out that Bob Hope, who has been one of the most successful comedians throughout the 1940s into the late 1960s, recording radio shows, filming motion pictures, and hosting television specials, has aged into nothing more than an unfunny has-been, an old man, who relied on a teleprompter to deliver his material. Decrepit, belonging to another age of entertainment, loss of memory, mental deterioration, senility, Alzheimer's Disease. Take your pick. Hope is quickly turning into nothing but history.

I had grown up in the mid-to-late 1940s listening to his radio programs and seeing his Road Pictures. In the 1950s, I watched his TV specials and the times when he hosted the televised Academy Award shows. Now, even I felt that the rumors flying around about his downfall had to be based on some truth, some reality. A doctor's report, stolen from a private file, perhaps?

Thank God that in January 1985 I am invited to the Moscone Convention Center in San Francisco for a special midnight comedy show. And you have to be invited; it is not open to the public. Because now I can come to my own conclusion about Hope's mental condition and performing capabilities.

At midnight sharp, I see the Bob Hope I have always appreciated as he does an hour-long stand-up comedy routine, his body upright (no nurses or nannies in sight, I note) as he holds a standard microphone. He is now eighty-three years of age, and he is absolutely perfect. Absolutely amazing as he delivers a flurry of one-liners. Not a single muffed punch line. Much of it is "blue material," the kind he couldn't perform on television. The kind, so they said, that Hope loved most.

The audience roars with laughter and applauds him as if he is the funniest man alive. As if he is still that young man of the 1940s,

This is the Bob Hope I remembered from that night in 1985 when he performed solo at the Moscone Convention Center—without teleprompter or nurses anywhere in sight.

funny as ever and always on the road to more laughter. To me, he remains the funniest!

Finally comes a phone call to remember, that precious moment when I will personally meet Bob Hope for a one-on-one close-up encounter. I am contacted by his personal Hollywood agent who tells me that Hope's ninetieth birthday is approaching and there will be a network TV special about his career, *Bob Hope: The First 90 Years*, to be aired on the night of Friday, May 14, 1993. Would

I consider coming to Los Angeles a few weeks earlier and do an exclusive interview with Mr. Hope? Guess what my answer is.

When I drive up to the Hope Mansion at 10342 Moorpark Street in Toluca Lake, a part of the San Fernando Valley, I park in front of a small building right next door to the English-style mansion that he built in 1939 in what had once been a walnut grove. I have been told to check in at the office. Hope's agent is waiting for me and he escorts me to the front door. I am utterly surprised when he tells me he won't be staying once he has introduced me to Hope. That's the way Bob prefers it, he adds. A moment later the front door opens. Here is what happens next:

Hope Springs Eternal!

Breaking bread at high noon with Bob Hope in his Toluca Lake mansion has to be the American equivalent of taking four o'clock tea with Queen Elizabeth in an opulent little nook at Windsor Castle.

Ironically, both are British born, but Hope is a form of royalty a bit different from the Queen. Although he slid from the womb of Avis Hope, an aspiring concert singer, into the world of London in 1903 as Leslie Townes Hope, he came to American in 1908 with Avis and her husband, William Henry Hope (a stonemason), and he became a king in this new land as the eternal stand-up, one-liner comedian, firing out topical gags. He would never relinquish his crown, always coming back decade after decade to perform in every media available.

I feel as if I am standing in front of royalty when we are introduced, and Hope, waving goodbye to his agent, leads me into a giant front room with a wall of glass that reveals an expansive back yard that includes a one-hole golf course. "See those trees in the back?" queries Hope. "Just behind them lives a very funny man. His name is Jonathan Winters." Hope, a geographic expert, among other things.

There is something very stately and palatial about this seven-acre spread with 14,876 square feet within the mansion, the very place where Hope hangs his golf cap and stores his irons, although there is not a trace of pomp or pageantry in how the legendary

This is the publicity photo Bob Hope signed for me on the day I dropped into his Toluca Lake mansion for lunch in 1993. Ten years almost to the day later, he would celebrate his 100th birthday.

comedian greets guests. Standing in the front room before high glass windows that afford a vast view of rolling lawns, an Olympic-size swimming pool, and that aforementioned forest of tall trees, Hope looks the essence of relaxation, casually clad in a white cotton golf shirt, brownish-gray slacks, and pristine white Reeboks. For a man who will be ninety in just a few weeks, he looks trim and fit, and he boasts that he has just returned from a robust round of golf at a nearby course.

Hope strolls across the room, his body loose and his chin tilted, that ski-jump nose upturned. He speaks proudly about his daughter Linda, who is producer of the three-hour special honoring his ninetieth birthday. "You know NBC," quips Hope in his familiar, happy-go-lucky way. "That's the network that knows only one thing: ratings. Linda, she's an amazing gal. She rounded up ninety guest stars. Imagine that. Must have had a large lariat and Roy Rogers' Trigger to help her. I just sit back and let her do the hard work. Old tapes, old film clips, friends from way back when. Times it's getting hard to remember." Hope sighs. "All those years. What a life it's been."

Indeed. A life of golf, radio, TV comedy, the Road Pictures with Bing Crosby, a slew of other Paramount movies that made him a box-office star of the 1940s and 1950s, the wartime USO entertainment tours (World War II, Korea, Vietnam, the Gulf War), hosting the Academy Award shows fourteen times, and the other milestones of a career that began in Vaudeville in 1924 dancing in a Fatty Arbuckle revue—all is to be recounted. On hand will be President Bill Clinton, the five remaining former White House chiefs, host Jay Leno, and guests Whoopi Goldberg, Tom Selleck, Lucie Arnaz, Gregory Hines, Tony Randall, Roy Rogers, Jane Russell, film critics Gene Siskel and Roger Ebert, Donald O'Connor, General Colin Powell . . . it's to be NBC's way of thanking Hope for the memories.

Hope sits at a table set for two near the massive window layout and waves his hand at the lavish grounds, where a gardener can be seen trimming hedges. "One time, I was rehearsing a show with Claudette Colbert and she was sitting in that same chair you're in now. She looked out and asked, 'How can you afford all that grass?' "

A light breeze wafts through an open pane as he laughs and begins a light lunch of diced chicken in a white sauce, a simple lettuce-tomato salad and a custard dessert, topped by a single strawberry. "You're lucky I'm eating today," he says. "Normally I don't have lunch. Gotta go light. Keep the tummy tight. It's the only way that makes golf right. And don't I sound a fright."

Occasionally, as the questions and answers flow for ninety minutes, interrupted only by a waiter's serving and the sound of a distant lawn mower, Hope shows he is hard of hearing by smiling warmly, leaning forward a bit and saying "Eh? How's that?"

Bob Hope in front of the NBC microphone doing a radio show, what became a "milestone" in his career as he developed the art of delivering topical one-liners by new, up-and-coming writers who went on to movie-TV careers as writers, producers, and directors.

He leans back. "What does it mean to be ninety?" he asks, in response to my next question. "Hah! I'm puzzled myself. I do hit the golf ball a little better than I did at eighty. I practice every day, either here at home out back or on a golf course, and I have no sore muscles. My knees still bend. I can twist my arms in circles. Even turn my head with my neck supporting me. Now that I'm old, I have to ask myself: When do I become decrepit?"

Bob Hope and Bing Crosby working together on radio, just one of the entertainment tools they pursued with a passion—each ridiculing the other about girth, size of nose, singing capability, age. Whatever the gag writers came up with-they loved doing it.

Asked about the milestones in his life, he laughs for a moment and refers to how lucky he's been—a key phrase he keeps reiterating. I mention radio, and he claps his hands. "My favorite, and it lasted decades."

It started in 1937 as *The Woodbury Soap* Hour, then in 1938 became *The Pepsodent Show* With Bob Hope, which lasted into the 1950s.

"All I know is, I had the greatest writing staff, all kids fresh out of college: [Norman] Panama, [Melvin] Frank, [Melville] Shavelson. And we did what people were talking and thinking about. Speed was one thing we concentrated on. Hit 'em quick. Hit 'em fast. Zoom. We were lucky. And so many of those writers went on to have fabulous careers of their own. Amazing, isn't it?"

In the zany Road pictures, Hope and Crosby were forever traveling to foreign countries to engage in a special kind of satire that spoofed movie genres, music and dancing. They ventured to Singapore, Zanzibar, Morocco, Alaska, Rio, Bali, and Hong Kong, always with Hope as the cowardly one and Crosby as the ladies' man.]

Inevitable is the topic of Bing Crosby—with whom he worked off and on for decades and who became an inseparable part of Hope's career. "We started out doing Vaudeville together in 1932 at the Capitol Theater in New York City. In those days, I was nothing more than a fast-talking vaudevillian. We did this act playing two politicians who meet on the street. We pretend to be glad to see each other but we're trying to pick each other's pocket. In another, we were musical conductors dueling with our batons.

Dorothy Lamour was Bob Hope and Bing Crosby's costar/love interest in the six Road Pictures they made together between 1939 and 1952. Known as the Sarong Queen, she once said, "I was the happiest and highest-paid straight woman in the business."

We got even better acquainted at a nearby pub called O'Reilly's, where we traded show-biz stories and made other drinkers laugh. It was the beginning of something good."

"We went on to do a lot of radio together, and of course the seven Road Pictures we made at Paramount. Those were the biggest money-makers of their day. See, there was a lot of chemistry between us. You know, Bing used to walk through his pictures a lot. But I'd show the screenplays to my radio writers and they'd make suggestions and I'd write notes on the script pages, and then show them to Bing and he'd always say, 'That's funny, that's great, let's do it.' In the beginning, we didn't tell the director our changes. We'd rehearse it his way and wait for the camera to roll, and then we'd do it our way. In the beginning the director didn't like it and complained to the producer. But when the producer saw the rushes he'd tell the director that our way was funnier. 'Leave those two guys alone and let 'em do it their way.'"

In *The Road to Morocco* (1942), the camera was running as Hope walked up to a camel. Suddenly, the camel snorted at Hope and he jumped back in shock. "Let's do that again," he requested. The

There was hardly a scene between Hope and Lamour in the Road Pictures when he wasn't trying to steal another kiss, or she wasn't using Hope to gain some nefarious step forward.

director, David Butler, shook his head and said no, this time he was going to use the take. "His way," explains Hope, "of getting back at me for the ad libbing."

One of the running gags in the Road Pictures was to break down the so-called "fourth wall," that which separates the actors from the audience. In one scene, Hope turned to face the camera and said, "Bing is about to sing a song so this is a good time to go out and buy some popcorn."

"For Bing, those pictures were a challenge. For me too. We were on our toes, always trying to top each other. But it wasn't malicious. We were playing to each other. And having a ball. One thing I remember vividly. Remember that sketch I told you about in which we played two politicians? When we did one of the Road Pictures, we redid the scene with Bing and I saying goodbye to each other as we tried to pick each other's pocket. It was amazing how we could steal from the past to enrich the present."

At first, while talking about Crosby, Hope's voice is filled with nostalgia, but it takes on a heavier tone when he describes how, a few months before the crooner's death in October 1977, Crosby was doing a CBS-TV special at the Ambassador Theater in Pasadena in May when he fell through a manhole on the main stage someone had mistakenly left open. "As he dropped, Bing grabbed a piece of proscenium arch made of wood and it helped to break his fall. I think it saved his life. After that 12-foot drop, he had head cuts and bruises. I ran downstairs and saw Pearl Bailey holding Bing's head in her arms, with Kathy [Bing's wife, Kathryn Grant] also hovering over him. Bing looked up at me and said, 'Jimmy Dundee couldn't have taken that fall better.' Dundee had been our stuntman at Paramount. I still think that fall was worse than we thought. I think it had a helluva lot to do with his sudden death from a heart attack."

Where was Hope at the time of Crosby's death? Hope looked me in the eye. "That's a very ironic question, given the sequence of events. The day that Bing dropped dead on that golf course in Spain, I was at the Waldorf Hotel in New York City, waiting to fly to England where, and here's where it gets coincidental, I was going to meet Bing in London. Why? We were scheduled to make our first picture together in fifteen years. *The Road to the Fountain of Youth*. I knew instantly there was no reason for me to go on to England. The project was over. My phone was suddenly ringing off the hook. Every reporter in America wanted to talk to me about Bing's death. Once I was over the initial shock, I told myself I had to get out of town before I went nuts. I went down a special service elevator, to the car, boom, right to the airport to catch the next flight back to L.A. Yeah, Bing. What a guy! And we never got to make that last Road Picture together."

When Hope talks about the USO shows he did for the military beginning in 1942 and continuing as recently as the Gulf War, he chuckles, shakes his head and says, "They were something. The shows, the boys. That was a great privilege to do those shows. I was so damned lucky to fall into that. When Phyllis Diller went on her first tour, I said, 'Now you gotta go through the hospitals.' On our first hospital visit, she came out in tears and told me, 'I don't

Phyllis Diller and Bob Hope as they perform together during Hope's 1967 Christmas Tour in Vietnam.

wanna do that again. I don't wanna see those boys lying in beds all shot to pieces.' I replied, 'You're gonna do it again. That's why we're here.' And Phyllis did it for the rest of the tour."

Next, he tells me about his own tough moment walking into a ward filled with wounded American soldiers. "It was in 1944 when we flew to an island in the Pacific called Pavuvu. The units there were preparing for what would become the battle for Peleliu. A terrible battle. Our military commanders miscalculated what it would cost. Turned out to be one of the worst in the Pacific War. We lost more than 2,000 troops. Thousands more wounded. Well, we did our show for those boys just before the battle. They really cheered us on. I can still see their faces and hear them shouting."

"A couple of months later," Hope continues, "we flew into Oakland, California, where we went to a military hospital. As I walked into the ward, a wounded Marine saw me and raised a fist. 'Pavuvu!' he shouted. Suddenly other men in the ward, who had been

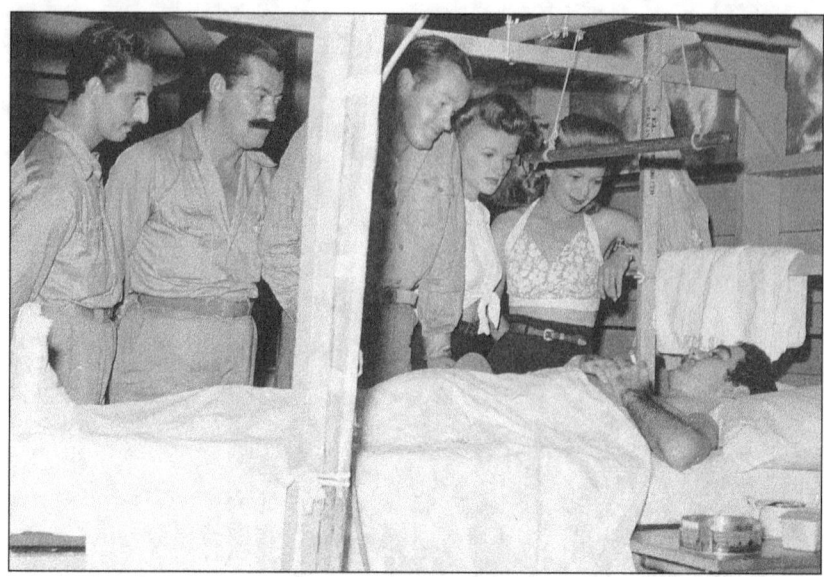

Visiting wards of wounded soldiers was always a must for Bob Hope and his fellow performers. In this 1943 photo, we see (left to right) jazz guitarist-singer Tony Romano, comedian Jerry Colonna, Hope, dancing "All American Girl" Patty Thomas and singer Frances Langford.

badly wounded and were missing arms and legs and God knows what else, shouted 'Pavuvu.' It was their way of telling me they'd been there and seen our show.

"Tears started running down my cheeks. I couldn't take it any longer and had to step out of the ward. In the hallway, I pulled myself together, and a couple minutes later went back in. That turned out to be the hardest moment for me during any of my tours. But, like I told Phyllis Diller, seeing the boys was something you *had* to do."

Hope also tells me about some dangerous moments. "One time, our radio went out when we were flying through the mountains up in Anchorage and this general, he put up the anti-aircraft lights. Our pilot, thank God, saw those lights and we landed safely. If you were gonna quit, you would've quit right then and there. You couldn't worry about the danger. Yeah, we were lucky to fly to so many faraway places with strange-sounding names and live to tell about all those trips."

Hope refers twice to a drawer full of letters sent to him by parents of soldiers killed in the wars. "They were so grateful that we'd

Ann Jillian, one-time actress and now a motivational speaker, appearing with Bob Hope during his 1983 Christmas tour of Beirut and Lebanon.

given their sons some fun, a little joy. But I can't read those letters anymore. I gave them all to Linda." Hope brightens when asked to reflect on his wealth, which includes large amounts of acreage in Palm Springs and the Santa Monica Mountains. (In 1984, Forbes magazine valued Hope's assets at around $115 million.)

It all started when an oil well hit a gusher in 1949. "It was the first well that came in Skoura County, Texas. Bing and I, we'd put up a few hundred thousand dollars each. I was there to see the gusher come in. God, we were lucky dudes." Lucky to the tune of about $4 million for each of them, which Hope then used to buy up large portions of California real estate.

Questions about Hope's so-called "hawkish attitudes" in the early years of the Vietnam War, about the unpleasant image of Crosby that has emerged since his death, about his differences with conservatives over the development of some of his land holdings—all wash over him as if they had never happened. "Naw, none of those things upset me. I made nine trips to Vietnam. A small majority thought I was supporting the Vietnam War. I was anti-war.

Who wouldn't be after seeing those wounded boys? As for the land, I gave some of it away [in 1990]. And I donated 80 acres for the Eisenhower Medical Center in Palm Desert [in 1966]."

Outside, someone is watering the expansive grass and another worker is covering up the chaise longues at the side of the pool. Hope watches, then turns back in his chair. "You know, money means one thing to me: doing the things I want to do, and helping people. If I didn't have that land, it wouldn't worry me."

Queried about the "ski slope" that is his nose, he burst out laughing. "Nothing ever happens to it. This is what mom and dad gave me." He shouts, his voice echoing through the large living room. "'Hey, Ski! Hey, Ski!' Bing used to call me that once in a while. 'Hey, Ski.'"

Does he attribute his great success to more than luck? "My knowledge of comedy," he answers. "Timing, definitely timing. In acting, everything is in the eyes. The eyes tell the story. When I see pieces of my old pictures once in a while, I realize I'm dreaming with my eyes on that screen. It makes me laugh, it's so silly."

Hope once said that laughter opens up all our arteries, and he still believes that. "Laughter is the greatest thing in the world for you. It gives us new, better personalities. Humor is something you turn to in a dark moment." Hope has also said, "A little love, a little laugh every day and you're way ahead of the rest of the world." That's a motto, he says, "I still believe in."

About his theme song on radio and TV, "Thanks for the Memories," which was introduced in *The Big Broadcast of 1938* IN A SEQUENCE ABOARD A LUXURY LINER. "SHIRLEY ROSS AND I SANG THAT TOGETHER AS A DIVORCED COUPLE RECALLING THE HIGHLIGHTS OF THEIR MARRIAGE. IT WASN'T INTENDED TO BE FUNNY, BUT VERY EMOTIONAL. THE WAY SHIRLEY AND I DID THAT SONG, IT WAS WELL REMEMBERED, A HIT. I DECIDED TO USE IT AS A RECURRING THEME AT THE END OF EACH OF MY RADIO SHOWS. AS IF IT'S SAD THAT I'M GOING OFF THE AIR. I SANG IT FOR YEARS, NOT ONLY ON RADIO BUT ON TV. OUR GAL FROM THE ROAD PICTURES, DOROTHY LAMOUR, SHE EVEN CUT A RECORD VERSION THAT WAS SWELL. YOU CAN'T HEAR IT WITHOUT

THINKING OF A GUY NAMED BOB HOPE. YEAH, WHAT A SONG."

Golf is a sport he has done much to promote and bring into the consciousness of America, especially in its early years, before it became so popular. "It's still a daily event in my life. It's a challenge you never completely conquer. You're fighting yourself on the golf course. When I shoot a good score, I feel great." He recalls his best golf game without a second of hesitation. "In 1951. A handicap of four. You know, we played, Bing and I, back when people didn't know anything about golf. Spectators used to stand on the sidelines and yell 'Sissy, sissy' when we took a swing. Later they didn't yell sissy when they had TV and saw that a four-foot putt could be the difference between $5,000 or $10,000 in prize money."

Lunch finished, Hope proposes a tour of his upstairs office. He would like to show me his new computer. He leads the way through a hallway off the kitchen, humming a little ditty under his breath. He waits for me up on the landing of the second floor, then whirls around and heads toward a room down the hallway.

I freeze at the top of the steps. Lining both sides of the corridor are glass-encased photographs of all the presidents since Roosevelt posing with Hope, all of them autographed. Harry S. Truman, Dwight D. Eisenhower, John F. Kennedy, Lyndon B. Johnson, Richard Nixon, and Gerald Ford. Further along the walls, signed photographs of all the generals and other military figures he met during his USO tours. Hope stands proudly, watching me as I pass from photo to photo. He doesn't bother to show me his new computer. That was just an excuse.

Hope leads the way back to the front room, ready for another appointment. Outside, the lawn is still being mowed. "Bought half this acreage for $12,500 back in '38. Offered the same amount for the other half, but got turned down. Ended up having to buy it for $40,000 a year later. What a lesson that was."

With so many milestones in his life, is there anything left to conquer at ninety? He thinks for a moment, the whirring of the lawn mower still audible. "Yeah, there is something. But what I'd like to do is impossible. I'd like, just once, to win a golf tournament... [or] how about hosting another Academy Award show?"

The photograph Bob Hope signed for our son Russ.

Before leaving Hope's home, I ask him if he would sign an extra photograph for our son Russ. He is more than willing. He hands me the photo, wishes me well, and opens the front door. One of my favorite interviews out of thousands has just ended.

Amazingly, Bob Hope lived to reach the age of 100 years. But just two months later, following a bad case of pneumonia, he died at his home in Toluca Lake. Shortly before death, when asked by his wife where he wanted to be buried, he was alleged to have replied, "Surprise me." He was interred in the San Fernando Mission Cemetery, in a section called the Bob Hope Memorial Garden. But I wonder if he was surprised . . . .

BING CROSBY
On the Road Again, For the Very First Time, To Meet The Crooner

In Hillsborough, California, on the first week of January 1970, I am still sobering up from the Christmas and New Year's holiday when I cautiously drive to Hillsborough, a posh district on the Peninsula south of San Francisco. Knowing that Bing Crosby lived several months of the year in the Bay Area, I had always wanted to meet and profile him, but there had never been an excuse. Now, with the 29th Annual Bing Crosby National Pro-Am Golf Tournament taking place in Pebble Beach very soon, and a publicist on my tail about covering it, I have my long-awaited invite.

The Crosby home on Jackling Drive, built in 1930, is a French Normandy-style 10,000-square-foot mansion with ten bedroom suites, a ballroom, and even a chauffeur's apartment, among many other classy things. *Plenty of class*, I tell myself, as a maid welcomes me at the door. Kathryn Grant Crosby, Crosby's second wife of thirteen years, is busy taking ornaments off a Christmas tree in the massive front room as I enter. Wearing a robe and her hair in curlers, she gives me a simple nod of her head as I start up a staircase leading to what the maid has described as "Mr. Crosby's office-study." (Kathryn will become a recurring figure, but more about her later.)

I notice two things when I enter the library-like retreat into which the maid has led me. A heavy rain is beating against the second-story window, and a Labrador Retriever is curled up at the foot of an orange leather chair.

The third thing I notice is Bing Crosby.

The singer-actor icon is seated at a large desk, hunched over a pile of paper work, and seems to be relieved he can now leave it all behind as he stands up to greet me and introduce his companion as Remus, "an excellent duck and pheasant-hunting dog." I am stunned for a moment, hearing for the first time one of the most

Bing Crosby's standard photograph at the time of my visit, which he signed to my wife Erica as our interview came to a close. It has hung on the wall of my den for twenty years and shows signs of deterioration: speckles cover Crosby's face and the inscription has blurred, proving even our favorite pictures sometimes show an age all their own.

famous voices in show business—in the world, often described as bass-baritone. As I stand with my mouth slightly ajar, Remus looks at me briefly with seeming disinterest, lowers his head to the hardwood floor with a light thud, and is soon back to sleep.

Crosby plops into a nearby couch, propping up one leg on a small table in front of him. The essence of leisure, the personification of casual. It is the Bing Crosby image he has portrayed for most of his career as singer, comedian, actor, TV star. I devour as much of the image as I can, knowing this will probably be the one and only time I will have an opportunity to probe him for good quotes.

Is this Bing Crosby trying to create that sound with a bubble in it?

The room has a masculine flavor with its ornate wood carvings and a shelf lined with twenty-two Decca Gold Record Awards, including the one for "White Christmas," which, to this day, according to Guinness World Records, remains the most popular recording of all time. In view are other impressive trophies, such as his 1963 Grammy Global Achievement Award, reflecting his career as singer and actor.

Historically, Crosby could wrap his velvety voice around a song, no matter how hackneyed the lyrics. The sound came out as fresh as new-baked bread pops from an oven. He gave those lyrics an enunciated clarity and explored gradations in projecting his voice. One observer said Crosby linked with "electric current as if he were making love to a woman."

Crosby brought a relaxed interpretation to compositions that created a new style and trend in singing popular music. His emotions seemed heartfelt, and that emotion was passed on to the listener.

I begin by reminding him that from 1934-1955, when he was under contract to Decca Records, he enjoyed 300 hits. Crosby did

"Play that thing, Pops," Bing tells Louis Armstrong during one of their musical production numbers done for Bing's TV series. Their best on-screen piece together was "That's Jazz," a brilliant combination of music and comedy in High Society (1956).

400 more recordings than Sinatra. He sold an estimated billion records and had more hits than even Elvis Presley, The Beatles, and Josie and the Pussycats combined.

Mentioning all these facts, I see a smile cross Crosby's face. "My notion of singing," he tells me, "was to make a sound that resembled the human voice with a bubble in it." As if he is putting me on, he adds: "I just sing the way it comes out when I open my mouth." (I had been forewarned that Crosby might underplay his incredible success in an effort to make sure his feet are still on firm earth.)

Orchestra leader Artie Shaw once called Crosby "the first hip White person born in the United States." Reminded of this, Crosby admits that jazz was something he learned growing up in Spokane. For one, Mildred Bailey, the Rockin' Chair lady. He also got to see Al Jolson, Eddie Cantor, Savoy and Brennan, the

That's Bob Hope on the left as a Cleveland Indian, pitching his jokes to Crosby, who has donned the garb of a Pittsburgh Pirate to field the jokes. Each owned a percentage of the team they are dressed for.

Avon Comedy Four. Jazz was something to emulate, but Louis Armstrong was the strongest influence. They made several films together, including *High Society* (1956), in which they performed "That's Jazz," describing the name and purpose of each member of Armstrong's *All-Stars* group. Louis also gave him the idea to do skat, making nonsensical sounds that often imitated musical instruments. (Crosby's *boo boo boo*, for example, can be found in his 1933 musical, *Too Much Harmony*.)

I ask him, with so much wealth and success behind him, why does he continue to work so hard? "Oh, I don't work that hard," he says, with a touch of laughter. "I spend maybe sixty days out of the year to do an average of fifteen shows. Jackie Gleason, Carol Burnett, Dean Martin, *The Hollywood Palace*. I've even resorted to being on Bob Hope's shows, even if it is a career comedown."

There's something, he continues, "inside an entertainer. Hard to describe. But we have to be turned on now and them. Take Bob Hope. I've seen him totally exhausted, yet a little applause and he'll snap back to full life with the energy of a child. Or, hand Hope a golf club at the end of an exhaustive world tour and he's ready to go again. You see, performing becomes a part of us we can never lose."

So relaxed, so at ease . . . I ask Crosby about comedy, a major part of his repertoire. "I just lean back and let that happy side wind its way out of me. Working with Hope, it all came so easily. I'd kid him, he'd kid me. Ad libbed or scripted, something worked."

They were also both instrumental in advancing the game of golf when he was still new to America. "It's a sport we both fell in love with early in our careers, and many of our best moments were clowning around from the first tee to the last, not to mention fun we had at the 19th hole. We loved sports, and that's why we each bought our own ball team. Bob, he came from Cleveland and that's why he bought a share of the Cleveland Indians. Me, I loved the Pittsburgh Pirates, so Bob and I would slip into our team uniforms and have as much fun hanging out in the bullpens as we did playing golf."

Crosby stares out the window at the rain, admitting he would rather be duck hunting today than staying home and doing paperwork. Remus raises his head from the hardwood floor as if to agree, then plops down with his eyes closed.

Crosby resumes: "I was very lucky through my years in show biz. Mainly because I was always willing to take a chance. A producer or director would come along and offer me something different, and I'd automatically do it, despite my misgivings." His cooperative attitude, he points out, really paid off big time when he went into a recording studio to record "White Christmas" for the very first time with the Ken Darby Singers and John Scott Trotter's Orchestra. "Several musical versions had been prepared with Irving Berlin's lyrics and they were piled up on a podium in front of me," Crosby recalls. "I was asked to check each and pick the one I liked best. I shrugged and said the one on the top would be fine. And that's the one I did, and everything was fabulous."

Crosby, Joan Collins, and Bob Hope in The Road to Hong Kong (1962), the last film in the Road Pictures series. It was directed by Norman Panama, who had started out as a writer for Hope's radio show in the late 1930s. A minor British starlet at the time, Collins later enjoyed great success in America on the TV series Dynasty.

If there was ever a guiding light in his career it had been Jack Kapp of Decca Records. "An utter inspiration, that man. He'd talk me into doing hymns, patriotic songs, marching numbers, light opera, country and western, hillbilly even. Anything and everything. I sang with every kind of band and every kind of entertainer, from Dixieland to Duke Ellington to cowboy melodies. And each one paid off. Because I had been willing to branch out, I would find an entirely new audience with each new piece of territory."

What is his best talent? Singing? Acting? Comedy? "That's just it," he answers, "I don't have a best. My greatest weakness? The fact I was never trained for any of the things I do. My greatest strength? The fact I was never trained for any of the things I do. I was always able to remain myself, or whatever Bing Crosby was supposed to be. But that really shouldn't be the key to success. A good actor should be many people, transporting himself into whatever personality a role requires. I still want to find out for

There was a constant change of costumes in the Road Pictures so Bing and Bob would fit into the culture they were traveling through. This obviously is a scene from The Road to Morocco *(1942).*

myself if I can play good character roles. And that's why, you see, I'm still a success."

About his movies with Bob Hope that came to be called Road Pictures. "I always tried to convey a sense of humor through my characters in the musicals I made as far back as the 1930s. When they brought Bob and I together for *The Road to Singapore* [1940], Bob would make changes to the script which, in most cases, were funnier than the original material. I never argued, we just did it and argued with the director later. We kept breaking down the fourth wall. In one scene, we were on a freighter shoveling coal into the furnaces. We're sweating like crazy and suddenly a well-dressed man wearing a top hat, who looks like he's on his way to the opera, steps up. We ask him if he's in this movie with us. He shakes his head and says, 'No, I'm taking a shortcut to sound stage six.' That's the crazy kind of stuff we used to do, and we loved doing it."

"Making feature films, I enjoyed that phase of my career. Most of my pictures were light- hearted, easy-to-forget romances. Who'd want to miss *Pennies From Heaven* [1936], *Rhythm on the Range* [1936], or *Waikiki Wedding* [1937]. But playing Father O'Malley in

Crosby in costume for the character of Doc Boone in the 1966 remake of Stagecoach, opposite Ann-Margret and Alex Cord.

Smoking a pipe and using it as a prop, Crosby always conveyed the pleasant image of a relaxed, unpretentious performer. It is the image I will always have of him.

Going My Way [1944], stopping to play baseball with kids on the street, singing 'Swinging on a Star' and 'Silent Night,' it was non-stop fun. What I was always looking for, though, was a role that called for real acting. Not just Mr. Nice Guy. I tried it in *The Country Girl* [1954] with Grace Kelly. I was a damn alcoholic showman and did my best. Got nominated for another Oscar, but didn't win that one. Then I tried it again in the '66 remake of *Stagecoach*, playing the gambler, a philosophical drunk. Well, it was pretty good while it lasted."

Was there any one piece of advice he would like to pass on to potential entertainers? "George M. Cohan gave me my best advice. He said, 'Get off the stage while they're still applauding.' Always try to give them not quite enough. And never sing the same things. A good singer moves in as many arenas as possible. Whether the parish hall, a picnic gathering, a revival meeting, the PTA or the Most Beautiful Theater in the World. *Get up off your butt and do the thing you do best.*"

Crosby walks over to the window as the rain continues to pound against the pane. Yeah," he says with a wink, "it's a great day, isn't it?"

Remus, still curled up on the hardwood floor, unfazed by nostalgia or memories of the good old days, just keeps on dreaming his way through heaven for canines.

Much to my wonderment, a few days after my interview with Bing ran in the Sunday section of the *San Francisco Chronicle*, I received a letter from the crooner himself. I filed it away with many other such collectibles and did not see it again until preparing this book. I was utterly shocked that Crosby had enjoyed the article enough to write me his thoughts about it, given the passage of forty-five years. Here is that letter:

Bing Crosby

Hillsborough
January 23, 1970

Dear John:

Thank you for sending me the tear-sheets from the paper. I enjoyed very much the article you did on me, and I think it's beautifully written, and certainly contained an accurate representation of my views - trivial as they are.

I've been interviewed a great deal in the last few years, and I always felt that it was more or less going over old territory, but you discovered some new approaches that made the article interesting and attractive.

Thank you very much -

Always yours,

Bing Crosby

BC:lm

Mr. John Stanley
Editorial Department
SAN FRANCISCO CHRONICLE
San Francisco, California

KATHRYN GRANT CROSBY

Okay, I'll be the first to admit that Bing Crosby's second wife never tried to be a comedienne, but she was an excellent mother, successfully raising two sons (Harry and Nathaniel) and a daughter (Mary Crosby, now an actress) and achieving in many different arenas of endeavor. One was becoming a TV hostess in the city of San Francisco. That's when I came along, and I will always remember her depth and beauty on the day we met.

Kathryn Grant Crosby was the electricity in Bing's life. It is one thing to be attracted to her beauty and charm; it is another to become the center of her attention, to feel her inquisitive brown eyes scan everything in sight like pieces of delicate radar equipment. You become data that is probed and quickly computed. When the scanning begins, suddenly that which was simply beautiful and decorative takes on a preciously human substance. Her curiosity and well-attuned senses crackle the air and bring everything about her to life. There is also a gentle smile that tugs at the corners of Kathryn's mouth, as if she knows your deepest and perhaps darkest secrets. You sense a touch of electricity and can only speculate (while examining those flashing eyes and soft-painted mouth) what thoughts are ruminating in that agile mind. I am before her to discuss a TV show she will do for a major San Fran-

Kathryn Grant Crosby, around the time of our rendezvous.

On the big screen, Kathryn Grant portrays a lovely princess, who is shrunken to peanut size by a wicked wizard in The Seventh Voyage of Sinbad *(1958), in which heroic Kerwin Mathews must rescue her from giant monsters created by special effects master Ray Harryhausen.*

cisco CBS-affiliate station (KPIX), but I am really before her to learn more about Bing Crosby, to whom she has been married since 1957. Make that seventeen years, for it is August 1974, at a time when she has earned her Registered Nurse certificate, when she has had three children with Bing, and when she has a certificate to teach elementary school. Now she's becoming a TV host.

Her relationship with Bing, she tells me, has always been "relaxed." In fact, she recalls, "the first time we met, I was interviewing him for a column I was writing for a newspaper, and he made me feel like a little girl from Texas again. He asked me to dinner—I accepted.

Swingers on a golf course: Kathryn and Bing, sometime during the 1960s when their marriage was at its height. He was producing songs, she was producing three children.

"I was fascinated by him, but it was not love at first sight, like many believe. The romance part grew over the next couple of years while I was starting to build a career in Hollywood, especially with *Anatomy of a Murder* [1959]. I don't know about love at first sight, but I do know there is strong attraction between the sexes, and it was certainly a case of that."

Bing, she claims, has refused to help her in certain situations. "So I've had to learn how to be many things. You have to respect that in a man, because it certainly contributes to the growth of our marriage. Bing is a special man, who would never impose his thoughts on me."

Kathryn prefers that you don't ask intimate questions about her and Bing, although she will confess to sleeping in "flannel granny nightgowns and tennis socks with the electric blanket turned to number 4, even in August."

As for the thirty-year difference in their ages, the only problem is "keeping up to Bing on the golf course."

My interview with Kathryn Grant Crosby runs on Sunday, and first thing Monday morning, when I settle behind my desk at the *San Francisco Chronicle*, I receive a call from Mrs. Crosby, thanking me for the publicity. Then she tells me the real reason: "This hosting business is going to be a big challenge to me, and I was hoping you might give me some advice. Since you meet and interview people all the time . . . please tell me, how do you host a TV show?"

I am totally startled, stunned, even shocked, by the question. Mrs. Bing Crosby, the one and only, is asking me how one goes about being a TV host. (For me, hosting *Creature Features* is still a few years down the highway, and at the moment I have a difficult time just hosting a Halloween party. So I try to think fast and give her some kind of help. And it comes to me! Bing, her very husband! He's the answer! How brilliant am I?)

I encourage her to speak directly to her husband, Bing, one of the great showmen of our time. After all, he's hosted radio and TV episodes by the hundreds. Surely he could advise her like no one else.

"Oh no," she instantly, flatly responds. "I already tried that with Bing. And he said there was no way on earth he was going to tell me how to run my life. I'm on my own!"

Even though I wasn't much help to her that day, a few weeks later I received an invitation from Kathryn to drop by the Crosby residence in Hillsborough to help her cook quail in the kitchen and eat on the terrace. Work, however, prevented me from at-

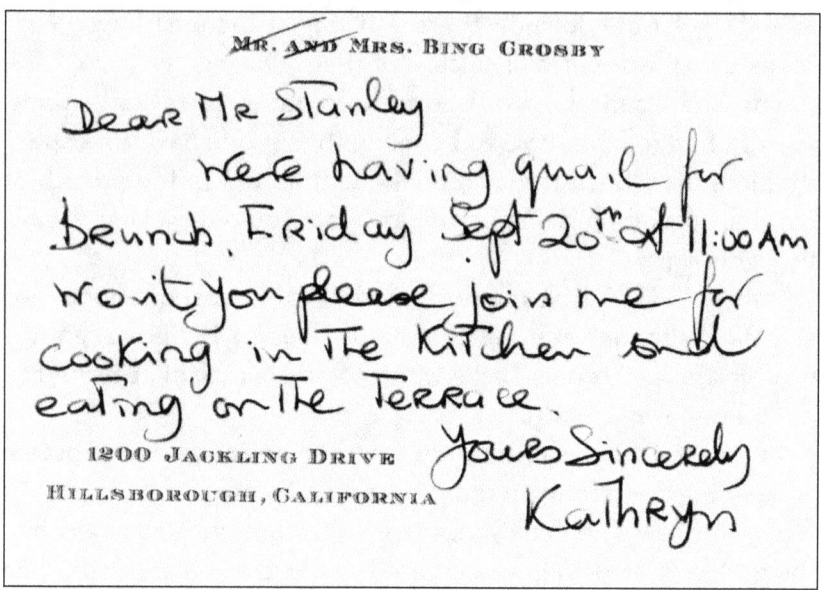

This is the invitation Kathryn Crosby sent me, but due to a conflicting work schedule, I could not break bread with her and Bing. A major disappointment.

tending and I missed a Golden Opportunity to meet the Crosbys one more time.

I will meet Kathryn Grant Crosby one more time in the late 1980s at the Fairmont Hotel. Singing star Rosemary Clooney opens her show one Thursday night in the Venetian Room and, as usual, Erica and I have been invited to attend the opening night. I am told in advance there will be a cocktail party on an upper floor after the show and to come on up, meet Ms Clooney, and get to know her a little.

Sounds good. So after her opening performance, Erica and I take an elevator up to the meeting room. It's low-key lighting when we enter, but I see Ms Clooney surrounded by other reporters, and I walk over and join the discussion. Suddenly, a woman stands at my side and asks if I would like a cocktail. I tell her that wine will be good for both of us but don't turn to look at her until she starts to walk back to a nearby makeshift bar. I freeze, not believing my eyes. Is that Kathryn Grant Crosby I see as she reaches the bar and begins mixing drinks? Ah, it can't be. I'm seeing things.

Bing Crosby's wife, relegated to being a bartender? I whisper to Erica what I think I've seen, and we turn and study her in the dim lighting. Erica nudges me. *"That's Kathryn all right!"* Before long she's bringing us our drinks and I don't have to tell her who I am, she remembers me as that "happy go lucky newspaperman" from those good old days. She and Rosemary Clooney, she explains, are the best of friends and she wanted to be here to help in whatever way she could—and that includes tending bar. What are old friends for, anyway? And she thanks me for helping her get her TV show started. And I remember how Bing had resisted helping her to deal with becoming a hostess. Life is certainly full of surprises!

Following Bing's death in 1977, Kathryn did more than help good friends serve cocktails. She kept herself busy by demonstrating a talent for oil paintings and by returning off and on to theatrical productions. That includes making her Broadway debut in 1996 in *State Fair*. She has also written two books, *My Life With Bing* and *Bing and Other Things*. Unfortunately, in 2010, her ten-year marriage to Maurice W. Sullivan, an educator that once helped the Crosbys raise their three children and who had become trustee of the Crosby estate after Bing's death—ended in a tragic accident on Highway 50, outside of Placerville, CA. Sullivan's vehicle went out of control and he was thrown from the car and killed. Kathryn sustained injuries and was hospitalized for a month before being released. Life, even for one as beautiful, hard-working, determined, and dedicated as Kathryn Grant Crosby, has never been easy.

GEORGE BURNS
Straight Man to the Comedy Bombardment of The Calmest Comedian Alive

"And if you should survive / To be 105 / Look at all you'd derive / Out of being alive / And here is the best part / You'd have a head start / If you are among the very young at heart."
–From "Young at Heart" by
Johnny Richards and Carolyn Leigh

    The words float smoothly and gently out of the portable tape recorder on George Burns' desk. In Hollywood, looking very alive at eighty-six—and here is the best part—he is seated on a chair on the side of that desk, having relinquished his command seat to yours truly in a funny way. A long cigar poised classically in one hand, he leans back and listens with a bemused, pleased look to the sound of his own voice. He might have just swallowed Tweety Bird. I lean back in the comedian's chair, but there's no way I am going to command the interview or wisecrack like he constantly does. Nothing comes out of Burns' mouth without passing through a filtering process that seeks out a comedic climax.
    It is April, 1982, and we are listening to a brand-new recording of "Young at Heart" for Burns' third album that was recorded in Nashville, Tennessee. Outside, rain is beating against the window, and the song's lilting melody cuts through the grayness of the morning. The setting is Francis Ford Coppola's Zoetrope Studios, purchased so he would have his own facilities to produce *One From the Heart*. (The film would fail at the box office and Coppola would soon lose the studio and return to his production headquarters in San Francisco.) Formerly known as National General, the studio has served as Burns' business headquarters since 1952, when he moved his TV series, *The Burns and Allen Show*, from New York to shoot their six remaining seasons on the sound stages nearby.

George Burns with his ubiquitous cigar, which gave him a relaxed, sophisticated look ... quite different from the image that filled the viewer's mind once he began delivering his one-liners.

(At one time, National General serviced TV producers who were not permitted to film in any of the major studios, an edict established when TV first came into being, and which wasn't broken until Walt Disney made a deal in 1953 with ABC for a series—all because Walt needed money to create Disneyland. Among those initial producers was Desi Arnaz, who had begun filming *I Love Lucy* on these very premises in 1951.)

Every morning, precisely at ten o'clock, Burns arrives here, meets his team of writers, and undergoes a two-hour brainstorming session (never longer than that, given the coming of the lunch hour and the "shortage" of brainpower). Today, those writers are "collaborators" Seaman Jacobs and Fred Fox, who have spent a good share of their time writing for Bob Hope, and an ex-Jack Benny gagman, Hal Goldman.

Their objective this morning is to create some sizzling jokes and zinging one-liners for a forthcoming Cary Grant dinner-roast Burns will host at the Friars Club in New York City. Burns stylishly flicks ashes off his cigar tip and points toward his writers. "We do everything off the top of our heads, which are mostly bald by now. Nobody comes in with anything on paper. If they do, I tear the sheets up. We start from scratch and kick each other around. I mean, we kick each idea around. Their ideas get kicked more than mine. Then we select the best stuff. Mostly my stuff. But I'm lenient with the boys. I allow them to work anywhere else they want after twelve o'clock for fifty-two weeks a year. Just so I get a piece of their action."

Also seated in Burns' office, mother-henning everything along with a light-hearted attitude, is Irving Fein, who handles all of Burns' business affairs on an exclusive basis. That means Fein has no other clients, and is available 24 hours a day to service but one living being, Burns.

Burns now smiles in Fein's direction. Fein sits silently, not responding facially or verbally, as if this is the way it always is with Burns. He does the talking, Fein plays the silent figure. "Irving Fein tells me what to do. If I like it, I do it, and if I don't like it, I make Irving Fein do it. Irving Fein and I've been together off and on for thirty years. A lot of it has been off. Irving Fein handled Jack Benny for twenty-five years. Toward the end of Jack's career, when Jack wasn't working as much, Irving Fein came to me and asked if he could handle my affairs. I said, 'Okay, but you better ask Jack.' Jack said, 'Sure.' That was nice of him. Even if I still had to pay Benny a ten per cent commission."

Burns' office suite, modest by most Hollywood-executive standards, is filled with memorabilia of his show biz career, which dates back to a Vaudevillian song-and-dance routine he did in his teens, followed by some trick roller-skating and stand-up comedy acts, before breaking into the big time. The cover of *Life* magazine for Sept. 22, 1958, announces the retirement of Gracie Allen, the comedienne who was Burns' costar and wife for nearly four decades in Vaudeville, radio, and TV, and who projected an endearing wackiness that was always a complement to Burns' laid-back straight-man style. Her reason for retiring at sixty-three: increasing bad health, a failing heart. That struggle continued until her death in 1964.

There are copies of his first two albums (*I Wish I was 18 Again* and *George Burns in Nashville*), and there are photographs of Burns dancing with Bing Crosby and Jack Benny in straw hats and spats. In one corner is Burns' Academy Award for *The Sunshine Boys*, the 1976 Neil Simon film comedy that marked his comeback following open-heart surgery two years earlier. Over in another corner, his Emmy for *George Burns' One-Man Show* (1977) and a cover of *TV Guide* dominated by Burns' head. Sure, they evoke old memories, but he says they have helped to keep him young and alive each morning that he comes here.

"Young at Heart" concludes. I ask Burns if he'd care to sing a few bars in person—just so we can see how the old tubes sound in the raw. He shakes his cigar. "I only sing to get paid," he says, "and you don't look like the type who can afford my extravagant price."

In the past he has always been put down as a warbler, but this morning he seems totally serious as he adds, "I have a whole new career as a country singer and I sing pretty good, and the songs aren't bad." He explains that he just got back from London, where he sang at a new music center that's even bigger than the one in Los Angeles. "I sang for Prince Charles and Lady Diane, for all those lords and ladies. But I didn't sing 'God Save the Queen.' It's not in my key."

George Burns was born Nathan Birnbaum in 1986 in New York City to parents from Romania. He was the ninth of twelve children (seven girls, five boys). "We were so poor," he reminisces, "we kids couldn't afford to have parents." His father was Louis Phillip Birnbaum, and his mother was Dorothy Bluth, who were victims of a prearranged marriage back in Europe, and hence not the most romantic couple of all time once all the children had been conceived and delivered. "My father," George pointed out, "should've been a watchmaker, because us kids, we came like clockwork." Louis pressed pants in a sweatshop and the family lived on Rivington Street. Not the greatest, as George and his brothers and sisters had to walk down three flights to an outdoor toilet.

Nathan joined with other Jewish children in the neighborhood to form what they called The Peewee Quartet. One day, they were invited to perform at a nearby Presbyterian church. "We opened the program with 'When Irish Eyes Are Smiling.' We sang so good each of us was given a wristwatch. I ran home to tell my mother, 'I don't wanna be Jewish anymore.'

"'Why not?' mother countered, shocked to the core of her soul.

"I replied, 'Well, I've been a Jew for seven years and have nothing to show for it. I'm a Presbyterian for one day and now I've got this wristwatch, which the church gave me.' Mom was so upset she sent me to bed without dinner. I came down for breakfast the next morning and rushed to find mom. 'I wanna be Jewish again,' I told her. 'Nathan, what is going on with you?' I pointed at my wrist. 'That watch I told you about? Last night it stopped working.' Mom sent me back to bed."

Nathan's father, never a very good provider, became so disenchanted with his work that he quit pressing shirts and pants and just wandered through the neighborhood or spent hours at the local synagogue. "One afternoon, papa came home very happy for having helped the rabbi hold a special event—for which papa had received nothing in return. Mama pointed this out to him. 'But,' said papa, 'they've invited me to come back for the next event.'"

In 1903, when he was forty-seven, Louis was to die during a flu epidemic, forcing Nathan (all of seven years) to take whatever job he could to help support the large family. Eventually he worked his way into Vaudeville and met a singer in The Four Colleens group.

She was a devotee Catholic, a lovely entertainer named Grace Ethel Cecile Allen, "Gracie" to her friends—and lover. She looked the part of the pert young Irish dancer she had been when she

George Burns and Gracie Allen during their early years in radio—proving to be a comedy team that would last more than thirty years.

sidled her way into show business in the years before World War I. She grew up on the stage, and was a seasoned show business professional when she teamed with Burns in 1922, in a conventional song-and-dance-and-light-comedy act.

"Came the day," says George, "when Gracie had to rush home and tell her mother she was going to marry a Jew and not a Catholic. Mother reportedly replied, 'Oh, don't worry about it, Gracie dear, I'm sure George will get over it.'

"January 7, 1926, was the most important day of my life. That's when audiences discovered I had a big talent, and I stayed married to that talent for thirty-eight years."

Audiences liked Gracie, liked her fresh-faced, open way with a line, to the point where her straight lines drew more laughs than George's gags. Burns was a canny enough performer to recognize her appeal, and switched the act around to make her the comic—and from there, Burns and Allen took off. But don't think for a moment she created all that comedy while George merely stood beside her. It was George who gathered with writers to shape the monologues for the stage, and later the comic exchanges for their popular TV series.

"Throughout the '30s," explains George, "we had a wonderful time making movies. *International House* (1933) with W. C. Fields, *Love in Bloom* (1935), *College Holiday* (1936). In fact, that decade was a holiday for us. One of those joys was making *Damsel in Distress* (1937) with Fred Astaire. Gracie and I had known the dancing team Evans and Evans, and we remembered they did a whisk-broom dance. One of the brothers came to our home and taught us how to use the brooms and we convinced Astaire to let us do it as a musical number in the film. We literally gave Fred the brush off."

Radio lasted for nineteen years, followed by the TV series for eight. "Freddie De Cordova was our director and he'd often argue with me, then go storming out, saying he would never return. So, I'd always send Freddie's mother a dozen roses." One day, George saw an angry De Cordova stalking across the stage toward him. "Before Freddie could say a word I told him I'd already sent his mother a dozen roses. A short time later, I found out that Freddie owned the flower shop."

Just because he's eighty-six, Burns points out, "that's no reason for me to be slowing down. If you slow down too much there's always the risk of your motor dying." So, Irving Fein is constantly getting offers for Burns' services. "I'm big in movies now. I'm a

A scene from the so-called "Brush-off Dance" in Damsel in Distress, *concocted by George and Gracie before they presented the idea to the film's star Fred Astaire, who loved it and incorporated it into the screenplay.]*

dramatic actor. I'm going to do a picture called The Old Detective. It's one of those murder mystery things. Who hasn't done a private-eye story at some time during a career? Even Bogart. He was a good actor. But even he wasn't a country singer." (No film matching his description of The Old Detective was ever made.)

When Burns underwent open heart surgery in 1974, he was to come out of it better in more ways than one. "You see," he explains, "Jack Benny was supposed to head to Florida to co-star with Walter Matthau in Sunshine Boys. But he had to drop out because of poor health. I'd been out of the hospital for two months when they asked me to take his place. Irving Fein advised me to do it, which I did. I went to Florida, and people were glad to see me. It was the first time I portrayed a character who was totally different from my comedy image. And it won me an Oscar for best supporting actor. So my advice to all young people, if they want to be successful, there is one thing they must absolutely

Here is George Burns reminding mankind of its virtues during his portrayal of the titular entity in Oh, God!, *which proved to be a cinematic high point in his career. He would have one Person to thank for that.*

do: have open-heart surgery. It got me started, and it'll get them started. You don't need jokes, you don't have to sing and dance. All you need is a damn good heart specialist. Make sure the surgeon is damn good, too."

When *The Sunshine Boys* (1975) proved Burns favorite axiom ("If you stay in the business long enough you get to be new again"), he was offered a script titled *Oh, God!*, which, at first, he didn't think much of. "What did I, George Burns, know about God? I'd never met him. (I may never meet him!) I couldn't even imagine what he would wear. But I finally realized, 'If you can't play God, who can you play?'

"So I just tried to be honest and believe the words." That film, made and released in 1977, helped Burns because "there were a lot of kids who related to me as God, and I discovered a whole new audience. They think I'm God. I am, you know. Irving Fein believes that."

Irving Fein's expression does not change nor does his body move.

"But now I only play God if I get paid."

Directed by Carl Reiner, Sid Caesar's one-time costar, *Oh, God!* was successful enough that Burns starred in a sequel, *Oh, God! II* (1980). Just prior to that, he had co-starred with Brooke Shields in *Just You and Me, Kid* (1979) and proved to be excellent as an octogenarian bank robber in *Going in Style* (1979), which co-starred Art Carney. "Given our ages," says Burns, "we did pretty good pulling off that daylight robbery."

A day in the life of George Burns begins at 7:30 a.m. with "lots of exercises, sit-ups, stretching maneuvers. A lot of touching the floor with my hands, if not my feet. Then I have breakfast. I don't eat any toast. Maybe some shredded wheat, a cup of prunes. It's been said of me often that I'm full of prunes. And always some coffee. Then I walk in my garden. I've been walking in my garden for forty-six years, which is how long I've lived in the same home in Beverly Hills. That's one year shorter than the age of the jokes I'm telling. So, I walk and I learn all my routines. My cook and butler follow along behind and have been trained to laugh in all the right places. Which is why I pay them.

"Then I come to the office for two hours. Then I have a light lunch at the Hillcrest Country Club: a cup of soup and an English muffin. I've been a member of the club for fifty years, and I used to sit at the Comedians' Round Table with all the great talents: Al Jolson, Groucho Marx, Jack Benny, Zeppo and Harpo, Eddie Cantor. Now the table is much smaller. Why did they die? Well, they'd died before. They'd died in Altoona, Schenectady, Scranton. Not to mention a few other places.

"After lunch? I play some bridge. Am I a good player? I'm not going to give up show business. Then I head for home for a two-hour nap. When I wake up I have a couple of martinis straight up. Usually I go out for a big dinner at Dominic's, Chasin's, Gatsby's, MacDonald's. I like to have at least one young woman with me. Tonight I have a date with three young women. All sing harmony. They're my backup singers. I will share a martini with each.

"They will light my cigar. I'll have a few more martinis. I'll enjoy my dinner. I do all the things other men do despite my age. Walter Matthau once asked me, 'George, when did sex stop for you?' I replied, 'Oh, about two o'clock yesterday morning.

"See, if you don't use it you lose it. I don't say I'm the world's greatest lover, but . . . well, I do come close. I feel fine about sex. I still enjoy it. I'm not going to give up anything, as a matter of fact. I was old when I was twenty-seven. Retirement is silly. What would I do if I retired? Play with my cuticles? I feel new and refreshed. I don't want to change that feeling."

Burns pauses to change the cassette in the small tape recorder residing on his desk. "This is one of the new songs in my album, written by the Gatlin Brothers. It says something about movies and why we're sometimes embarrassed to take the kids to the movies. What I mean is, innocence in movies has fled with the approach of blatant sex." He pushes the start button, leaning back in his chair. His eyes almost seem to twinkle. As his recorded voice drifts out accompanied by a country rhythm, he begins to look very pleased with himself and flicks the ashes off the end of his cigar toward his three gag writers, who have been sitting silently, listening to me and Burns exchange comments. Irving Fein still hasn't moved. And what I hear is this:

"Whatever happened to Randolph Scott, riding the trail alone?
Whatever happened to Gene and Tex, Roy and Rex and the Durango Kid?
Whatever happened to Smiley Burnette, Tim Holt and Gene Autry?
Whatever happened to all of these
That happened to the industry?"

George Burns promised several times he would live to be 100, and do a standup performance to prove he could still stand on his own two feet. But in 1994 things started to go bad when he fell in his bathtub and damaged his head so badly he had to undergo a major operation. Just a few weeks before his 100th birthday, he attended a Christmas party at the invitation of Frank Sinatra, but that night caught the flu. So, when that 100th birthday occurred on January 20, 1996, he was unable to attend any ceremonies. "If only," he joked, "I could have spent that day with Sharon Stone!" On March 9, 1996, he died of cardiac arrest. Just prior to death, he had commented that he was looking forward to the moment. After all, he and Gracie would be together again.

George and Gracie together for eternity.

LUCILLE BALL
A Phone Call to Remember
For Out-of-Town Press

I am about to leave my room at the Beverly Hills Hotel and rush to Santa Monica, to a place called Lawrence Welk Plaza, for I am scheduled this morning, in the summer of 1975, to interview the popular TV orchestra leader himself. Suddenly, the phone rings. It is Axel Peterson, my main contact at the CBS Television Network, informing me that if I am free for the evening, there is a very special story I should cover. The publicist can't tell me whom I will be meeting, but he guarantees it will be a moment to remember.

The only reason I'm being invited is because I'm "out of town press"—an entertainment reporter who does not live within the Los Angeles area. I will be one of only a handful of visiting columnists. I scribble down the North Roxbury Drive address and the time—5 p.m.—and my wife, Erica, and I head for Santa Monica, where we meet Welk in a corner suite within a 22-story office building next to the Pacific Ocean. If that's music to your ears, wait until you find out what happens next.

Late that afternoon, at the appointed time, we drive into Beverly Hills, where we are to meet an unnamed TV star. As I park on the street, I realize it has to be someone really topnotch, for only a few doors away, at 918 North Roxbury, is the home of James Stewart.

A ringing of the bell brings a middle-aged man to the door wearing a chef's cap. He introduces himself as Gary Morton and says we are the first to arrive. Axel Peterson is bringing the other reporters as a group, and Lucy is on her way home from the studio. Should be here in a minute or so. Lucy? Not Lucille Ball?! Then it hits me: one-time comedian Morton married Lucy shortly after her divorce from Desi Arnaz. For a moment, I am breathless, as "Mr. Lucy" escorts us into the two-story home. I am about to meet the greatest comedy star of television. The funniest of the funniest!

This look of the sophisticated lady equipped with a lengthy cigarette holder couldn't come closer to matching exactly how Lucille looks and poses herself when you are standing beside her next to her swimming pool, learning all you can about her new TV adventures.

Auntie Mame, (or call her Lucille Desiree Ball, whichever you prefer) strolls with theatrical decadence into the back yard of her mansion, made soft and bluish by the late afternoon light and the chlorine water of a free-form rock swimming pool. She flicks ashes from her cigarette with an air of disdain, like someone flipping off the Surgeon-General, and sips a martini just handed to her by a bartender stationed at a nearby makeshift bar. "Boy," she says, carefully tasting the martini, then stirring it with her olive stick, "did I need that!" She takes an immediate second swallow. And soon, the olive is gone.

Lucy has arrived first, followed shortly by Axel and the other reporters. We now surround Ms. Ball, who has had, as the old saying goes, a hard day at the studio. But not so hard that she can't face us gooey-eyed entertainment writers in her never-ending search for publicity. For not one brand-new TV special is coming this fall on CBS, but two! She is co-producing them with Morton, who is standing on the sidelines near the barbecue pit. (There is a former husband from another glorious time, named Desi Arnaz, but he hasn't been around since their divorce in 1960.)

A long-sleeve blouse of purple-green-red, a three-tiered necklace hanging to her waistline, and dazzling ornaments on her wrists clash for one's attention, but the eyes go immediately to the most famous face in television. The face that first made television history in 1951 with the most popular show of the time, and the face that continues to predominate the viewing habits of millions that perennially return to reruns of *I Love Lucy*.

Because she has driven straight from the studio, Lucy is still wearing a black wig and heavy theatrical make-up. Remarkably, she has retained her youthful figure and still knows how to show it off; this evening the lower half is sinuously encased in tight-fitting slacks.

Sure, Lucy looks tired and there are the unavoidable traces of aging which her make-up people constantly fight against, but this is a sixty-four-year-old, who is warm, receptive, and pleasantly kooky. Call her urbane, an extrovert who greets each newspaper reporter with eyes that sparkle with curiosity. She even pauses to kiss her husband, Gary Morton, as though they have been separated for too long. The smack resounds across the backyard. Morton, that chef's cap still sagging atop his head, turns and goes back to the barbecue pit to cook burgers and hot dogs for us reporters.

There is a very sexy side to Lucy when you are in her presence, as this older publicity still from her early days as a studio contract player demonstrates.

A poodle named Ginger dances at Lucy's feet, constantly demanding attention, unwilling to settle for anything less than total adoration. Lucy does her best to ignore Ginger to keep the conversation going, but one can tell she wishes she could pause and give Ginger more scratches on the top of her little head and goofy-voiced mutterings of reassurance.

Finally, it's time for why the reporters have come—to discuss the new Lucille Ball TV shows she is making back-to-back. She plunks into a deck chair, flicking a long stem of ash into a tray labeled *Auntie Mame*, a souvenir from her 1974 portrayal of the exuberant sophisticate in an updated musical film version called simply *Mame* (but never quite as good as Rosalind Russell's in the 1958 original.)

Neither special, she claims, is a variety show, neither is a straight situation comedy the likes of *The Lucy Show* and *Here's Lucy*, her follow-ups to *I Love Lucy*.

The first, *How Are You, Catherine Carter?* (to be aired on CBS in November)

Here are Gleason and Ball in a production still from their TV special Three for Two.

will costar Art Carney. "It's about a woman newly divorced who suddenly realizes how alone she is, and knows she can never be a swinger. It's bittersweet material broken down into three parts: her first night alone, her first affair, and her first new love. Carney," she says with a wink, "is my lover."

The second special, which she is just wrapping, will be entitled *Three for Two* and co-stars Jackie Gleason. "It's told in three parts," explains Lucy. "An adventure set in Rome, another about a couple meeting illicitly in a restaurant, and the third is a married-couple sketch."

Lucy takes a moment to look into the faces of the reporters, including mine. The smile that went with her description of her new shows is gone, replaced by a look of total seriousness. "Now

Gary Morton, one-time stand-up comedian, shown here with Lucy after they married, turned out to be a good hamburger flipper and hot dog roller.

listen carefully," she says. "I really mean this. I don't want to do any more Lucy TV comedy series. I've had too many seasons of that. The people can have me that way in reruns for the next hundred years. If I'm going to do something, I want it to be different. Gary [Morton] is producing these shows and refused to put them on tape. He feels too many productions on tape look like high school plays, so we're making them like motion pictures with a single camera."

Morton, standing by the barbecue pit, gives Lucy a little wave, as if to thank her for mentioning his name. She might have also mentioned that it was her first husband, Desi Arnaz, who came up with the idea of using film in the early 1950s, thereby assuring the worldwide syndication of *I Love Lucy* for decades to come and assuring enough money to allow him and Lucy to buy a film studio in 1957 called RKO Radio Pictures, which they renamed Desilu. Ironically, RKO had been where Lucy had worked as an ingénue contract player in the late 1930s.

After she and Desi divorced in 1960, Desi eventually sold out his interest in the studio. One morning, Lucy drove through the studio gate to realize she was now the major stock holder and chief on the Board of Directors. She would spend the next seven years running Desilu. She would be responsible for green-lighting *Star Trek* at a time when NBC wanted it but her financial advisers didn't. They all feared that Gene Roddenberry, a wild man when it came to spending money, would quickly bankrupt the studio. Six months to a complete financial collapse. She would confess that she didn't have the heart to fire Roddenberry, Leonard Nimoy, William Shatner, and all the others, so she okayed the series. Eventually, she would sell Desilu to Paramount for an estimated $10 million profit.

I study Lucy in the diminishing light, curious about how this redhead not only had the most successful TV series of all time but had become a major Hollywood figurehead, making decisions that would in retrospect seem monumentally historic.

"I never wanted to run a studio," she says in response to my query. "I hated having to do all that terrible stuff. I hated making decisions. Trying to balance budgets. Because I didn't want money to get on top of the fun of a show. I love acting and don't want to put anybody out of work. That's why I wanted *Star Trek* on the air. God knows I've had my ups and downs in this town. But you know what? All I ever really wanted to be was a mother and raise my children in peace. And act. Do all that funny stuff. That's what I loved. Acting. Being funny. And the kids. I loved raising the kids. Forget all that damn studio stuff."

Ginger, with yellow ribbons entwined in her hair, rolls over at Lucy's feet. The actress reaches down and scratches the upturned tummy. "Now," she says, putting down her empty martini glass, "I've got a surprise for you all." She makes a sweeping motion with her arm, as though someone is about to make a grand entrance. And someone does.

Anyone who has watched *The Honeymooners* and enjoyed the whacky character of Ed Norton, sewer worker, can see that the figure emerging into the back yard from the kitchen is Art Carney. He steps into our view as Lucy explains he is fresh from the set of *Won Ton Ton: The Dog That Saved Hollywood* (a spoof of Rin Tin Tin co-starring Teri Carr and directed by Michael Winner, but it

Never did a smile cross the face of Art Carney during our encounter in Lucille Ball's back yard.

would not be a winner among the critics.) He shakes hands with the reporters, but he doesn't smile.

Carney, during the rest of the evening, makes no attempt to be friendly or open. In fact, he looks preoccupied, as if he wishes he was elsewhere. At fifty-six, Carney looks older than one might expect—perhaps it's the failing light or maybe it's the dark glasses he is wearing. He gives Lucy a kiss and asks her, "Am I a good kisser or not?" He finally allows a minimal smile to brighten his face and sits by the side of the swimming pool.

"I'm a better kisser," replies Lucy, informing the reporters that Art is hard of hearing and we should speak up. Someone asks him

Jackie Gleason was alive and living with a sense of humor and charm not often found so easily in an individual you are meeting for the first time. Life was a never-ending party for Gleason.

about the Hollywood producer he plays in *Won Ton Ton: The Dog That Saved Hollywood*, but, suddenly, Lucy swings her arm as if she wants to strike the reporter. "Stop asking questions about *his* movie and start asking questions about *my* TV specials. This is my home. This is my back yard. This is my party."

The way Lucy says it, she means business. Nothing funny about this Lucy. No twinkle in her eyes as she asks for another martini. Ginger barks, as if to scold Lucy. Lucy baby-talks back to Ginger. "Coochi coochi coo. Goopsie poopsie."

Carney sits in the gloom and doesn't say much. His preoccupation has carried him away into an isolated world that only he knows exists. He stares out across the swimming pool as if there is no one else in the back yard. Nobody asks any more questions about *Won Ton Ton: The Dog That Saved Hollywood.*

Suddenly, Lucy sweeps back her arm again and says another surprise is approaching. An "ah" leaps from the mouths of two female reporters and the male reporters all look up from their cocktails. Someone drops a ballpoint pen and stops taking notes. Ginger dances with joy.

A new guest is walking up the driveway. Anyone who has watched *The Honeymooners* and laughed at the character of bus driver Ralph Kramden can see that it's Jackie Gleason. He passes through pools of light as he approaches our group, looking as if he just stepped out of a haberdashery shop. His gray suit is tailor fit, adhering to a body that must be a solid 210 pounds. The striped tie complements him perfectly; there is a handkerchief stuffed into his breast pocket and a red carnation shoved into his lapel.

Gleason's face is well-tanned and the hair and mustache are suavely in place. It appears he's recently lost weight, but he still has that rotund look we associate with Ralph Kramden, the Poor Soul, Joe the Bartender, Reggy van Gleason III, and other colorful characters he played on his long-running 1950s TV series. I am also reminded of Minnesota Fats, the pool hall champion, in his 1961 movie hit, *The Hustler.*

Gleason pauses, sizing up each individual, then he proclaims, "*Mmm, you're a good group.*" Gleason and Lucy kiss. Someone makes the crack that maybe Carney kisses better. "Yeah," says Gleason, "Carney has a kisser all right." He whirls toward the man manning the makeshift bar. "Where's the man with the wrinkled apron? It's the drinking hour. Bring me a double, triple time."

For a while, Gleason and Carney talk about *The Honeymooners* days. You would like to see Carney leap up, scream "Hiya Ralphie!" and rush to the frig to steal a snort of milk, but he stays seated and stays sedate and distant. Not even Gleason can seem to cheer him up. What comes out is reminiscent talk, nostalgia-hour conversation. Audrey Meadows, Alice, what ever happened to her?

Ah, she's married to some millionaire now. Making a bundle off oil, not comedy. "I'm making scale," says Carney, glancing down at his feet. One doubts he means that.

"You made that Oscar, too, Art, and you deserved it. You worked a lot of years to earn that Oscar." Gleason is talking about *Harry and Tonto*, a 1974 feature that earned Carney the best actor award. Oddly, Carney says nothing, gazing into nothingness.

"Hell, we make movies," continues Gleason, "because we're show-offs. Anyone who comes on being humble, that's phony. How can you command big salaries and make big demands and be humble. Hell, I was never humble a day in my life."

Ginger, the poodle that loves Lucy, sniffs at Gleason's highball glass. "No, bad dog," scolds Lucy. Gleason scowls. "Nothing worse than a drunken poodle. Keep that dog sober, Lucy."

Darkness falls over Beverly Hills, but not over Lucy and Jackie, who line up next to the pool in deck chairs to discuss the art of comedy. "Anybody can play dykes and gays to get a laugh," says Gleason. "Yeah," replies Lucy, "but few can tell a good solid joke."

"Our shows," says Gleason, "they had believable premises. The people were believable. Ralph Kramden's apartment was run down. You believed in those people. They weren't rich; they didn't have a *Brady Bunch* mansion like you have, Lucy."

"I refuse to go back to series comedy," vows Lucy. "There's too much realism in TV today. What people need more of is escapism. Comedy. Real entertainment."

"Then you should go back and give them that," says Gleason. "Who else can give it to them like you can? I don't want to go back because I'm too damned disciplined. I stick by discipline and that makes working too demanding." Lucy's follow-up silence suggests she is thinking that one over.

"Listen," says Gleason, "I'd go back if I could play Joe the Bartender. I could do that standing on my head. But I wouldn't want to do a sit-com and have to learn a new script every week. I'd hate like hell to get stuck in a rut, no matter how golden it was."

I ask Gleason where some of his catch-phrases originated. The ones he always used on his Saturday night show: "How sweet it is . . . and away we go!"

This is the photo given to me by CBS' Axel Peterson. While I'm not in it, the major characters of the evening are. My wife Erica is surrounded by Jackie Gleason, Lucille Ball, and Art Carney. Not a boring bunch to hang out with when you're passing through Beverly Hills.

It's a question he loves to answer and he bursts out immediately: "Back in my New York days, I used to take my friends out drinking to Toots Shor's, our favorite watering hole. We'd line up at the bar and belt them down. Toots always let me sign the check so when the bill came, I'd hold it up and say 'How sweet it is,' meaning ain't I sweet?

"Then we'd be in Toots' drinking until all hours and then I'd suggest we should hit some other spot and I'd say 'And away we go!' Meaning finish your drink, we're out of here, and we're going to another joint for additional belts. Later these little expressions became naturals for television. Shtick sticks. Once we were doing *Honeymooners* and I was really feeling Kramden's frustration with

Alice, so I blurted out 'Pow! Zoom! To the moon!' just like that. And that stuck too."

"Do you need another belt, Art?" asks Lucy.

"No," he says, "but I'll tell you what's wrong with the business today—"

"Demographics," interrupts Gleason. "That's what's wrong today. With show business. Everything today is based on Demographics. Statistics. Age groups. Where are there real people in statistics?"

"That's not what I was gonna say," replies Carney. "What's wrong today is, there isn't enough good pure comedy."

"I'm tired of comedy, that's it," says Lucy. Ginger barks and wants Lucy to play. Lucy doesn't.

Gleason slaps his own knee. "There's only two things I watch anymore on TV. Sporting events and Sherlock Holmes."

"Gees," says Carney. "Sherlock Holmes. Yeah, Sherlock Holmes."

A reporter asks Gleason to define comedy. "If you define it, it isn't. It's something that makes you happy. Don't try to analyze it. What you need is characterization to make the comedy pay off. If you have the character, you'll find the comedy."

"Stop analyzing it," warns Carney.

"I'll never go back to TV full-time," vows Lucy.

"I'd go back," says Gleason. "For the right money. It's always about money."

Carney slips off into a new reverie of silence. Gleason gently sips his drink. Lucy plays with Ginger. The darkness is complete now. The hotdogs and burgers have been served and eaten. For a moment, it was the history of three popular comedy entertainers. Now they are just three figures at the side of a swimming pool, thinking their private thoughts, like ordinary people.

Finally, Gleason glances up. "Hey, my glass is empty. Must've been that poodle of Lucy's. Someone find that guy with the wrinkled apron. Double, triple time."

All the other reporters head for home. Gleason and Carney slip away together, chattering, heading up the driveway. While Gary Morton cleans the barbecue grill, Lucy invites me and Erica into her home to play backgammon, a card game she loves with a pas-

Lucille Ball enjoying a round of backgammon at her home table, which will become part of her memorial at Universal Studios Theme Park.

sion. She spends the next hour teaching us how to play . . . and then, suddenly, the evening is over. And it's time to leave.

By the next morning, it all seems like a wonderful dream. An evening with Lucille Ball, Jackie Gleason, and Art Carney. And you know there'll never be another evening like it.

Flash forward to summer 1996, seven years since the death of Lucille Ball, who has died at the age of seventy-seven. I am at the Universal Studios Theme Park in North Hollywood, visiting "LUCY: A TRIBUTE," a walk-through museum dedicated to the *I Love Lucy* series. Behind a glass-encased display, against the wall in a corner, stands Lucy's backgammon table, and suddenly that night in 1975 washes over me and I am with Lucy again, Ginger is dancing around her feet again, Gleason is laughing his head off, while Art Carney stares off into nowhere.

I think about the irony of Lucy running a studio and never enjoying a minute of it, yet she had made *Star Trek* possible by ignoring all her advisers and telling NBC to go ahead and put it into the 1966 fall line-up—all because she didn't have the heart to tell Roddenberry, Leonard Nimoy, William Shatner, and all the others they wouldn't be working anymore at Desilu. Soft-hearted Lucy, who a year later sold Desilu to Paramount for $18 million, and Paramount got the *Star Trek* franchise, never realizing until later how many billions it would earn from a movie series and several TV spin offs, more than enough to pay for buying Desilu.

Lucy, the funniest lady in the world, the lady who never wanted to be part of the business of Hollywood, up there right now, knowing she had made it all possible, laughing her heart out and playing another round of backgammon.

One of my favorite Hollywood publicists was Axel Peterson, who had invited me and Erica to Lucille Ball's home. Thanks to him I covered countless other celebrities associated with CBS-TV series, as he was a longtime employee in that network's Media Relations department. After retiring from the network, he died in 2002 of cancer in Blaine, Washington. Gone, so young, at seventy.

Gary Morton had been asked by Lucy to give up his comedy career to help her run Desilu, but after Lucy's death he was no longer wanted as a producer and disappeared from the entertainment scene. Aka Morton Goldaper, the one-time stand-up comedian died at seventy-four in Palm Springs in 1999.

As for Art Carney, it was revealed that he had suffered from alcoholism, barbiturates, and depression for many years before giving up drinking around the time he appeared in *Harry and Tonto*. There were definitely signs that his depression might have still been working on him that night at Lucy's. He kept busy until his death in 2003, only a few days short of his eighty-fifth birthday.

What about Jackie Gleason, you ask? Our paths would cross once again. Another moment to remember . . . .

JACKIE GLEASON
Standing With "The Great One" On the Edge of a Precipice –He Will Fall . . . But Recover

In the words of Jackie Gleason, the Fox Theater at Seventh and B Streets in the downtown area of San Diego, California is "cavernous . . . if you want to arch your eyebrows, you also have to perform a body flip. No wonder they rent binoculars in the lobby. It's murder, playing a big house like this."

Not even Gleason, the king of television comedy, dwarfs the enormous stage of this opulent theater to which I have been invited so I can hang around the edges of an afternoon rehearsal. I watch bemused as he turns and walks through a Gay Nineties parlor bedroom in the style of a hungry, 200-pound polar bear searching for delicacies to carry back to his den.

Dressed in a bright blue jumpsuit with white trimming and Pat Boone loafers, "The Great One" is rehearsing a farcical play, *Sly Fox*, with Cleavon Little and Irwin Corey. His character, Foxwell T. Fox, is the inspiration of Larry Gelbart, famed for writing material for comedians Red Buttons and Sid Caesar, creating the 1962 Broadway hit, *A Funny Thing Happened on the Way to the Forum*, and writing and producing the TV version of *M*A*S*H*.

Standing on the set and directing Gelbart's comic play is Arthur Penn, better known as a film director through *Bonnie and Clyde* (1967), *Alice's Restaurant* (1969), and *Little Big Man* (1970). At the moment, he is smoothing out some rough edges to *Sly Fox*, an updated stage version of Ben Jonson's *Volpone*. (No longer set in Renaissance Venice, it's now San Francisco-based.) It's Gleason's first play since *Take Me Along*, which was a musical version of *Ah, Wilderness* that was a hit at the Schubert Theater in 1959-1960.

In March 1978, almost three years since my initial meeting with Gleason in the backyard of Lucille Ball's home in Beverly Hills, I have flown to San Diego for the day for just one reason: to nail

That's Jackie Gleason dressed as the character of Foxwell T. Fox in the stage version of Sly Fox, *in which director Arthur Penn allowed him to use some of his classic gag lines. It is early 1978, when Gleason was sixty-two.*

down Gleason for an interview before the comedy play comes to San Francisco for a two-month run at the Orpheum Theater. From there, *Sly Fox* is set to move across the country, concluding in Florida in November. It isn't going to quite happen that way, for at this very moment Gleason is standing on the edge of a cliff,

Jackie Gleason, a pool hustler in his youth, brought his skills with a cue stick to the 1961 hit The Hustler. *His portrayal of Minnesota Fats was to earn him an Oscar nomination. One thing about Gleason: He was never behind the eight ball anytime in his life.*

from which he is going to fall. (How someone will catch him, I'll explain later.) For today, I'm there to do my journalistic job.

Gleason listens courteously to the suggestions of Penn and also makes several comments of his own, which Penn accepts or modifies. In one scene, Gleason has to slip into a coat, and he complains that he needs more time. "I get the damn thing on backwards . . . I can't get the buttons fastened . . . and the tail gets caught up my . . . ."

Penn laughs so hard I figure he might include Gleason's ad lib as dialogue. Gleason turns to tell me and says, "You think this is bad! There's one act where I gotta make five changes. Five!"

A little later, Gleason bellows like a bull for the show's publicist and rushes off the stage. Minutes later, he reappears on the far aisle and signals that it's time to leave for dinner. Clutched in his fingers is the first of many ubiquitous cigarettes I will see during the rest of my visit. (Four packs a day is Gleason's estimated usage.) He tells me he likes an early break from rehearsal so he can have a little booze, a little food, and then take a rest before tonight's eight o'clock curtain call.

Waiting at the curb is a symbol of Gleason's affluent lifestyle: a gleaming Cadillac limousine equipped with TV, radio, and a bar. Strangely, since Gleason is the major passenger, that bar is dry of any booze. I expect to hear "Umm, you're not a very good provider" flow from Gleason's lips, but he sits silent as the Caddy pulls into rush-hour traffic. "Don't worry," he finally says, "the cocktail waitress pops out of the cabinet after the first mile." He orders the driver to head for Casa di Baffi. "That's the Toot Shor's of the West," he proclaims proudly, as if we are headed for afternoon tea with Queen Elizabeth.

At my first meeting with Gleason, when he turned up as a total surprise, there had not been time to ask all the questions flowing through my mind, but now I've had time to research his background. Herbert John Gleason was born in Brooklyn into a family that, eight years later, broke up, his father literally deserting his mother. He would proclaim years later that "I grew up in pool halls"—an ironic fact if you recall that he was to play Minnesota Fats in the great pool-hall drama, *The Hustler*, for which he was nominated for the Oscar. He would break into show biz at the age of fifteen in an amateur-night contest, and go on to perform in Vaudeville, carnivals, nightclubs, and road houses. Gleason even had short flings as a boxer, a pool hustler, and a stunt driver out of Atlantic City.

In 1941, he was signed to a movie contract (he was billed as Jackie C. Gleason), but not much happened. You can catch a glimpse of him as a member of Glenn Miller's band in *Orchestra Wives*

Gleason as Chester A. Riley and Rosemary De Camp as wife Peggy in a scene from the TV comedy The Life of Riley. For Gleason, it turned out to be a "revoltin' development" in the ratings.

(1942), and he was in *Springtime in the Rockies* (1942) with Betty Grable. Another role, though largely forgotten, featured him with Rock Hudson and Yvonne De Carlo in *The Desert Hawk* (1950), portraying none other than Aladdin.

It was the coming of television that gave Gleason his ultimate success. Although his first effort, *The Life of Riley*, flopped during the 1949-1950 season, probably because the role really belonged to William Bendix, he found a home on *The Cavalcade of Stars* from 1950-1952, and CBS lured him away to do his own one-hour show in 1952 by paying him $8,000 per episode—an increase of nearly $6,400 per week from what he had been earning.

Broadcast on Saturday nights, *The Jackie Gleason Show* was a smash hit. I grew up in my early teens watching it almost weekly.

This is the body movements Gleason would make whenever he did his "And away we go!" In this photo he's in the costume of his character, The Poor Soul.

Like Red Skelton, he filled each hour with a plethora of colorful characterizations: Reggie Van Gleason, the spoiled rich kid; blabbering Joe the Bartender; the Poor Soul—a loveable bum wandering the streets and parks of New York; the destructive Ruddy the Repairman; and ultimately New York City bus driver Ralph Kramden in a series of sketches with their own title, "The Honeymooners," which in 1955-1956 became a half-hour series of its own. Gleason's theme song, which he wrote himself, was "Melancholy Serenade."

There were those wonderful catchphrases he had told me about at Lucy's home three years earlier: "Umm, you're a good group" . . . "And away we go!" . . . "Pow! Zoom! To the moon." Portly, brash, and uncouth, Gleason's characters almost always had giant egos, but somewhere in all that was hidden away a soft side. (Can I possibly uncover it?)

When we arrive, Casa di Baffi isn't open yet, but owner George Pernicano, who also holds a controlling interest in the San Diego Chargers, eagerly shows Gleason to his favorite table. "This is the only restaurant in this town that I bother with," he tells me, ordering two glasses of booze. (One is for me.) He leans back, lights up a fresh cigarette, and sighs. "I don't know why I'm doing this play. I sure didn't need it. I was playing golf in the sun, and who in hell needs to show up somewhere every night at eight o'clock?

"Hell, I'll admit it. *Sly Fox* was written by Gelbart for me, but at first I refused to read it. I told them not to bother even sending me a script. So in '76, George C. Scott played my role at the Broadhurst on Broadway. About a year later, I found a copy of the damn thing in my den. I don't know where the hell it came from, but I opened it, and I started to read it, and suddenly I was hooked. It was perfect for a guy like me. So, I got on the phone and I was making demands. I wanted private jets, penthouse suites, limos. They kept saying yes, yes, yes, and I ran out of things to ask for. And it was too late to back down. I stepped right into the part but I've added some refinements and some shticks. See, Fox is a rich guy who cons San Francisco into believing he's going to die, so he can have fun with those who think they can inherit from his death. Cleavon, who knocked 'em dead last year as the lawman in *Blazing Saddles*, he plays my servant, and we've been having some fun with that.

"Penn's a marvelous director, and I'm sorry I've never had the chance to work with him in movies. He separates the actors; he never allows them to cluster up. He's a genius at blocking and staging. And he's willing to listen. He doesn't believe his word is the final one. He's willing to bend a little. He even lets me use

Jackie Gleason in his bus driver's costume, portraying Ralph Kramden, central to "The Honeymooners" segments in his one-hour comedy series.

some of my better-known lines from my TV show, just to remind the audience who Jackie Gleason really is."

"See, *Sly Fox* is an opportunity for me to show off. Hell, all actors are show-offs. Any of them who come on being humble, that's phony. How can you command big salaries and make big demands and be humble? Hell, I've never been humble a day in my life."

There are many myths about Jackie Gleason and he says nothing to dispel any of them. "If people want to believe I'm afraid to fly, let them. Then here's this business about what a great ad libber I'm supposed to be. Hell, when I do a play I impose a discipline on myself that would turn a monk pale. I stick to the dialogue. I don't do business unless it's been okayed by the director, and I know exactly what the writer intended with every line and I stick to it.

"Let me tell you what can happen when you ad lib. We were doing 'The Honeymooners,' and at quarter to seven I threw away the script. Now, we were going on the air at eight. Everyone was going crazy, and I said to Art Carney, 'Let's go up to my apartment and we'll come up with an idea.' I put some paper in the typewriter and typed the words 'The Honeymooners.' Then I said, 'Christ, let's have a drink and loosen up a little,' and so we belted down a couple and then it got close to eight and we still had nothing on the paper but the title.

"So we rushed back to the studio without a story. I told Audrey Meadows to ask me, 'Did you stop at the bakery?' Well, we created the rest of it right on the spot. We went off that stage thinking it was the end of our careers. One of the producers rushed over and told us it was the best show we'd ever done. 'Thank you,' I said, 'now would you mind leaving us alone for a while.' I said to the cast, 'Never again. We were lucky once and we got away with it.'

"That's how that terrible thing starts. You think you can get away with it all the time. But you can't get away with it. It can destroy you. That's why an actor needs discipline. And as much as I hate discipline, I stick by it. That's why I don't like to do television any more. Because it demands so much discipline."

Gleason still does frequent *Honeymooners* specials, but hasn't had a regular series since 1970. He is still trying to sell the networks on his private detective concept Panama Fargo, but so far "they won't allow me to do it my way so the hell with them. I might need to be a little bit hotter before I connect with something."

All his characterizations—the Poor Soul, Reggie Van Gleason, Fenwick Babbitt, Rumdum, Joe the Bartender—were "psychological constructions. They were all based on people, or personality traits, I had seen in action." (A new character he had added, only a year earlier, was Sheriff Buford T. Justice in the comedy hit *Smokey and the Bandit*.)

What about his image as a boozer? "I've never had a booze problem. I drink to get bagged like the next guy. The trouble with too much drinking is that the blemishes, pimples, and blackheads on the people you're drinking with start to vanish, and you lose perspective. When that feeling starts to creep up on me, that's when I stop drinking." (By this time, he has had his second, and final, drink of the afternoon-evening.)

And his extravagant living habits? "I've always spent money like I was a millionaire, even when I didn't have much. I've always been accustomed to the good life and that's part of me that'll never change."

Any regrets? "My only regret is that I was immature when I married my first wife. She wasn't responsible for our divorce; hell, she was an excellent wife. But I was a young kid who wanted to have nothing but a good time. I didn't know how to handle all my mistakes. That led to some unhappiness that came later in life when the Church wouldn't grant us a divorce, and I couldn't remarry. But otherwise, I've lived the way I've always wanted to live. And there's no regrets."

Just two weeks later, Jackie Gleason was a sensation on the stage of the Orpheum Theater in San Francisco. Whenever he would slip in one of his famous lines ("... how sweet it is!") the audience really cracked up. *Sly Fox* moved on to other cities and was in Chicago in June when Gleason suffered chest pains and checked into a hospital. Before long, he underwent a triple by-pass heart operation that lasted for six hours. (Doctors had discovered his coronary arteries were 80 per cent blocked.) Sly Fox was cancelled and his version of Foxwell T. Fox was dead forever. Panama Fargo? It never materialized.

Amazingly, Gleason recovered and life continued as before. He made two sequels to *Smokey and the Bandit* and starred with Karl Malden in *The Sting II* (1983). There would also be the TV movie, *Izzy and Moe* (1985), in which he and Art Carney performed together for the last time.

Gleason lived out his remaining years at his $2 million mansion in Lauderhill, Florida, with his third wife Marilyn (sister of June Taylor, who had been his choreographer during his best TV years). When he was seventy-one, death came on June 24, 1987, from colon and liver cancer, and he was entombed at Our Lady of Mercy Catholic Cemetery in Miami. There was an inscription on his tomb: "AND AWAY WE GO!"

After his death, it was discovered that there was a film vault that contained a kinescope copy of every episode of *The Jackie Gleason Show* from the 1950s, provided to him by CBS through a contractual arrangement. Thus it was that MPI Home Video was able to extract all episodes of "The Honeymooners" into a 15-disc set in 2011.

AUDREY MEADOWS
Pow! Zoom! How Sweet It Is When Alice Kramden Returns From the Moon to Prove That She's the Greatest!

Once upon a time back in 1951, when television was still a fledgling medium, a pretty young woman auditioned for a role that was important because it was destined to become one of the best

This is the photo Audrey Meadows signed for me in 1985. At the age of sixty-three, she is still looking great, and in no way dresses as Alice Kramden.]

This is how gorgeous Audrey Meadows looked in 1951, just on the eve of trying out for Jackie Gleason's TV show. Too gorgeous, according to Gleason, who turned her down until she willingly stripped away her beauty to capture the drab Alice Kramden look.

acting roles of its time, and it would make history for years to come. In fact, it is still making history.

In 1951, the beautiful twenty-nine-year-old actress wasn't thinking about history, just about furthering her career. So far she had made it as a regular on TV's *The Bob and Ray Show*, but she desperately needed another stepping stone. The major network star auditioning her had already interviewed and rejected many big (and little) names in the business, and finally he rejected the pretty young thing on the grounds that she was "too pretty" and "too young."

She went home distraught. She had wanted the role so desperately. She stood in front of her mirror for a while studying her features. Then she began messing up her expensive hairdo, wiped off her makeup, rubbed off her lipstick, put on a ripped blouse, and returned to the mirror, studying the less beautiful image. *Good*, she told herself. *I no longer look "too pretty" or "too young."* She hired a photographer, who snapped a series of photos of her in her disarray, and she had the audacity to send the drab photos to the TV star without identifying herself.

The TV star—"The Great One" aka Jackie Gleason—saw the photos and his mouth fell open. "That's her!" he shouted. "That's my Alice Kramden. Get her on the phone right now!" And when he learned he had already turned the actress down, he said, "Any dame with a sense of humor like that deserves the job double."

And so, Audrey Meadows ("Raggedy Audrey" as she had thought of herself) became Alice Kramden in a single comedy sketch on *The Jackie Gleason Show*, which was already a major hit that year on CBS. In time the recurring albeit brief Kramden vignettes, called "The Honeymooners," grew in popularity. It was all about a loud-mouthed, ego-driven Madison Avenue bus driver, who thought he had all the answers to life's problems and his plain, long-enduring, haggard wife Alice, who just wanted things to be a little bit better. Would the cheapest pair of high heels be okay with you, honey?

Unlike other sitcoms of that period, which dealt almost exclusively with middle-class American families, these characters were depressed, lower-class citizens living in a dreary section of New York: specifically, at 328 Chauncey Street in the Bensonhurst district of Brooklyn. The only part of their world that the audiences saw each week was a bleak, almost barren kitchen with the cheapest-looking stove and icebox imaginable.

Meadows' Alice would often freeze in place, armed crossed, as Gleason's Ralph went off on a tangent, usually with upstairs neighbor Ed Norton (Art Carney) standing by, ready for more comedy action.

"The Honeymooners" was live television with a remarkably talented ensemble. Gleason was a sensitive actor, who could successfully segue from threatening Alice with a fist ("Oh, are you gonna get it! One of these days, Alice! One of these days! Pow! Zoom! To the Moon!") to suddenly becoming a softie who would proclaim "Alice, you're the greatest!" before sweeping her into his arms and giving her a matinee idol's kiss.

Meadows was often clad in a plain house dress, apron, and flat shoes, enduring Ralph's moments of unparalleled rage and quickly seeing through his schemes to get rich ("Forget it, Ralph, it'll never fly!"), but she was always ready to take Ralph back once he had learned his lesson and had returned to the reality he lived in.

Art Carney and Joyce Randolph co-starred as Ed and Trixie Norton, the upstairs neighbors (he was a municipal sewer worker, which allowed for some hilarious jokes; she was an ex-Burlesque dancer.) They were always getting involved in Ralph's schemes for social climbing and quick riches. Invariably Ed got Ralph into deeper troubled waters, while Trixie sided with Alice.

These four characters came to dominate the one-hour Gleason show as its most popular characters just as Alice Kramden would dominate the career of Audrey Meadows throughout the 1950s, when the characters became popular enough for their own show. Thirty-nine half-hour episodes were produced in 1955-1956, filmed before live audiences on the very same set used for the one-hour show. Despite its popularity, it was not brought back for a second season, and soon even Gleason was off the air. However, there were four one-hour *Honeymooners* specials produced in the 1970s.

It is finally in 1985 that Meadows comes to the Bay Area to promote the fact that all of the original seventy episodes from the one-hour shows are being replayed for the first time since their initial broadcasts on the Showtime network.

"After the Showtime run, the episodes will be sold into syndication," says Mrs. Robert Six, aka Audrey Meadows, as she enjoys a modest breakfast of hot tea and rolls in her suite at the Four Seasons Clift Hotel. "And we have Jackie to thank for saving those episodes from oblivion. You see, his contract with CBS contained a clause that he was to receive a kinescope copy of each and every one of his shows from the 1950s. So, when he retired and moved to Florida, he took all those shows with him, and he carefully preserved them in an air-conditioned storage room."

Red-headed Meadows, who has been married to the one-time owner of Continental Airlines since 1961, and who is the sister of actress Jayne Meadows, still has the beauty, charm, and carriage that graced her early days on Broadway opposite Phil Silvers in *Top Banana*, her one crowning achievement before appearing as Alice Kramden.

As she drinks her tea, she seems glowing and vibrant, dressed as she is in a multicolored flared skirt and a bright blue blouse draped with a bow and string of pearls. Her high heels are a matching bright blue. She turns in her chair often, possessed by a nervous energy, her skirt swirling around her.

"What keeps these old shows alive?" she asks herself, pondering the never-ending popularity of The Honeymooners. "I think the reason is, they dealt with the American Dream, and that doesn't change generation to generation. And our shows were never topical. They'll never be dated. They're about people wanting more from life, and everyone wants something they don't have. New furniture, a better car, a paid mortgage, a refrigerator with a freezer in it. Ralph and Alice fought about the same things that our viewers fought about. We dealt with eternal verities: we played for the truth. And you get an appealing reaction because everyone identifies with that and recognizes it is the truth."

She digresses for a moment to explain that *Dynasty* and *Dallas* are at the opposite end of the spectrum, presenting "the images of our fantasies and not our realities; things beyond the grasp of the average viewer who doesn't drive gleaming limousines or live in rooms with crystal chandeliers or wear gorgeous gowns.

"Can you image Jackie trying to sell *The Honeymooners* to CBS today? Four people with no money, no glamour, living in a barren apartment with just a kitchen table, a two-burner stove, an icebox, a sink, and a bureau over in the corner? Without any T & A?" She laughs uproariously at her joke.

What did Audrey Meadows think of Alice Kramden? She lights a cigarette but does not put the lighter down, turning it endlessly in her fingers. "I feel that Alice was the most beautiful character who ever lived theatrically. People loved her because no matter how much pain Ralph brought her, she still understood him and loved him deeply, and realized all he really wanted was a better life for her. A life where there were curtains on the windows and a better coat and something more than $62.50 a week. Did you know that's how much Ralph was making in the 1950s?"

She looks upon Ralph and Ed as "complete innocents, always being taken by the con men and bringing home vacuum cleaners

Could you live on $62.50 a week? Well, the Kramdens did, but no matter how desperate things would look, an episode always ended with Ralph and Alice kissing and making up. Otherwise, how could there be another episode next Saturday night?

that never worked. But no matter how frustrated Ralph became, no matter how many times he said 'Pow! Zoom! To the moon!' or 'You're gonna get it Alice, oh, are you gonna get it!' he never harmed Alice. It was his way of letting off steam. He was tender and touching, and it gave the show an underlying theme of love."

The cast never rehearsed the show. In fact, Gleason prided himself on never doing a scene more than once. This threw off many actors who needed rehearsals, so for the bit parts the producers depended on what they called "Gleason Actors," those capable of stepping in with no trepidations.

Was the cast close? "Yes," Meadows replies, "but we never socialized. We never went to parties after the show like Sid Caesar and his cast. We were a team that supported and respected each other."

Meadows remembers Gleason, who always called her "Aud," as "kind, decent, sensitive—so professional, he would never leave another actor hung up." Art Carney was "shy, quiet, his own person. I was painfully shy myself as a child, so I always sympathized with that. Art was a private family man. I saw him only on Saturdays when we did the shows." (I am reminded of the cool, almost unfriendly manner Carney had displayed in Lucille Ball's back yard back in 1975.)

The least-known member of the group, Joyce Randolph, is something of a mystery to Meadows. "We'd known each other from the start. We'd worked together as chorus girls in a production of *No, No, Nanette*. I think she did some commercial that Jackie saw, and he hired her on the spot. She was a fine actress but not very outgoing. She came to work very serious, you could say she was tense. After five years on the show, she married and had a baby, and I think she finally put family over career because she didn't do much after that."

Since she did her last *Honeymooners* in 1957, the year Gleason's CBS show left the air, Meadows has continued her acting, though never again attaining the high profile of Alice Kramden. She has been in six specials with Sid Caesar, has appeared with Carol Burnett and Tim Conway, and has taken assorted dramatic series roles, proving she has a wider range than many give her credit for. And she has been a regular on the Ted Knight sitcom *Too Close for Comfort*, as Mrs. Iris Martin.

There have also been periods of time away from show business to travel extensively with her husband. She has served as a director of the First National Bank of Denver and as an advisory director of Continental Airlines. However, she has never been able to resist the lure of show business.

Meadows hopes that the *Honeymooners'* characters are not left open-ended, that Gleason will eventually see his way clear to do a final chapter. "With this recent rebirth, we owe our viewers a finale." She suggests a story line in which Ralph and Alice have reached retirement age and moved to Florida, but they face what many senior citizens are facing today, a shortage of money to live comfortably. And then Ralph dreams up one of his schemes....

"So what if the characters have aged," she says. "If they're still believable and true to character, they're acceptable. Real people get older too. How sweet that is!"

Audrey was reported to be a chain smoker, and I saw her go through several cigarettes during our interview. She was to die of lung cancer just ten years later, at the age of seventy-three. The story goes that her sister, Jayne, was at her hospital bedside, and that her last spoken word was, "Jayne." And then ... it was over for the Kramdens.

MILTON BERLE
A Child's View of the First Major TV Star in History

By spring 1949, Milton Berle was the hottest comedian in America—the first entertainer to become a TV star when the medium was still an enigma on the horizon of American pop culture. Berle struck his success almost overnight, after just a handful of one-hour shows, becoming popularly known as *Uncle Miltie* and *Mr. Television*. In just a few months, he rose up to become a national institution, even if only 1 per cent of the U.S. population owned TV sets. With no standards yet established, TV was the perfect medium for Berle's visual comedy, boundless energy, and super-zany craziness.

When he became one of several rotating hosts for *The Texaco Star Theater* in the summer of 1948, TV was a brand new medium that had yet to be explored and exploited. There were absolutely no standards; there was no level of "taste" to which producers could aspire. It was the Wild West of video, the unexplored frontiers of a new visual medium. Berle exploited that virginal territory for all it was worth, and so outperformed his co-hosts that NBC signed him in September to a thirty-year contract, paying him $100,000 annually whether he worked in front of the cameras or not. He became the solo host for the weekly show, now titled *The Milton Berle Show*, which was to evolve into the most watched program of its time, winning an Emmy in 1950.

From the beginning of that unique TV fame, I was one of the faithful who always watched. We didn't have a TV at home yet, so I'd get to my aunt's home in Napa Valley faithfully every Tuesday night just before 8 p.m. and settle down in front of her small-screen set. My dad and I would speculate about what crazy costume Berle would open the show in. One night it was nothing but a barrel—an IRS agent had taken everything he owned. Another night Berle came out as Lady Godiva and pranced around

This is Milton Berle during the 1940s when he starred in radio shows of varying degrees of success, and appeared in person on Broadway in the Ziegfeld Follies of 1943. Television was just beginning in America, and Berle would almost immediately rise up to become one of its first major comedy stars.

on stage in a white, tight-fitting body stocking while behind him, prancing across the stage, was a whinnying white charger.

I vividly remember the goofy night that Berle, opening the show in a caveman's costume, rushed into the audience and plucked a

A glimpse of what Cleopatra might have looked like the Tuesday night that Milton Berle donned "her" costume and headpiece . . . "going drag" became one of his recurring themes during the dawn of television, with an impression of Carmen ("The Lady in the Tutty Frutti Hat") Miranda also one of his personal favorites.

fur coat off a lady's seat, returning to the stage to prance about in the glittering piece like a sales model; or the time he emerged from behind the curtain in a Cleopatra costume; or the night he spoofed Carmen Miranda while Tony Martin provided the singing. It was all bizarre and spontaneous—aspects that made his comedy so wonderful to one as young as myself. Yet if you looked closely at the format, it was nothing more than an old-fashioned Vaudeville potpourri of Berle, guest stars, comedians, singers, ventriloquists, acrobats, and jugglers [what *The Ed Sullivan Show* would become years later, but without a slapstick comedian as host]. Berle relied mainly on put-down ad libs and slapstick comedy enhanced by outrageous costumes, often those "drag" costumes. (Down the road, he and Bob Hope would both go "drag" in a comedy sketch about two lady supermarket shoppers.)

Berle held this #1 position for the next seven years, but by the mid-1950s, some standards of taste had been established, and Berle's star began to dim quickly, so that by 1956 he had seen his glory days. He attempted two comebacks in 1958 and 1966, but these failed. Audiences expected more sophistication and taste, and that was not Berle. He would never again attain such a high level of stardom.

I'll be the first to recognize the corniness of Milton Berle. There are many who think he was not funny at all. That there was a crude edge to his work that didn't allow it to hold up over time. Tastes change, but there was a day when he was king of that kind of comedy.

I was never more excited about meeting a celebrity than on the day we spent two hours together discussing all the elements of his career. I was reminded of this over the years whenever I was asked, "Whom did you enjoy interviewing the most?" I would immediately answer, "Milton Berle! Without a doubt! It was more like he was putting on a show for me than doing an interview." He was, in the final analysis, unforgettable.

An eye doctor opened the door to my rendezvous with "Mr. Television." Oddly enough, my adventure with "Uncle Miltie" doesn't begin as a routine *San Francisco Chronicle* assignment; it starts one afternoon when I see an optometrist about a new pair of glasses. When the eye doctor learns I am a *San Francisco Chronicle* writer, he suddenly forgets about examining my eyeballs and their sockets and begins enthusiastically telling me that he is on the committee for the Congregation B'Nai Emunah, a synagogue located in the outer Sunset District, not far from the Pacific Ocean.

The eye doc rattles on as fast as he can, as if he has suddenly mutated into a religious salesman, that the committee is currently

Milton Berle was rarely seen in public without a cigar clutched in his fingers ... and he had one he was waving through the air on the day we met, the usual kind eight inches long.

raising money for renovations and has contacted Milton Berle's agent in Hollywood. An agreement has been reached that Berle is to perform his comedy in two shows in San Francisco's large Masonic Auditorium atop Nob Hill. What the committee hopes is that Berle will draw a giant audience, with the net profits going to help restructure the synagogue. Will it be possible, the optometrist-pitch artist asks, for me to interview Berle in advance of his shows so there is a story in the *San Francisco Chronicle*? That will help to attract a big audience and get the synagogue up and running again.

Remembering my enthusiasm as a kid watching his shows in the late 1940s and realizing he was really television's very first comedy icon, I am more than enthusiastic to tackle such an assignment, and so it is that Milton Berle and I are destined to meet.

I experience the comedic force field of "Uncle Miltie" in March 1982, when I arrive at the Friars Club on Santa Monica Boulevard in Beverly Hills, a very famous watering hole and social club for show business personalities. The unique individual I am about to meet had actually begun the non-profit organization as far back as 1947, one year before he became a major TV star. The organization, famous for holding countless "roasts" of major celebrities, had attracted such members as Robert Taylor, Bing Crosby, Al Jolson, Frank Sinatra, Lucille Ball, George Jessel, Eddie Cantor, and Jimmy Durante, to name but a handful.

In 1961, Berle moved the group's meeting location from the old Savoy Hotel on Sunset Boulevard in Los Angeles to its present location, where for the past six years, Berle has not only been the group's president but also the official greeter at the main entrance to the Friars Club dining room. (This is now considered one of the more prestigious dining sites within the Hollywood community.)

Every noontime (assuming he isn't out of town or working on a project), Berle can be found seated in a corner booth in the main dining room, or he is rushing to the front entrance to greet the greats and near-greats as they arrive. Always, he is flitting about like some official gadfly, cracking jokes, being festive and friendly, and bringing an aura of dancing electricity and sense of humor to an otherwise somber-looking dining room.

I have been warned in advance that Berle will very likely be greeting me at the entrance. Sure enough, there he is, eight-inch cigar in hand, beaming broadly. After I introduce myself, he continues to smile and blurts out, "So, you're the kid from San Francisco. I've been expecting you, Johnny. Look, it's very busy today, but I promise we'll have plenty of time to yak." Waving for me to follow him, he leads me to a table on the far side of the room. "I have to greet folks, but I'll be back in a flash." As I take a seat, he rushes back toward his corner booth.

I have also been told in advance that there is never a shortage of fame and talent at the Berle table. Today, Berle is rubbing elbows with comedian Jesse White; Berle's twenty-year-old son, Bill Berle (author of the book, *My Father, Uncle Miltie*); and writer/producer Buddy Arnold, who for forty years has hung out with Berle. On more luminous days, one might expect to see Frank Sinatra, Bob Hope, George Burns, Red Skelton, Buddy Hackett, or Jan Murray drop in. Maybe all on the same day. Cracking jokes and breaking bread with the one and only, Milton Berle.

Berle, that ubiquitous eight-inch cigar forever in front of his face, is really never out of a self-produced spotlight. He seems trapped in a force field of his own energy, darting to the door to greet new guests, hurrying back to his table, and then rushing madly back to my table, to which a waiter brings Berle a hot tamale for his lunch.

He insists on personally setting up my tape recorder directly in front of him (stopping and starting the tape will be done on his explicit command). He offers me a Havana cigar, which has been especially rolled for him with tobacco he purchased from the estate of long-dead comedian Ernie Kovacs. I decline, having never smoked anything in my lifetime, including reefers.

He keeps referring to me as "Johnny," urgently gives signals to the waiters, asks for another tamale because the one in front of him has turned cold, and is always aware of who is entering and leaving the dining room. As often as he dashes back and forth, he never seems out of breath. Energy, gallons of it, drives Milton Berle.

Berle looks uncommonly healthy for a man of seventy-three years. His complexion is ruddy (when you can see it through the cigar smoke), his eyes sparkle behind his eyeglasses, and occasionally he checks his countenance by glancing into the huge mirror behind my booth. He slouches down in his seat and frequently scratches at his eyebrows. The movements never stop coming.

Yeah, he looks great, but he admits he should work out more. So much time spent at the Friars Club, at the expense of things he loves—golf, exercising, strolling—but he watches his food. Yeah, he watches it but he doesn't eat it, even when the waiter brings him a warm tamale. There is a sense of legend and history that instantly rubs off Berle as he flings his one-liners hot and fast. Always on, always the showman, he is laughing his way through his sixty-fourth year in show business, and people still come up to the table and call him *Uncle Miltie* in reference to the days when he was TV's first big star on *The Texaco Star Theater*.

There is also a sense of urgency about Berle. In the style of some fidgety ingénue waiting for a return call from a producer, Berle is never more than a few feet from a telephone, which a waiter has placed on our table. He pounces on it at least five times during our two hours together, and each time the bell rings, Berle signals for my tape recorder to be shut down.

First things first. "San Francisco," he begins ebulliently, "is one of my favorite cities. I first played there in 1922 at the Golden Gate Theater in a straight dramatic act with a girl named Elizabeth Kennedy. That was Vaudeville. A beautiful city, San Francisco. I was up there in 1980 for several weeks in a production of *Guys and Dolls*. In case you missed it, I was one of the guys."

He pauses, giving me a chance to laugh at his gag, then stares with greater intensity at me. "Say, Johnny, how long have you been doing these interviews?" He leans in closely so he can look me squarely in the eye. "What enjoyment do you get out of doing these things? How come you've spent all those years talking to guys like me? You must get something out of it."

Suddenly, I realize that Berle has switched roles and now is interviewing me. Me doing most of the talking isn't why I am here, so I truncate a fast answer about having wanted to be a journalist from the time I was fourteen. To get things back on track, I ask him to give me some personal background, a history in his own words, life on Earth for "Uncle Miltie."

"Promise not to fall asleep?" asks Berle, jiggling his elongated cigar. "Just keep in mind that Gregory Peck once introduced me to the world as 'the five-star general of all the armies of funny men.' Still awake? Okay, I was born in 1908 in New York City, only they called me Milton Berlinger, seeing as how my mother, Sarah, was Jewish. From the beginning, she being star-struck, she pushed me through the swinging doors of show biz. I was all of five when I won a contest impersonating Charlie Chaplin. That got me kiddie

Famed orchestra leader Glenn Miller confers with his publicity agent (played by Milton Berle) in this production still from Sun Valley Serenade (1941).

roles in movies at Biograph and other studios. Proudly, I can say I got a leading role opposite Chaplin himself in *Tillie's Punctured Romance* (1914) and that memorable serial, *Perils of Pauline* (1914). [Berle's roles in both films were actually brief bit parts, not leading roles.] And they were calling me 'The Boy Wonder' in those days. But Mama, around 1923, really wanted me to tour the country in Vaudeville."

At the age of twelve, Berle tells me, he made his Broadway debut in *Floradora*, followed by appearances in *Life Begins at 8:40* and *The Ziegfeld Follies*. A lengthy run in the 1943 *Ziegfeld Follies* established him as a brash, broad-minded (ha ha!), wise-cracking comedian. "That's when I became known as 'The Thief of Bad Gags.' Johnny, the names never stopped comin.'"

He made his adult film debut in *New Faces of 1937*. His roles began improving in 1941 with *Tall, Dark Handsome* and *Sun Valley Serenade*. In the latter, he played a cigar-smoking public relations man for the Glenn Miller Orchestra. Over the years, Berle told

One of Berle's more offbeat films was Always Leave Them Laughing *(1949), a dramatic biography of what a Vaudevillian goes through for fame, with Berle portraying a personality who lies, cheats, and anything else to hit the top, and Ruth Roman as one of the performers caught in his various traps.*

me, "I'd had some success with radio, and in 1947 I had my own series, but it was cancelled in early '48 and it looked like things were going into the sinkhole for me. Some critics were saying that my career was at an end. Splat!"

Then he was signed to appear in *The Texaco Star Theater* for that summer, and he became so popular that by September he had that thirty-year contract signed and sealed. "It was my experience in Vaudeville that really made the show work," he reveals. "Did you know the studios suddenly realized that movie theaters weren't selling as many tickets on Tuesday night as they had been, once the series was sailing? A lot of Emmy nominations for me and the show, and that's how it went until around 1955, when things dwindled away."

One of the lobby cards for Always Leave Them Laughing *(1949).*

What has life been like for Berle these last few years? "Different, very different," he replies. "I don't have to push like I used to. In the early days of my career, there was only me. I was a factory working single-handedly. Now, I have others working for me through my own production company." He writes, produces, and directs, as well as performs. "Now I pick my spots." He says he has two shows right now on cable TV: *Magic of the Stars* with Walter Matthau and Lucille Ball performing magic tricks, and *Milton Berle's Mad Mad World of Comedy.*

He also does benefits and roasts–sometimes three or four in one week. He made five appearances recently on the *General Hospital* soap opera as a theatrical agent, and he does the college circuit, delivering seminars on comedy, a cross somewhere between a monologue and a lecture. He's also done *The Best of Berle*, an upcoming 90-minute prime-time special featuring kinescopes and tapes from his old Texaco programs that first aired on NBC.

Berle isn't worried about any of this old material going out of date. On the topic of comedy, his speech slows somewhat, as though he is carefully articulating his thoughts before speaking. This is Berle the astute thinking man. "Funny is funny, whether it's in color or black and white. Fans like you, who remember me from the 1950s, will wax nostalgically while a new wave of young people will be discovering me for the first time.

"There is no such thing as an old joke," blurts Berle, the world's greatest self-confessed joke stealer. "There're only older audiences. A comedian is a guy who isn't afraid of silence. For example, the timing of the great late Jack Benny. He believed in silence . . . he could take those pauses and wasn't afraid of losing his audience. What do I owe my success to? I'm a stand-up comic. Joke, joke, joke . . . fast one-liners . . . rapid-fire non sequiturs. But to be a comedian you have to be an actor if you want to sustain as a personality. It's the same as sustaining in any other form of entertainment.

"You have to ask yourself three questions. 'Who am I?' 'What am I doing here?' 'Why?' Example: I've seen some comics (I won't mention their names) but afterward there was nothing to take home with me, there was nothing about them to remember. Let's talk about style: It must be indelible. We know what Woody Allen stands for. He's the modern-day Walter Mitty; he's an incongruity. And [John] Belushi, the guy they just buried, he was magnificently crazy, irreverent, a wild mad hatter. He was gloriously fresh to his generation." (Belushi had died only a month earlier, at the age of thirty-three, of an "acute" heroin and cocaine overdose.)

"I see young comedians at the improv shops—Comedy Star, Rising Star, Laugh Stop—and they ask me what I think. I have to say the same thing over and over. Your material, what you're doing, doesn't befit your look. You've got to look in the mirror and ask, 'What should I do? What should I be?' You must have a definitive style. Just like you can't try to be someone else. There's only one Sinatra or Streisand or Garland. They threw the molds away. And when a singer goes out to do 'Over the Rainbow' or 'You Made Me Love You,' that's a mistake. One has to search for one's own song. One's own routine, whatever it has to be.

"Now, Johnny, let's talk about Milton Berle. You saw me as a young fella growing up on TV. So you know I deal in brashness. I know who I am. Right now, as I'm talking, I'm dissecting myself. I deal in flippancy. I'm a wise-guy comedian, a put down artist.

Another one of Berle's unusual roles was portraying Louie the Lilac, a criminal trying to gain control of the America flower market in four episodes of the Batman series (1967-1968) starring Adam West.

I take care of hecklers. I walk on the sides of my feet. I say tag lines and make funny faces and do physical things. Shtick, Johnny, that's me, shtick. Purely."

Suddenly, Berle leaps up and rushes back to his table to receive new guests. In his absence, an old friend of his, John Francis, stops at our table to tell me he will be producing the upcoming show at the Masonic Auditorium. Francis points his finger at Berle and shakes his head. "That man, he's a pain in the ass. He's such a damn perfectionist that when we get to Frisco he's gonna inject himself into every phase of the show. I'll tell you something: he saved this club from obscurity. Six years ago it was much in the red. He appointed committee heads, he built a rescue crew, he was ship's captain. Now he's always here and keeps this place alive and living. But still, what a pain in the ass!"

Francis scurries off furtively when he sees Berle returning. Berle sits and opens fire immediately to my question about retirement. "I wouldn't be in any other business. It's too late to open a used car lot. Or a hamburger stand. Someone asked George Burns when he was going to retire. George answered, 'To what?' I have the same answer. See, I'm still stealing other comedians' material.

"Hey, Johnny, you need a joke? I have the largest file of jokes in the U.S., in the world. In my office, six and a half million jokes, indexed and cross-indexed on cards. I have every Burlesque scene ever written. Off the top of my head, I can remember 200,000 gags."

About his thirty-year exclusive contract with NBC, which expired only the past August, there is an unusual degree of melancholy and disappointment in his voice. "My contract stated NBC could use me as a producer, director, writer, executive, consultant. But they blew it, Johnny. They never once called upon me for anything other than my acting. They never put me upstairs as an executive in charge of comedy shows, or asked me if a script was suitable for a week, four weeks, or a series. I was never used, yet I could've given the network so much more than I did."

But hell, that contract and NBC were behind him, he says, becoming more light-hearted again. "My philosophy is simple, Johnny. To live and enjoy, day by day. To always have my work and my family." He smiles and looks very contented, and waves across the room at a new arrival. "I only hope that I live to be as old as Henny Youngman's material."

Then came the surprise ending: Berle puts on his show at the Masonic Auditorium, the one produced by John Francis, that guy who had stopped at my table at the Friars Club. In addition to Berle ("I'm going to be the emcee for the entire show. How can you stop me? That's a joke!"), there is singer Billy Daniels, tap dancer Arthur Duncan (from Lawrence Welk's TV show), a juggling group called The Saxons, magician Mercer Helms, and Manny Harmond's 21-piece orchestra.

As I recall, it is a pretty lively show, with some individuals in the audience calling out with derogative remarks and Berle responding to them with his own put-down replies, a form of ad libbing for which he had become famous—or infamous. I don't think much more about it... until I arrive a few days later at my optometrist's office to pick up my new glasses.

The eye doc looks very sad and sounds depressed when I ask him how everything turned out with the Berle event. "Well, things went south," he says. "The turnout wasn't so hot, and we didn't make the kind of box office we'd hoped for. So a member of our committee got on the phone to Milton and asked him if he'd be willing to forego the $60,000 fee we'd all agreed upon. Otherwise, the Congregation B'Nai Emunah was not going to have the funds for renovation.

"But, Berle refused to give up his fee. He said he had properly earned it with the show he had presented. He had lived up to his end of the bargain. And that was that."

Suddenly I realized there was one subject Berle had never joked about—money.

In 1984, Berle was inducted into the Television Academy Hall of Fame—the first of seven of his peers. He stayed busy until he was diagnosed with colon cancer in April 2001. He refused any kind of treatment and died eleven months later at the age of ninety-three.

JACK BENNY
Jack's Still Thinking It Over: How He Used the Violin To String Us Along Into A Fabulous Comedy World

The gum is the sugarless kind, fruit flavored, and even a man of seventy-seven years can still chew sugarless gum vigorously enough to get it stuck to the roof of his mouth. Benjamin Kubelsky has just done that, but think of him more as Jack Benny, the name he assumed when he went into show business.

He stands near the front door of his 2.5-acre mansion in Holmby Hills, designed in the style of an Italian villa, trying to be graceful about the "irritable wad" as it interferes with our initial meeting. He says "Pardon me a moment, if you don't mind, please," and removes the gum from his mouth, wraps it up into its original wrapper, slips it into the pocket of his jacket, and rubs his hands together as if to get rid of any remaining remnants.

"Never," he tells me, "let anything go to waste." Especially if it's in "good taste."

That, after all, fits the penny-pinching stage image of this straight-faced man, who had started out in show business at the age of eighteen, playing his violin under the stage name of Ben K. Benny, until he joined the U.S. Navy in 1917. He served his country best, as it turned out, when he played his violin as part of the U.S. Navy's "Great Lakes Revues." In fact, during one of these concerts his playing was so poorly-received that he decided to make some wisecracks, and they evoked such laughter that he was convinced it was time to put the violin aside and become a comedian. That's when he did the final name change to the plain Jack Benny. Put the violin away? Never. That would become another instrument of comedy that he would employ forever.

The gum disengaged and tended to, Benny proudly announces he will be coming to the San Francisco-Bay Area soon to perform

This is almost the image of Jack Benny that greeted me at the door of his home in 1971. Well-dressed in suit and tie and looking relaxed. No sign of a penny-pincher anywhere in sight, and certainly not somebody who would drive a 1916 Maxwell.

Here's the image of Jack Benny playing his violin—the instrument he took seriously until he was booed by a concert crowd. From then on, he used it as a comedy tool. Sweet music it would never be, but it would bring him tons of laughter. "I love to string the public along," he would often joke.

at a theater in San Carlos, and pauses to brag about the fact that Hugh Hefner's Playboy Mansion is just across the street. He jokes about having telescopes hidden at various windows upstairs. "It's all part of my learning curve," he jokes, leading me into a living room where he plops onto a sofa. "Think of it," he says, "as a joining of the flesh and the devil."

"I hope you appreciate the fact," he tells me, "that despite my age I still do four to six benefit concerts a year, and I was recently awarded a Presidential citation for raising millions of dollars for symphony orchestras through my personal appearances and violin playing for the past fifteen years." He dusts off his hands again, as if to cement what he has just said into fact.

"Concerts are important to me," says Benny, establishing a somber tone, which he will maintain throughout our meeting, even when he makes a joke. "I thrive on a live audience—and I enjoy being back on a stage just as I was in the days of radio and television. These things become an integral part of you, and you never feel the same again without them."

This love for work is exemplified by the fact he will have another TV special with movie composer Henry Mancini, and has been scheduled to do shows in Las Vegas and at Harrah's Tahoe. He has also recently completed trips to Israel and England. "Don't worry about those long distances," says Benny. "I still know how to travel cheap."

Even so, Benny admits he feels the strain. "I get too worked up about things and end up overextending myself. Pushing myself harder than I would really like to. But that's the kind of animal I am. Glad I don't feel cooped up about that. Then there are times when I'm taking it easy and enjoying myself, but still feel a bit restless. It's hard to find a happy in-between."

On his recent trip to England, Benny met with some London reporters and, during the interviews, mentioned he was seventy-seven. While the British just buried that fact, the American press jumped on it and made a big to-do about Benny publicly admitting he was no longer thirty-nine, one of the longest running gags any comedian has perpetrated on the American people. ("Benny Confesses His Age!" screamed one newspaper headline. I wonder if one day Benny will be called "ageless.")

Portraying himself as thirty-nine through three decades of success in Vaudeville, radio, TV, and movies was just one shtick that turned Benny into one of America's most popular comics. Others included pretending he was cheap (or thrifty, as he often called it), smarter than everyone else, and never giving up on his 1916 Maxwell, no matter how dilapidated the car got. (Noises of deteriorating pieces of metal and screeching tires, donated by Mel "Bugs Bunny" Blanc.)

Suddenly, Benny begins humming the tune and some of the lyrics of "There's No Business Like Show Business." "Boy, when Irving Berlin wrote that number he really knew what he was doing. I remember when I made up my mind to go into Vaudeville. I had just graduated—and didn't feel like going on to high school." He pauses as I burst out with laughter, realizing Mr. Benny isn't always as serious as he may sound. I ask him about Vaudeville. "What memories those early shows bring back. Two or three a day on Broadway, at the Palace. Rubbing elbows with Jimmy Durante, Georgie Jessel, Johnnie Wilkes Booth . . ." He pauses so I have a chance to laugh again. "I did that very joke on radio. Some pieces you never forget." He chuckles, staring out through a window for a bit. As an afterthought: "I paid for it so why shouldn't I use it more than once?"

He continues: "Then Vaudeville began to be killed off by a new medium, radio. I wanted to do radio, but knew I needed a surefire formula and character. I decided I'd play a tight, miserly skinflint. The public got a million—or is it a trillion?—laughs out of that character, and so do I every time I count the money, I'm saved."

While verbal was his power during the radio era, he turned to more visual designs with the coming of his TV series in 1949. Such as giving a "slow burn" look when someone said something derogative or revealing to him. He would stand silently, turning left and right to look at his audience (call the pause "pregnant"), as one who has been left speechless. "Yes, silent," he emphasizes. And then remains silence for the next twenty seconds, first looking left, then right. An amusing sample I can still visualize. "I hope that's an image," he says, "that burns into your soul and you never forget it."

After I stop laughing, Benny says he stays in shape by playing golf, exercising, walking "an awful lot" and "running to the bank." He watches what he eats and smokes only cigars. Any charges of senility he hastily discounts, contending he's as sharp as ever. Among his weaknesses he lists "procrastination," although "for some reason or other it always seems to work out to my advantage. Never put off until tomorrow what you can't do today."

As for his act, he says he still "spends more time preparing and editing my material than anything else. Once a routine's right on paper, it never bothers me. I've always been a firm believer in sticking to the script. Ad libbing is fine if done in the right place. Of course, the real secret in comedy is to make it seem impromptu when it's really been carefully planned. Sometimes ad libbing can damage a routine.

"I think I know how to prepare a good show. I know how to stay on subjects pretty well. Timing is the important key here. I talk slowly, but that isn't always the reason for good timing. Timing . . . no, pacing is a better word. The hardest part is trying to keep up to the times as much as possible. Each year, you have to be a little more sophisticated, and just a little smarter. You have to be a judge of what is unusual. In the Bay Area, for example, I'll be doing some old things, but I'll also be doing some new stuff. After all, you do have old and new people to contend with."

Benny admits that he always surrounded himself with good writers. "Ask me for my favorite line and it was something I once said to Fred Allen. It was during one of his radio shows when we were carrying on our infamous feud. 'You wouldn't talk to me that way, Allen, if my writers were here.' I also insisted to my writers that I be surrounded by colorful characters. And they were to receive as many funny lines as I was. It took some of the stress of starring in a show off my shoulders. And those characters became as beloved as the Jack Benny character I was playing."

Benny is referring to several memorable contributors to his success. There was Phil Harris, his band leader, who would eventually develop his own series playing an orchestra leader with his real-life wife, Alice Faye. Also bragging, even on the air, that he had two shows while Benny had only one. There was Mel Blanc, best-known as the voice of many popular, now classic, Warner Bros. cartoon characters, who occasionally portrayed Benny's violin instructor Professor LeBlanc. Blanc also played a Mexican character, whose name was Sid and whose "Sí" when asked a question became a recurring gag line. Sid's sister, of course, was Sue. Blanc was also the station announcer's voice who repeatedly said a train was leaving for "Anaheim, Azusa, and Cucamanga."

That's Eddie Anderson cranking up Benny's 1916 Maxwell Touring Car while Benny waits patiently. Eventually the car was put on display at the Universal Studio Tour Plaza before becoming privately owned.

Eddie Anderson played the valet/butler Rochester, and was always the driver whenever Jack went anywhere in his Maxwell. Don Wilson was the show's salesman/host who was often the brunt of jokes about being overweight. One of the most endearing was tenor Dennis Day, who could produce as many laughs as musical notes as he and his mother—played by Verna Felton—feuded and argued and put down Benny. Day would develop his own radio show after World War II and become very wealthy from it, and, like Phil Harris, constantly remind Benny he had one more radio show than Benny.

Then there was a very important lady, Mary Livingstone, who was really Sadie Marks. "She was a hosiery clerk I met at the May Company one day. One year later, in 1927, we married, and she became one of the most popular voices on our radio show." (Because of stage fright, Sadie had stopped appearing on Benny's TV

Jack Benny with his co-star wife, Mary Livingstone, aka Sadie Marks. Oddly, the e at the end of Livingstone was dropped so her name on air was pronounced Livingston.

The husband-and-wife team of Benita Hume and Ronald Colman, who became regular comedy characters on Jack Benny's radio show after moving into his neighborhood in 1947. They are the key to understanding the famous "Your Money or Your Life" routine.

show in the mid-1950s and officially retired at the same time that Gracie Allen left her TV series because of failing health.)

The most famous moment on radio occurred on March 28. 1948, when Jack paid a visit to the home of Ronald Colman and his wife Benita Hume, who had become regulars on the show, having been good friends of Benny for many years and having just moved into Benny's neighborhood. (The gag was that Benny was always intruding into their nearby home to borrow things. Colman and Hume pretended to accept Benny, but they really abhorred his presence.)

Colman had just won an Academy Award the week before for his performance in *A Double Life* so Benny had told his staff writers to work that fact into the plot of the show. Which is, one evening Benny borrows Colman's Oscar so he can show it to his valet, Rochester, and is walking home through the darkness with it when, suddenly –

A Voice Out of Nowhere: *"Hey bud . . . hey. Got a match?"*

Benny: *"Match? Yeah, I have one right here in my—"*

Voice: *"Don't make a move! This is a stick-up."*

Benny: *"What?!"*

Voice: *"You heard me."*

Benny: *"Mister, mister, put down that gun."*

Voice: *"Shut up! Now, come on! Your money or your life!"* (long pause) *Look, bud, I said your money or your life!"*

Benny: *"I'm thinking it over!"*

While there is a pause, it is not as long as some have said, and hence the sequence has become surrounded by a certain amount of myth. Still, it ranks as *the* classic Benny moment.

However, the gag isn't over yet, as Benny reminds me during our meeting. This part, he claims, has become largely forgotten, but the routine is turned into a running gag for the next few weeks. Here's what happened, according to Benny: He tries to replace the stolen Oscar by visiting the home of Bing Crosby, who had won an Academy Award for *Going My Way*. Crosby is smart enough not give Benny anything but some sass. Three episodes later, Jack almost convinces Frank Sinatra to let him borrow his Oscar (won for the 1945 musical short, *The House I Live In*), but at the last second Sinatra is sucked away into a vacuum cleaner operated by house cleaner Mel Blanc. (It was never revealed how Sinatra crawled out of the device.)

Finally, Benny informs me, the running gag is brought to a close on May 9, 1948. At their breakfast table, Benita Hume excitedly tells

Here's Jack Benny, as a band's third trumpet player, cutting loose in a scene from The Horn Blows at Midnight *(1945), the most talked about movie of Benny's career, as its alleged incompetence became a recurring gag on his radio shows.*

hubby Colman that Mary Livingstone has revealed that the Oscar Benny borrowed was stolen on his way home. Colman orders Benita to calm down, there's nothing to worry about because when he gave the Oscar to Benny he feared he would never get it back, and thus ordered the family chauffeur to hold up Benny and take it back. The Oscar has been safely at home all this time, and the alleged hold-up man is simply a sweet, endearing family employee.

Although few of us think of Benny as a film actor, he says he appeared in twenty-four pictures–"all of them successful." I remind Benny of a few of those titles, having listed them before our meeting. I mention *Buck Benny Rides Again, George Washington Slept Here,* and *Charley's Aunt.* He laughs. "You haven't mentioned anything yet. Let me tell you about my movies. I made

This unusual production still is from one of Benny's lesser remembered films, George Washington Slept Here (1942), in which he and wife Ann Sheridan move into an old farmhouse in Pennsylvania and discover it's full of bizarre history. Benny first saw the play version on Broadway (written by George S. Kaufman and Moss Hart) and insisted that Warner Bros. produce the film and give him a starring role.

them year after year, and nobody said anything about them. But let me tell you, you make one stinker and you're through."

But Mr. Benny," I almost shout, "didn't you make one *stinker* in 1945?"

"Hah! If you're talking about *The Horn Blows at Midnight*. I can honestly say I never heard from more than ten or twelve people who didn't like it. Come to think of it, I never heard from more than ten who even saw it." He waits for me to finish laughing. Then: "Yeah, that was one of our greatest on-air running gags,

Jack Benny was never more dramatically powerful than in Ernst Lubitsch's To Be or Not to Be (1942), in which he portrays a member of a Warsaw theatrical group that is doing a comedy play about Adolf Hitler, shortly before the invasion of Poland. In this scene, he's dressed as a Nazi officer as he converses with his wife (played by Carole Lombard, in her last screen role, as she died in a plane crash shortly before the film opened in American theaters.

and it lasted not for weeks or months but years. Every joke was like the one I just threw at you. That *The Horn Blows at Midnight* did lousy business at the box office, that it was completely awful, that it was the greatest stinkaroo of all time, and I was the star, cast as a trumpet player who dreams he's a trumpet player up in Heaven. It was all for the sake of a laugh, and it was completely ironic, because *The Horn Blows at Midnight* did okay at the box office. Once again, I laughed all the way to the bank."

One of Benny's best performances is to be savored in *To Be Or Not to Be* (1941, in which he portrays an actor in a Warsaw theater group spoofing Hitler's Third Reich. [It has remained popular enough that in 1982 Mel Brooks produced a remake, no doubt in part as a tribute to Benny.] Newfound audiences are also appreciating *Love Thy Neighbor* and *It's in the Bag*, the latter a 1945 comedy that highlights the famed Jack Benny-Fred Allen feud.

But all that is largely forgotten by Benny. "I always like the next thing I'm supposed to do better than what I've done in the past. I've never been interested in things from the past. Unless, of course, it's a check that came in yesterday's mail. I'm not much for nostalgia. In fact, the hell with nostalgia. I don't enjoy keeping old memories and old things. Wait a minute! Who just said I was old?"

Perhaps Jack Benny didn't put that piece of gum in a little wrapping paper, after all. Maybe he just stuck it under the nearest table top and forgot about it.

Jack Benny lived just three more years. Diagnosed with pancreatic cancer, he fell into a coma three days before Christmas, 1974, and died one day after Christmas at the age of eighty. During those days when he was unconscious, some of his best friends paid him a visit, including Bob Hope, George Burns, and Frank Sinatra. At his funeral, Hope said: "This is the only time when Jack Benny's timing was all wrong. He left us much too soon."

DENNIS DAY
Gee, Reader! It was the Night I Spent With Day,
The Comedy Sidekick of Mr. Benny...
Who? Me?

On a Saturday night in Sparks, East Reno, Nevada, in the spring of 1963, I am seated in the Circus Room of John Ascuaga's Nugget Casino in a suburb of "The Biggest Little City in the World." It's called The Circus Room because nightly an elephant named Bertha and her daughter, Tina, perform on stage. Dare I say it's a giant act in which both are wearing trunks during each performance?

Also entertaining on that stage this weekend is a forty-six-year-old comedian-singer showing signs of tension. Back in Los Angeles, his wife, Peggy, is expecting their ninth child at any moment. I ask the entertainer if he would prefer a cocktail to soothe his shattered nerves rather than the cup of coffee he has been nervously sipping on. "I know I may look a little jittery, but I'm really okay, but thanks anyway." (The baby won't be delivered until two days hence, and it will be a boy called Daniel.)

Dennis Day will always be best remembered as the tenor on Jack Benny's radio and TV shows, portraying a shy adult trapped in the clutches of a domineering mother named Lucrezia Day (voiced by Verna Felton). A naive pipsqueak, Dennis would wander into Benny's home with a high-pitched "Yes, please. Who, me?" or "Gee, Mr. Benny," deliver some utterly ridiculous lines, and then sing popular, nostalgic songs. He became an expert at both singing and comedy.

In 1946, after serving for two years as a lieutenant in the U.S. Navy, he returned to Benny's program and he soon began his own radio comedy series, *A Day in the Life of Dennis Day*. So he would often, during a broadcast, tell Benny that, while he, Dennis Day, had two shows, Benny had only one. As Day frequently put it, "Gee, Mr. Benny, I must be the best." Whatever, he had

Dennis Day during his successful years on The Jack Benny Program *as not only its singing star with a powerful tenor voice but one of its comedic characters.]*

become "America's Favorite Irish Tenor," singing such classics as "Clancy Lowered the Boom," "Dear Hearts and Gentle People," and "Mona Lisa."

While millions of Americans were guffawing at Day and making him the brunt of their own jokes, he was busy raking in a fortune. After his show left the air in 1951, he stayed with Benny on his TV series, but Day was smart enough to form his own corporation

Caption: Dennis Day and Jack Benny.

and produce *The Dennis Day Show* for NBC-TV, making a fortune that Benny had never brought him.

"It was a profitable characterization, that goofy guy, and it all happened through an odd set of circumstances." Day (born Owen Patrick Eugene McNulty to a New York family of Irish immigrants) was attending Manhattan College when he became a member of the glee club. "I had done some singing," he explains, "with the St. Patrick Choir. I'd vocalized on a few local radio stations, and I'd worked with Larry Clinton's Orchestra. But—and this was a big but—I never imagined I'd make a permanent living as a performer. I originally had my eye on criminal law as a vocation."

Along the way, McNulty had cut a record, "I Never Knew Heaven Could Speak," and it was heard by Mary Livingstone, Jack Benny's wife, just at a time when Benny was about to lose his regular tenor, Kenny Baker, who had been offered his own program. She approached McNulty and talked him into auditioning for the part. "A few days later, I was sitting in a tryout room and there was Jack just a short distance away, talking to other tryouts. Suddenly, without any warning, Benny called my name. I was shocked. Instinctively, I leaped to my feet and turned toward Jack, spontaneously muttering 'Yes please. Me?' "

Day couldn't have sold himself better. "That's our boy!" shouted Benny. "We'll play him just like that—a shy, utterly sincere boy." And so, at the age of twenty-one, McNulty became Dennis Day, radio star. "But," continues Day, "it is one thing to be the silly fool on the Benny show and another to be inept when I do a show like I'm doing tonight. The public is smart; it knows I've been in the business for a long time, and knows I'm more than a one-dimensional personality. Here and now, they want to see what the real Dennis Day is like. And that's the challenge I face today."

Nevertheless, between songs in the Circus Room, Day had told plenty of jokes. "I don't mind sharing the bill with Bertha the Elephant—but dressing rooms, too?" Because he was especially talented at doing voice imitations on Benny's show (James Stewart and Ronald Colman were the most frequent), tonight he has imitated Lawrence Welk. He also tries out a few accents ranging from a Japanese Justice-of-the-Peace ("Marriage in bathtub is double-ring ceremony") to a British dentist ("Water from the River Kwai is good for your bridge").

The interview must end, as Day has one more late show to perform. He finishes his cup of coffee, reiterating we should not worry about his wife's ninth delivery. "I'm so used to this sort of thing, I could phone this one in."

Not long after our meeting in the Circus Room at the Nugget in East Reno, Dennis Day took time to write a short thank you postcard to my wife, Erica, and I:

"Dear Erica and John: My sweetest thanks for your kindness to me. All the Warmest and Every Good Wish. DENNIS DAY."

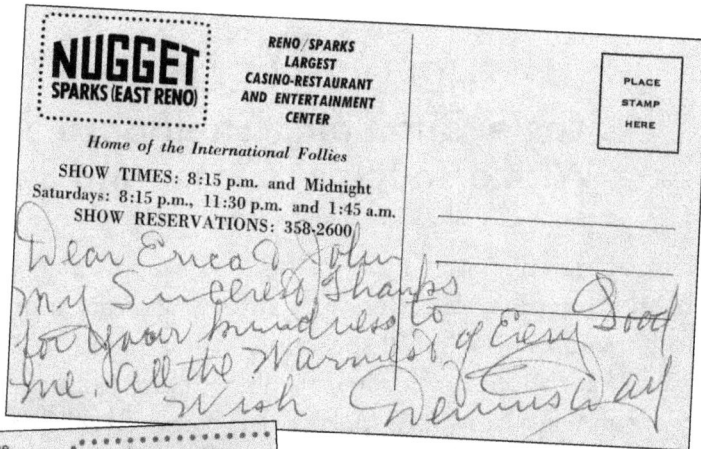

Front of Card and Back of Card.

Day will continue to perform on Jack Benny's TV show until its final season two years later, still playing "the kid" (at forty-eight) who is always cracking wise when not singing a popular number. He would also make an occasional public appearance, although he preferred to spend more time with his ever-growing family. Wife Peggy would have a tenth child before life ended for Day from Lou Gehrig's Disease in 1988. He was seventy-two.

SHELDON LEONARD
Stogie-Chomping Sheldon, a Mug With a Touch of Class—and Sass

In September 1975, I am in the Hollywood office of Sheldon Leonard, another Jack Benny favorite, a racetrack tout who loved to horse around. He will soon be starring in a new CBS sitcom, *Big Eddie*, about a reformed gambler trying to begin a new career running a New York sports arena. Leonard will bring all those traits he's famous for in creating this latest of the many "mugs" he has portrayed on radio, TV, and in the movies over several decades, including his comedy character contributions to Jack Benny's radio show. In short, "like dis," chomping extra hard on a stogie with the bite of a Great White Shark and talking "outta da side of da mouth, like dis."

While I have no doubt at the moment that playing Big Eddie should come second nature to Leonard, I ask him to focus on the colorful Runyonesque characters he has played since 1939. He will always be remembered for his New York accent coming out of the corners of his mouth. He tells me how, in the movies, he gave his strong comedic support to *Lucky Jordan* (1942) as Slip Moran, *Stop, You're Killing Me* (1952) as Lefty, *Guys and Dolls* (1955) as the unforgettable Harry the Horse, and *Pocketful of Miracles* (1961) as Steve Darcy. "Yeah, Harry the Horse, that's the guy I loved the most," he says proudly, straightening the cuffs of his dress jacket. "And Slip Moran, he wasn't *that* bad!"

Leonard points out that he has had his serious side, too, displaying the kind of villainy you didn't laugh at. A classic example was his Joe Portugal in the Film Noir classic *Decoy* (1946). Others: *Somewhere in the Night* (1946) and *Come Fill the Cup* (1951). In *Sinbad the Sailor* (1947) and *The Diamond Queen* (1953), he showed his stuff as the evil caliph but with a touch of satire. He could also appear to be outright mean, like the way he threw Jimmy Stewart into the snow in *It's a Wonderful Life* (1947). "Me? Throwing Jimmy

Sheldon Leonard, around the time he was struggling to be a producer and also trying to start a new TV series as Big Eddie.

Stewart around like that? What a moment! It comes only once in a lifetime."

I am more excited about finding out what Leonard has to say about the classic characters he performed on radio for Jack Benny, Phil Harris, and Bob Hope, those named Louie the Louse, Larry the Lip, Marvin the Moose, and Dirty Ernie.

"Hey, Mr. Stanley," he tells me, "you left out one of the best, one of the funniest, and it was on Benny's show. Remember the

Sheldon Leonard as he looked back in his tough-guy days in the movies, playing Louie the Louse and Marvin the Moose. That was before he became a successful TV producer.

racetrack tout? He was simply called 'The Tout.' Benny would be in a public place somewhere, innocently shopping, and suddenly I'd say 'Psst, hey bud, come here a minute." I'd follow up with inside information based on jokes about horses and racing. It was ridiculous, but fun to do, week after week. One time, Benny was

Robert Culp, Sheldon Leonard, and Bill Cosby on location making an episode of I Spy *in the mid-1960s. Credit Leonard for being the first to hire a Black actor to star in a network TV series.*

shopping in a market, in the vegetable department, and I warned Benny not to bet on a horse named Bananas. 'Why not?' he asks me. And me, The Tout, tells him: 'Bananas always tends to bunch up on the rail.'"

What many may have forgotten about Leonard was his great success as a TV producer, winning five Emmy Awards in the process. Of course, he had to stop talking out of the side of his mouth to do it. Among his hit shows were *Make Room For Daddy* with Danny Thomas, *The Real McCoys*, *Gomer Pyle, USMC* with Jim Nabors, and *The Dick Van Dyke Show*. He really made news with *I Spy*, becoming one of the first producer to cast a Black actor—Bill Cosby—in a leading role, even if some NBC affiliates threatened to boycott the series. While making *I Spy*, he was also the first to take his production to foreign locations, introducing to the industry the compact Cinemobile, a studio-on-wheels that enabled him to reach locations with a minimum of trouble and equipment.

About those days, Leonard explains, "A lotta people thought I just got tired and quit acting, or went to Palm Springs to play a little golf. It was none of those things. When I started out in the early 1950s, it was a seller's market. Out of eighteen ideas I attempted, sixteen were accepted by the networks. I had guarantees from sponsors going in, and there were no money problems. But that's all changed now. Producing has turned into a difficult and often unpleasant experience. The Feds have cut down on prime time and there are fewer series. Everyone's making pilots and trying to sell them. It's no longer profitable to produce except under a major studio, which can afford to charge a large overhead. The independents have been hurt. Severely!"

For a time, Leonard tried to make feature-length films, but "that was a complete disaster. I kept losing out to other producers when it came to buying properties. I wanted the original screenplay for *M*A*S*H*, but Ingo Preminger [brother of director Otto Preminger] aced me out. For a whole year, I drank martinis and had lunch at the Polo Lounge, trying to swing a deal. But no matter how many times I got smashed or ate too much, nothing. No luck."

Finally, he decided it would be better to return to acting than rust away in Leisure Village. "So I have this *Big Eddie* concept. But . . ." I can tell there is an uncertainty about his choice. In his eyes is the question: *Will the character of Big Eddie, so true to the Leonard canon, be a hit or an anachronism?* Ultimately, all Leonard can do for me is shrug and chomp ever harder on that big black cigar of his, and pray Damon Runyon characters are still popular, and his show can compete with Redd Foxx on the NBC network, and folks will never forget The Tout or Harry the Horse.

Big Eddie lasted for a whopping three months before it vanished into the graveyard of failed comedy series and was Leonard's last major effort as actor and producer. He died in 1997 at the age of eighty-nine. No more Pretty Willy (*Tall, Dark and Handsome*, 1941), Lippy Harris (*Jinx Money*, 1948) or Jumbo Schneider (*Money From Home*, 1953).

Meet Chief Ogone, one of Sheldon Leonard's more offbeat colorful characters from his feature film The Iroquis Trail.

MEL BLANC
The Looney, Looney, Sometimes Tuney, Tuney
Beep Beep Beep King of Animated Voices

Although it will take you a while to find out how it came to pass, believe me when I tell you this next comedic personality was very helpful to the career of Jack Benny. "That's . . . that's . . . that's not all, folks!" His face is hardly known to the public at all, even now in the month of November 1981, yet any living being who has seen a Warner Bros. cartoon will know *that* voice, possibly the most often heard voice in the entertainment world. His voice has given dimension to the gregarious carrot-chewing Bugs Bunny, to the shotgun-packing, rabbit-seeking Elmer Fudd, to the stuttering loveable Porky Pig, to the rootin'-tootin' cantankerous Yosemite Sam, to the naive Tweety Bird, and to his nemesis, sloppy slurry Sylvester the Cat.

Mel Blanc doesn't mind that most people don't recognize him in restaurants or department stores. He has made enough fortunes for several men during the four and a half decades he has provided voices for cartoon characters, radio shows, commercial messages, and movies. At seventy-three, he is busier than ever—the demand for the Blanc sound has grown greater with each passing decade. If it isn't a TV commercial, it might be a Saturday morning cartoon (right now he's Barney Rubble on *The Flintstones*, Spacely on *The Jetsons*, and Heathcliff the Cat on *Heathcliff*), or maybe just a live appearance. He has just completed speaking at his 125th college audience, showing some of the old cartoons and describing how he helped to create a unique sound for each character.

Blanc could go on doing this potpourri forever, but it's doubtful he would ever attain greater notoriety than that which the Warner Bros. cartoons have brought him. They continue to live on in reruns and in occasional film festivals, such as *Friz Freleng's Looney Looney Looney Bugs Bunny Movie*, a current composite of

Mel Blanc, the face you hear a lot about but never see. He was a unique creator of sound.

old and new material that is making the rounds of motion picture theaters throughout America.

Blanc is in his office at Blanc Communications, a Los Angeles-based corporation co-owned by Mel and his forty-two-year-old son, Noel. The company is mainly designed to handle the worldwide demand for Blanc and a series of commercials that all have one thing in common: the voice of Mel Blanc.

"Warner Bros. cartoons were ahead of their time," he tells me, an unmistakable note of nostalgia permeating *that* voice. "Every film was fully animated, every frame was drawn. There were none of the money-saving techniques they use today for the Saturday morning shows. It used to take 125 people nine months to complete one seven-minute cartoon short and it would cost nine times more than they spend today in limited animation. Loving care went into each little cartoon."

In addition to twenty minutes of newly animated material about the life of Bugs Bunny, the *Looney Looney Looney* film features two Academy Award-winning cartoons in their entirety: *Knighty Night Bugs* is a takeoff on King Arthur and His Singing Sword, in which every voice belongs to Blanc, and *Birds Anonymous* is a spoof on Alcoholics Anonymous, in which a cat must train another cat not to eat birds.

Although the Oscars for the cartoons went to their producers and directors, and never to the voice creator, Blanc today owns the Oscar for *Birds Anonymous*. He explains: "Ed Selzer, one of the producers, was sick, and though he was dying, and he called me up. He told me to take one of his five Oscars because I deserved it. I refused to take it, but he vowed he was going to will an Oscar to me. Well, two years later Ed died, and sure enough, he lived up to his word."

Blanc, a native-born San Franciscan who was raised in Portland, Oregon, first started fooling around with dialects by imitating the thick Yiddish accent of a grocery store owner in his neighborhood. Jobs in Chinatown also gave him a range of Asian accents. Pretty soon he was performing on local radio with a one-man show. His wife, Estelle, urged him to move to Hollywood in 1935, and they went to face some difficult times.

Blanc might have never been heard had one particular casting director had his way. "I went to see Leon Schlesinger, who had a small studio. But the man at the desk wouldn't listen to me. For two years I would go back to Leon's every two weeks, always to be turned down. Finally, that man died and his replacement, the first time I saw him, agreed to audition me. I was asked if I could do a drunken bull. I said sure. What would a drunken bull sound

In order to create all those wonderful cartoon voices, Mel Blanc would occasionally have to move his lips in peculiar ways.

like? I was asked. I replied, 'Hick I'd sound a little hick loaded, looking hick for sour mash.' Someone laughed, and I was finally on my way."

From that point on, whenever he was asked to create a new character, he would first study the characteristics of the animal. "When they showed me a drawing or a storyboard, I'd always ask myself, *If that animal could talk, how would he sound?* For Woody Woodpecker, it was a silly 'hee hee hee hee' laugh. Bugs, he was a tough little stinker, so I blended a Bronx and a Brooklyn accent. If a pig could talk, he'd talk with a grunt, so when I created Porky Pig, his words would start out with the grunt, giving a stuttering effect. For Pepe Le Pew, the French lover skunk, I gave him a Charles Boyer accent. 'Ah, my lovely one, I'm crazy about you; you crazy pussycat, I want to hold you in my paws and kiss you.'"

Originally, they weren't going to bother Blanc about doing the "beep beep" of the Roadrunner . . . until the producers lost the mechanical car horn they had intended to use. Blanc has done every "beep beep beep" since, and also designed the articulate, suave British voice for Wile E. Coyote.

Yosemite Sam was a tough one for Blanc because "he was this cantankerous character only two feet high with a red mustache, and I had to make him noticed on the screen. So I gave him a gravelly, deep voice, boisterous and like a cowboy. 'Ya ornery critter, I'm gonna blast ya.' For Tweety Bird, the baby canary, I needed a babyish sound, and for Sylvester the Cat I needed a sloppy 'Sufferin' succatash.'"

Blanc was a bit thrown when they showed him a drawing of the Tasmanian Devil. "I asked if anyone had ever heard a Tasmanian Devil, and they hadn't. So I created this crazy ongoing growling that sort of sounds like words, and I defy anyone to tell me that's not the way a Tasmanian Devil sounds."

Despite all the characters, Bugs Bunny remains his personal favorite. "Bugs has done a lot for me. I'm recognized immediately when I use that voice."

Blanc's involvement in radio during the late 1930s and throughout the 1940s is a major footnote to his career. He became the sound of a duck on *The Joe Penner Show* (whose familiar line was "Wanna buy a duck?") and anonymously provided sound effects and dialects. His radio career, however, really blossomed to its fullest when he became associated with *The Jack Benny Program*. One of his memorable characters was the railroad conductor, whose voice would boom from a loudspeaker: "Train leaving on Track Five for Anaheim, Azusa, and Cuc–*long pause*–amonga." He was also the voice of Benny's snotty Polly the Parrot, often taken to a psychiatrist where the bird character would have to answer questions. He will also always be remembered for having an emotionally sad voice for Benny's "long-suffering" violin instructor Professor LeBlanc, who ultimately, on one of the shows, was "driven insane" by Benny's incompetent playing. Then there was the store clerk who would have a nervous breakdown before the show was over, all because he had to deal with Benny always changing his mind about how he wanted his purchases to be gift-wrapped. There was also a Mexican character named Sid,

Mel Blanc during a rehearsal session for one of Jack Benny's shows. Standing behind Mel and Jack are announcer Don Wilson, he of the wide girth, and valet-butler Rochester, played by Eddie Anderson.

whose usual response to a question was "Si," and whose sister was "Sue." Sue? Si!

Two of Blanc's other memorable achievements during those radio years were on *The Judy Canova Show*. He was the lazy, slow-speaking hillbilly named Pa ("Ma, I think there's a fly in my soup and I think it's lookin' right at me!") and he portrayed Pedro the Mexican ("Pardon me for talking in your face, senorita"). For Burns and Allen, he was the sad-voiced Happy Postman who would bemoan, "Keep smiling, Mrs. Burns."

The thing to remember about Mel Blanc is that there was always a microphone just inches away as he sat in studios and recording booths creating the voices of Bugs Bunny and countless other cartoon characters.

During this period, Blanc was also Botsford Twink on *The Abbott and Costello Show,* August Moon on *Point Sublime,* and Floyd the Barber on *The Great Gildersleeve.* He even had his own show in 1946 as the owner of a fix-it shop, doing voices for himself, as well as a stuttering character named Zookie, who sounded very close to Porky Pig. The fix-it character, unfortunately, was on the wimpy side, and *The Mel Blanc Show* lasted only one season.

Of all of these radio moments, his work for Benny remains his most historic contribution. "Benny and I were very close during those years. In 1961, I was in a near fatal car crash and had been in a coma for twenty-one days with a triple skull fracture. When I came out of it, the first person I saw was Benny, standing beside my bed. He'd come to see me each day I'd been unconscious."

Although Blanc may have been unconscious for those twenty-one days, another part of him wasn't, if we are to believe his story. "A doctor kept trying to wake me up, but I wouldn't respond. Not until he decided to address me as Bugs Bunny. According to my wife, who was at my bedside, I blurted out 'Eh, what's up, doc?' It was at that moment the doctor changed his mind and decided I was going to live. Turned out he was right."

At one time, Blanc did around 80 per cent of the Warner Bros. cartoon characters. Today, he has a contract that assures he will do *all* the voices. "I've trained my son, Noel, how to do every voice, and he can duplicate them exactly. I guess we have the same genes and the same kind of throat. Even after I'm gone, there'll be no noticeable change. All those characters will live on."

"The Man of a Thousand Voices" began to suffer from throat pain when he tried to do some of his famous characters, and his last Warner Bros. cartoon was 1988's Daffy Duck's Quackmasters. One year later, he was diagnosed with coronary artery disease and within two months died on July 10, 1989, at the age of eighty-one. His gravestone in the Hollywood Forever Cemetery reads, "That's All, Folks."

HILLIARD MARKS
Brother-in-Law to Jack Benny Writes Revealing Book With Help From Sister Mary

I find it ironic that so many connected to Jack Benny crossed my path during my years at the *San Francisco Chronicle*. My final encounter related to Benny was with one of his major producers, who had written a book with Benny's wife, Mary Livingstone Benny. Oddly enough, it was entitled *Jack Benny* (Doubleday, 1978).

I have devoured the contents of *Jack Benny* when I have lunch with Hilliard Marks in the summer of 1978. Mary Livingstone (always introduced on the show without the final e pronounced) was married to Benny for almost forty-eight years, and Hilliard, brother to Mary, was the producer of Benny's radio and TV shows for nearly fifteen years. (Helping them write the book was *Hollywood Reporter* critic Marcia Borie.)

Hilliard immediately points out that their book follows in the wake of Milt Josefsberg's *The Jack Benny Show*, published in 1977. Then there was *Jack Benny: An Intimate Biography*, written by talent agent Irving Fein, who spent twenty-eight years as Benny's publicist and advertising director. (See my George Burns interview for more about Fein, who was in Burns' office the morning we met.)

"That Fein book," insisted Marks, "wasn't so fine. It was loaded with discrepancies and was unsettling to me and Mary. Our book, on the other hand, will be of special interest to old-time radio show collectors and those seeking an in-depth, not always flattering study of the popularity that Jack built up over the years. We wanted to point out that much of Jack's success in Vaudeville happened by pure chance, and we describe how Jack mastered the techniques of radio and TV when each medium was in its infancy.

"One key element was his understanding in the early '30s that you couldn't just keep repeating yourself week after week, as one could do in Vaudeville as you toured the country. Jack saw some entertainers dying [being cancelled] after a few weeks or months,

This is the book I carried with me to my luncheon with its author Hilliard Marks.

and told his writers to keep things fresh each week. And create new characters that could surround him. And don't hesitate to give those characters lines as funny as Jack's."

So it was that even Benny's orchestra leader, Phil Harris, became a recurring character on the show, always cracking jokes

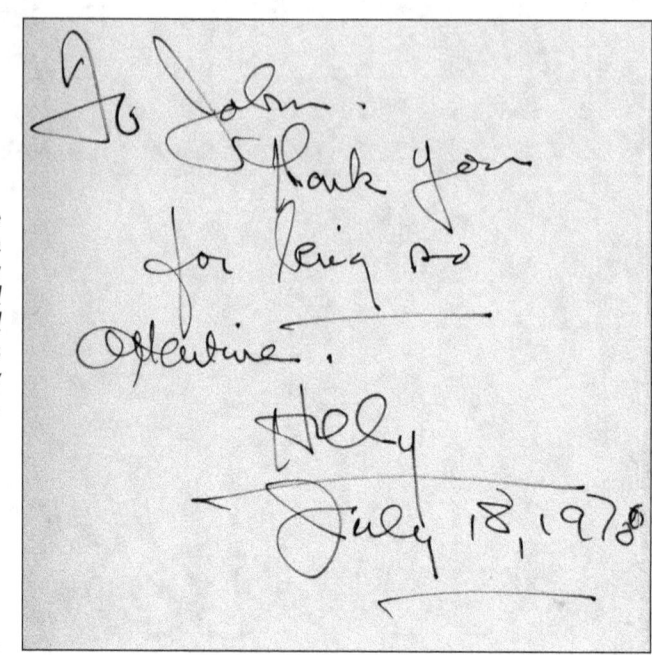

This is the title page from Jack Benny that Hilliard Marks signed for me as our interview ended.

about band member Frank Remley's need for booze. (This role was taken over by Bob Crosby in later years, who became a regular voice on the radio series until it ended in 1955.) Don Wilson was the announcer about whose heavy weight Jack was always cracking jokes. Rochester Van Jones (Eddie Anderson) was Jack's valet/chauffeur who became one of the most familiar voices on radio. Frank Nelson never played a character by name, but was always the train station manager or department store employee who would address Jack with "Yeeee-esss?" and proceed to insult him in various ways. Joseph Kearns, who occasionally showed up as an IRS agent examining Benny's 1040s, became the voice of the security guard Ed, who was stationed 24 hours a day in Jack's basement, where he kept all his money locked up in a safe. Then there was Mr. Kitzel (Artie Auerbach), a hotdog salesman who would always ask, "Do you want the pickle in the middle with the mustard on the top?" Eventually his lines became famous on a best-selling record.

Hilliard continues, "We also shed light on Jack's movie career, which is largely forgotten today except for his role as the Polish actor in *To Be or Not to Be* [1942]. Of course, jokes were made

The only photograph of Hilliard Marks from his own book is this 1958 shot, taken the night Jack Benny fondled an Emmy that had just been presented to Marks as Best Producer of the Year for his work on The Jack Benny Program. *That same year, four more Emmys went to Benny's writers Hal Goldman, Al Gordon, Sam Perrin, and George Balzer.*

for years about how bad The Horn Blows at Midnight [1944] was, especially on the evening when Jack L. Warner, the film's producer, was his guest. And we've got enough anecdotes and extracts from radio scripts to make it lively reading. Excuse us if we get a little sentimental now and then."

Hilliard Marks and Benny had been working on an autobiography when Benny died at the age of eighty. Hilliard kept the project alive, but after a year of research, he realized he needed a collaborator, so he joined forces with Borie. Then Mary Livingstone (nee: Sadie Marks) said she wanted to open up and tell the story of her marriage to Jack for forty-seven years, including how they first met when she was seventeen but didn't marry for a few years. The running joke on the air was that she was working in the hosiery department of the May Company when they first met, a situation that was repeated over and over again.

"What I really wanted out of all this was a book that was objective. Jack was often a moody man and I wanted to capture some of his complexities. I wanted more than a eulogy. And I didn't want merely to glory him: he was too unassuming for that.

"People are always asking me why Jack was such a unique man and I think there were several reasons. But I thought it would be unfair of us to try and articulate all those things alone, so I went to a jury of his peers." Among those quoted at great length are Bob Hope, Wayne Newton, Dennis Day, Johnny Carson, and many close family members.

Hilliard remained close to Benny over the years, often sending phony telegrams that would throw Jack into a tizzy. The stories he relates depict Benny as a self-assured man who still suffered from a streak of naiveté right up to his death in December 1974. Hilliard retired from the Benny production staff in 1959 because "there were too many people between us and the finished product." Marks had a successful mini-career in real estate but would still return on occasion to assist Jack's production team.

Hilliard Marks, who in the final count had helped Jack Benny with his shows for forty years, lived just four more years, dying at the age of sixty-nine in Portland, Oregon. Mary Livingstone lived five more years after the book's publication, dying of heart disease in Holmby Hills at the age of seventy-eight. There would be another book about Jack Benny entitled *Sunday Nights at Seven*, written by his daughter, Joan, with portions of the manuscript written by Benny shortly before his death on Dec. 26, 1974. Before closing the book on the Benny clan, I would like to share one of my favorite moments on a 1954 program, demonstrating Mary Livingstone's comedy ability:

Dennis Day: "There's a slot machine at the Sahara [in Las Vegas] with my name on it."

Mary Livingstone: "That's nothing. There's a slot machine at the Flamingo [Hotel] with Jack's blood on it."

Jack: "To show you I'm sincere I'm going to give you a kiss, Mary." (A pause . . .) There, Mary, how's that?"

Mary: "You lost more blood in Vegas than I thought."

Mary Livingstone and Jack Benny.

RODNEY DANGERFIELD
Comedy: A Field of Danger for Rodney, Most 'Disrespected' Funny Guy of All Time

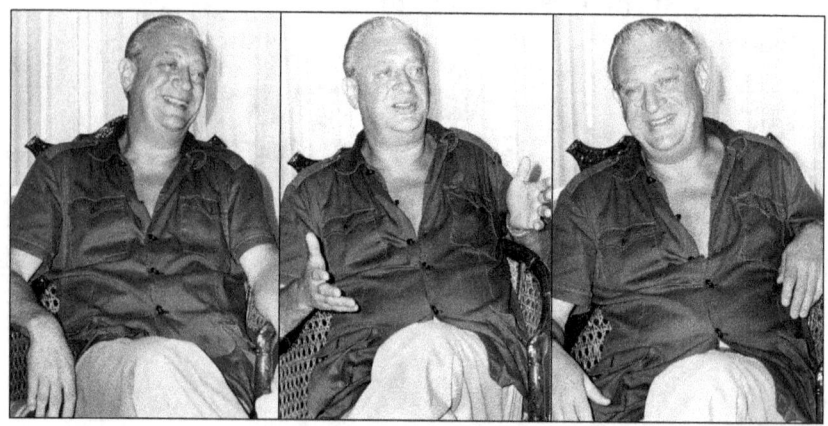

This is how Dangerfield looked during our interview. He was constantly motioning with his hands and animating himself, with his booming voice in a fast-talking style, just like when he did stand-up comedy.

Let me tell you about this comedian I run into. This man, who is considered a king of putting down himself and all other Earthlings, looks like a walking, talking midlife crisis. On this memorable day in August 1983, when he is promoting his first starring role in a feature film, *Easy Money*, Rodney Dangerfield appears agitated, a man whose nerves have been completely shattered. His body is soaked with perspiration and he keeps wiping his neck and brow with a white handkerchief. Frequently, he pats each of his flushed cheeks as if to awaken some secret energetic force within, waiting to be released on an unsuspecting world.

The setting is a posh Hollywood hotel, where critics from all over the country have gathered to see *Easy Money* and converse with Dangerfield, who in the comedy portrays a professional photographer (a specialist in taking baby pictures) set to inherit $10 million. First, he must give up pot smoking, heavy drinking (as in

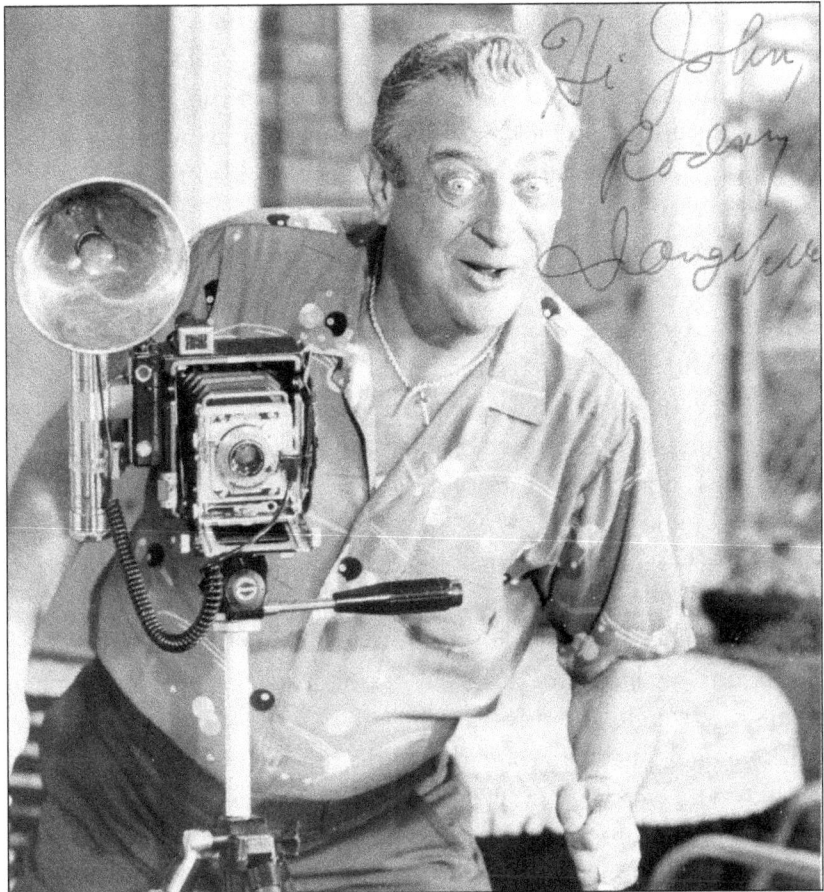

Dangerfield signed this publicity photo for me on the day we met. It depicts him as the photographer in his first starring picture, Easy Money.

crazed alcoholism), and an uncontrollable urge to gamble that has him so deep in debt that IOU notices are dangling from each ear.

Nervous, neurotic, nagging . . . Dangerfield is self-effacing, but he also makes jokes about his wife, his friends, and his co-workers, as the "Lost Soul" who gets no respect. To hear him put it: *"I DON'T GET NO RESPECT AT ALL!"*

No respect . . . a catch line that had become as firmly attached to Dangerfield as stinginess once became attached to Jack Benny, or Bob Hope's "ski-nose" was attached to his face on a peculiar angle. Here is the image of Dangerfield: baleful eyes, underscored by woeful bags filled with distressful wrinkles.

He opens up by telling me how much he hates his first starring-role movie, coming in the wake of *The Projectionist* (1971), in which he portrayed the owner of a movie theater, and *Caddyshack* (1980), in which he portrayed an obnoxious member of a golf club—a role that brought him considerable attention within the film world.

Hate for *Easy Money*? Isn't that why he's here? To sell his movie with adoring adjectives? "Ahh," he replies, "making films is terribly hard work. It's not what I'm really looking to do. I'm never pleased with anything. I see a thousand things I woulda done differently. When you have all kinds of people around you, it never comes out as you intended. Some things work, some things don't. Hey, relax, don't look so nervous. I don't carry a gun or nothing. I don't get violent about it."

As time wears on, Dangerfield admits—as if he really is the character he plays in *Easy Money*—to too much "overeating, overboozing, oversexing, oversmoking, and overflowing on the scales." He describes his life as "a gruff experience, hardened by too many years of struggle and adversity."

Once again, he pats the sides of his face. "I been clobbered by it all. Am I a happy guy? Are you kidding me? Life isn't all laughter and comedy. Life has its serious side; as a matter of fact, I'm a very serious, miserable guy." And for just a moment he looks miserable, to prove what he says.

Dangerfield doesn't stop. He cannot be stopped. Here is a comedian who wants to prove what he has just said is true. "People associate money and success with happiness. It doesn't work that way. You're born a certain way, you are what you are. You have an attitude, you stay that way. Inwardly, you don't change."

In his own words, Dangerfield was born into poverty. "On Long Island, in a place ironically called Babylon." His name then? Jacob Rodney Cohen. "From the beginning, a sense of inferiority smothered me. I was selling magazines when I was only six. I was running a newsstand for a whole stinkin' buck a week before I went to school. Each morning, I was doing everything to make a lousy buck. The whole survival thing for a measly dollar.

Dangerfield early in his career, when he was performing as Jack Roy.

"Did my parents support me? Hah, they were separated. My father, a Vaudeville actor, I hardly ever saw him. My mother gave me nothing. Zip. Zilch. They took what I gave them, okay? Finally, I graduated from high school. Then drove a laundry truck. Then a fish truck. Finally, I started writing jokes two days a week. Are you beginning to get the picture?"

But young Rodney was not writing those jokes out of any feeling of gaiety or happiness. "I was writing to escape reality, to create my

Nobody in show business could widen their eyeball sockets quite the way Rodney Dangerfield did it. Forming a circle with his fingers was a visual trademark he used in scores of publicity photos taken along the way.

own fantasy world that blotted out the hardships of my split home." Dangerfield's heritage, he exclaims, is that of "social horror!"

As much as he hated his father, who was billed as Phil Roy, Rodney started performing stand-up comedy at the age of seventeen under the name Jack Roy, as if following in his father's footprints—the father he hated so intensely. At nineteen, Jack Roy transmutated into a singing waiter, then morphed back into a comedian again. "I was doing things for five bucks a night and my agent was getting 50¢ commissions. They were tough nightclubs, where the bouncers would say, 'Hey kid, I think you stink. Whattaya gonna do about it, you worthless punk?' So, I learned humility. I learned to be a nice guy. A humanitarian. I learned this:

You have to be well-liked. Part of being a comedian, they *must* like you. Otherwise your body will go flyin' through the sky headfirst."

"Nowness"—that's what he had to create. "You gotta have just the right routine, just the right material, just the right timing. In later years, Dustin Hoffman hung around me before he filmed *Lenny* [the story of Lenny Bruce], and one night he asked me, 'How do I do standup?' I told him, 'I can't tell you. You have to go out and walk the boards for twenty years. Nobody can tell you. Here's some good advice: Work in a joint as a comic, and then maybe you'll learn something."

Eventually, Jack Roy became Rodney Dangerfield on the marquees. I point out that Rodney was his real middle name, but where had Dangerfield come from? "Jack Benny first used that name on a radio show, where he was posing as a cowboy hero, in the early 1940s. And it was used again by Ricky Nelson on [*The Adventures of*] *Ozzie and Harriet* TV series. It's a name I fell in love with and I'm never giving it up. Think about it. Danger in a field. Comedy. So, Dangerfield! Rodney Dangerfield!"

It seems important that I ask Dangerfield where the "No Respect" gag came from. He smiles, relaxes a bit, and doesn't wipe at his face for the next few minutes. "I wrote this one-liner: 'I played hide-and-seek but nobody came to look for me.' When you write a joke, you have to put something in front of it, as a way of introducing it. That's when I thought of the tagline, 'I don't get no respect.' And I started writing hundreds of jokes with that same line." I asked for his favorite example. "Thanks for asking. 'If it wasn't for pickpockets, I'd have no sex life at all.' " And, "My parents hated me. My bath toys were a toaster and a radio."

One night Jack Benny came into his Manhattan nightclub (called—would you believe this?—Dangerfield's) to watch the show, then came backstage afterward to tell the comedian that while the Benny image was "cheap and thirty-nine," the Dangerfield image "looked into the soul of every man. Every day something happens to a guy. He gets cut off in traffic or a girl stands him up. We all get treated wrong and that's something everyone can identify with. In short, the whole world can relate to you, Rodney. Never forget that."

These photos were taken of Rodney and myself during our interview, and later sent to me by the studio's publicity department.

Even though there is more I want to learn about Dangerfield's career, I'm told my time is up. "Wait," says Dangerfield, before I leave the room. "I want you to have this tape. It has a little poem on it that I wrote just for you. An exclusive for you and your paper. Nobody else gets it. I mean, nobody anywhere! It's all yours."

Later, back at the *San Francisco Chronicle*, I listen to the recording. It's Dangerfield's voice, singing to a disco beat. And these are the exclusive words he spits out, just for me and my paper. And now, just for you:

"I was an ugly kid, I had no fun.
They took me to a dog show–and I won!
I'm getting old, it's hard to face.
Why, during sex I lose my place.
My car broke down, I called Triple A.
They left the car and towed me away.
I can't take it no more, I'm getting too old.
I called Suicide Prevention . . . they put me on hold.
I don't get a break with nothin' . . . .
I don't get no respect at all."

Dangerfield went on to appear in fifteen more films, some of which he also wrote material for. One of the highlights of his career was his own comedy club, Dangerfield's, located in the Upper East Side of Manhattan. The club, co-owned by Anthony Bevacqua, opened in 1969, still showcases top comedians, and is still rated one of the most successful clubs of its kind. Rodney continued to entertain America with his negative-powered sense of humor until October 2004, when he died of heart problems just short of his eighty-third birthday.

JOAN RIVERS
A Torrent of Comedy—and Talent!

This interview with Joan Rivers took place on January 27, 1983, when I paid a visit to her home in Beverly Hills and met her and husband, Edgar Rosenberg, also her personal business manager. Rivers had risen to become one of America's leading comedy star thanks in part to Johnny Carson allowing her to guest host his show for two decades. One professional disaster and one personal loss would have a grave effect on her four years after we met.

Can we talk about Joan Rivers for just a moment? Can we talk?

You know I mean the perennial guest host on *The Tonight Show* when Johnny Carson is off slumming. She is the guest hostess with the long eyelashes and pretty blonde hair and what might be a good figure if she didn't hide it all the time beneath beautiful flowing gowns and suits that make you want to peek around her corners. The crazy, fastest-talking American comedienne, who sounds like she has two mouths in gear at all times, though never quite meshing either one. She talks so fast during her stand-up comedy club routines that rare is the sentence that is uninterrupted, coming at you from five directions at once.

Joan Rivers loves to make sport of her gynecologist, her pantyhose (or her panties, depending on what she is wearing at the moment), her eternally-suffering husband, Edgar Rosenberg, her size 34-long "boobies" being so thin that they fall down to here, and other regions of the female anatomy that might be of interest to those watching. Bazooms, that's what men like, according to Joan. Oh, you better believe Joan when she gets philosophical . . .

The sex jokes. Oh, you don't know? Did you hear the one about the tramp who had to have her thighs paved? Did you hear that when that tramp took off her braces, the entire football team sent a thank you note to her dentist? How about this one: "Puberty hit me late. My hair came into my armpits a color gray." Or, "I'm so flat-chested people have to look at my shoes to see which way I'm facing . . . I'd show you my cleavage but I'd have to sit down first

An autographed photo from Joan Rivers, which she signed to me during my visit to her home. It reads, "To John: A pleasure meeting you. Good luck." Dated January 27, 1983.

... My husband Edgar took me to an auction and the auctioneer said, 'What am I bid for this old chest?' And Edgar shouted back, 'My wife is not for sale.'"

The outrageous, the raging Joan Rivers, a torrent of comedy that's given us so many blatant undressing room gags and jokes, both pubic and private. Okay, the sexual side to her is walloping, yet beneath the surface of the flowing rapids is an insightful understanding of women and the daily appointments and disappointments that await them—and their bodies.

Maybe that's what makes Joan so popular—her ability to give you a one-liner that is more than an imitation Henny Youngman; that probes the nerves that most tickle us and make us sensitive to the human condition; maybe even make us like ourselves and understand ourselves a little better, or remind us that although life's expectations often fall down, there's still something to laugh at. No matter what.

We get the message. It isn't easy being a woman, and there's something frenetic and frantic about Rivers that touches everything she touches. She had recently given one of eleven one-night-stand performances in San Francisco's Warfield Theater. Each show was in a different American city, night after night with no breaks. She called it her "manifest destiny," moving east to west like some pioneer of humor. Who would want to submit to such a rigorous schedule? She does it for the challenge, she'll tell you, but you also get the feeling she does it to satisfy an out-of-control compulsion to be everywhere at once. But it's something not even eleven cities, or a hundred cities, or even a thousand cities, or a million cities, could ever completely sate.

After seeing her one-woman show, I knew that I had to meet this woman face to face. However, in order to talk to Rivers in person, I would have to journey to the heights of Southern California living, to her Beverly Hills New England-style mansion on a hillside that turned out to be as coiffed as Rivers during her act. Joan may not look vulnerable on stage, but here at home she is protected by an electronic gate and barking dogs behind a wire fence.

Although she's suffering from the last remnants of a flu bout (and if you think she looks not as good as usual, she replies, "You should have seen the flu!"). She scurries to the front door, all sound and fury, looking like no ordinary woman who just hangs around the house. She is wearing this fabulous black mink housecoat. Beneath the mink is a pink blouse; beneath the blouse are black pants. At the bottom, black high heels, even at noon. Her cheeks are flushing in contrast to her Nordic-complexioned skin, set off at the neck by a string of white pearls. Flu or no, her eyes seem to sparkle like some of the diamonds and other baubles she keeps around the house.

"Show business," she says, leading the way into a library, where coffee and coffeecake are waiting, "is one big party and I'm the hostess. It's a tremendous responsibility I don't take lightly. Where does my energy come from? From being scared to death all the time. I'm always terrified before a show. The more I do, the more terrified I get. My nervousness has never gone away. I've always been insecure and I always will be. And I hope I stay that way. Being frightened makes me try harder. I never take any of this for granted."

Joan sits surrounded by fluffy pillows, which have been inscribed, just for her, with oddball sayings: "It's Just as Lonely at the Top, Only You Eat Better" . . . "It is Better to be Nouveau Riche Than Never Riche at All" . . . "Vacations Are for Amateurs" . . . "I'd Rather Be Me With Only $10 Million and a Lot of Friends Than $60 Million and No Friends at All."

She pats the $10 million pillow lovingly. "Money is divine, isn't it? It solves a lot of life's problems and paves the way. That's what it should be used for, not hoarded or kept. When you're sick and need a nurse, you can have a nurse. You can send a gift to a friend. I'm sending some relatives through college. Money doesn't change people. If you were cheap when you were poor, you're going to be cheap when you're rich."

If Joan is rich, it doesn't show in the character she portrays up on stage. Rather, she epitomizes the average American housewife who is fascinated by the stars and their private lives and eager to put them down with a cattish sense of humor; the kind of woman who reads the *National Enquirer* and can't wait to spread the gossip. Elizabeth Taylor's thighs have gone condo, or the woman who went to a plastic surgeon and asked to be like Bo Derek was given a lobotomy. Always she seems irresistibly drawn to the human anatomy.

"When you're coming out and making fun of other people like that," she explains while serving coffeecake, "you have to let the audience know you think you're not such a hot potato either. I tell them what's wrong with me. That makes everybody feel better and laugh. I was buffeted about too much in life to be a sex symbol myself. Last night, I asked my husband, 'What's your favorite sexual position?' and he replied 'Next door.' After we made love, he made a chalk outline of my body on the bed. 'Just so I won't forget,' he said."

There constantly spews from Joan a battering-ram of new material—her opening monologues for the Carson show never repeat the same jokes twice. "I work constantly at it," she explains, pounding a pillow that has been inscribed with: "Don't Expect Praise Without Envy—Unless You're Dead."

"Comedy is such a slow process. Out of twenty jokes, if two work you're lucky. And if those two work consistently, wow! You've had a bonanza. It's like God gave you a gift. Comedy is slow, slow, slow."

This is one of her weeks to host the Carson show (Johnny is slumming again) and she's been "constantly working the local comedy clubs, just to try out new material." What is approved by the Los Angeles nightclub crowds she takes to the Carson show. What does make her humor work? She really looks baffled for a moment, but then answers, "Who knows? I asked that same question of Woody Allen once, and he said, 'Just fall on your knees, Joan, and thank God that someone laughed, and go on to the next joke.' Some people analyze humor. I don't analyze it. If it works, thank you, thank you, thank you. Certain words are funny. Banana is a funnier word than apple. Who knows? You've got a great joke if it's going to work with apple."

Despite her abundance of risqué material, Joan feels that George Carlin, Richard Pryor, Bette Midler, and Lily Tomlin are bluer and wilder. She also feels she's really "a tiny nipple in the Sexual Revolution." She claims, "I just missed that part of comedy history. I'm so mad. Seriously though, the Sexual Revolution went too far. The straights now have herpes and the homosexuals have gay cancer. I think man was meant to be monogamous. He wasn't meant to screw everything that came down the pike. He went too far. It's taken all the romance out of life."

Joan tells me she came "from a background where you were courted by men, you went to dinner, you got the flowers the next

A light-hearted moment for Joan Rivers, seen here with a personal friend, while making the only film she ever directed, Rabbit Test.

morning. Sex wasn't always automatic. Before I was married, every affair was a love thing with a relationship. I hope it goes back to that. I see so many of my friends pulling off one-night stands and not happy with them, not fulfilled."

Joan, who is now forty-five, was brought up in Brooklyn's Eastern Parkway, the daughter of a doctor whose family consisted of Jewish immigrants from Russia. "I was about ten years old," she recalls, "when I first became aware of the importance of humor. I was on a fishing trip with my father and mother off Long Island, and I realized adults were laughing with me, not at me. It was wonderful! I remember their laughter so vividly. I knew I had a gift, something special. Comedy is something you can't learn. You must innately have the ability to deliver it with a personal style."

Does she consider herself an aggressive broad? (I just thought I'd ask.) "Oh," she answers, laughing, "you better believe it. Nothing has come to me, nothing has come to me. I've had to be aggressive. And yes, I'm a broad. I have to have twelve projects going at all times because I know that eleven will fall apart. Talk to me on Wednesday and I've got a movie and Broadway show and six books going. Talk to me on Thursday and I've lost them all. You must be yourself starting in this business.

"I had to start up my own [1978] movie, *Rabbit Test*, which I wrote, produced, and directed. [The film, about the world's first pregnant man, would be her only directorial credit.] They told me I shouldn't do it, but it was successful and established a whole new trend in movies. I love film. Put me in an editing room with 500 cans of film and I'd come out a year later very happy. I just finished a film, *Rich Girls*, with Lily Tomlin. We play a couple of middle-aged ladies. We think we're still glamorous and sensual and decide to go to New York to find new husbands. There are other projects, but who knows yet which will work. You just keep praying and working." [Oddly enough, I could find no film entitled *Rich Girls* among her credits or the credits of Lily Tomlin.]

Joan Rivers hugs her $10 million embroidered pillow and considers herself the luckiest woman on earth. "I have a positive attitude about myself and my work. I have a lot of friends who don't know they're lucky. They're sitting in big homes in Bel-Air with Mercedes in their garages, and they're complaining. I don't care if I lose nineteen out of twenty projects. I have no complaints. I want to enjoy life now. I want to work until the very end. I plan to fall off my stool and hit the stage dead. And I don't care about anything after I'm dead. I've already told my daughter [Melissa Rivers] to write a *Mommie Dearest* and make a lot of money."

And she hugs that pillow again, the $10 million pillow, and pounds on it a little bit and looks like the happiest comedienne in the world.

Four years later, in October 1986, Joan would host a brand-new late-night talk show on the Fox Network, proving she was an ex-

Before I left her home, Joan also signed a photo to my wife, Erica. She wrote, "To Erica, with all good wishes."

pert at her job. The first woman entertainer in history to have such a nightly program! Having her own show absolutely pissed off Johnny Carson (jealousy?) and he never invited her back to host his late-night show after that, and their friendship fell by the

Joan Rivers giving a loving smooch to her husband, Edgar Rosenberg, for handling her business affairs—and other non-public, up-close-and-personal matters of the heart.

wayside. She claims she called him twice on the telephone, and Carson hung up on her twice.

Soon after that, another professional disaster befell her. Her German-born husband, Edgar, had been working as the series' producer, but suddenly, after only eight months on the air, Fox wanted to fire him, feeling he was not suited to the job. Joan argued to keep him, and suddenly both Edgar and Joan were fired, even though the show continued with rotating hosts.

Then, three months later, in May 1987, Edgar committed suicide in a Philadelphia, Pennsylvania hotel room by taking an overdose of prescription drugs. Joan blamed his firing as the cause of his depression and subsequent death, saying he had been humiliated beyond repair. Not only did Rivers face getting over the grief of her husband's death . . . but there were personal problems between her and daughter Melissa, which in 1994 were portrayed in the TV-movie *Tears and Laughter: The Joan and Melissa Rivers Story*. Cast in the two leading roles? Joan Rivers and daughter Melissa, who else?

Nevertheless, Joan had the strength to make a comeback after a long absence from the stage. She knew that her husband's death had thrown a pall over her as a comedienne, so her first joke when she resumed her career was to tell the audience: "From now on, I'm going to be spending time with my late husband every day. Yes, I just had his ashes scattered at Neiman-Marcus." Later, she said that the wall of sorrow between her and the audience crumbled away and she could be comedienne Joan Rivers once again, with nothing between her and laughter.

Life would continue successfully and include her own afternoon talk show in 1989 that would last for five years and win her a Daytime Emmy. Then came that fateful day in August 2014, when she reported to the Yorkville Endoscopy in New York City, an outpatient clinic, where she was to receive a "minor throat procedure."

The "procedure" turned into an operation during which her blood pressure dropped and she suddenly stopped breathing. However, she was kept alive, though unconscious, for the next few days at Mt. Sinai Hospital in New York. She died on September 4, 2014, reportedly of "brain damage" caused by the initial "procedure." She was eighty-one.

After a two-month-long investigation, the clinic was charged with malpractice. As Joan might have summed it up, "Not a very funny way to die." Ironically, in her book, *I Hate Everybody . . . Starting with Me* (2012), one of twelve she wrote during her lifetime, she insisted that "my funeral . . . be a huge showbiz affair with lights, camera, action! . . . I want to look gorgeous, better dead than when I was alive . . . I want Harry Winston to make me a toe tag." Only from the mouth of Joan Rivers. She couldn't have been funnier, even talking about death.

WOODY ALLEN
The Night Woody Allen Didn't Want to Talk . . .
But Hey, Come Back Tomorrow Night . . .
He'll Have . . . His Manifesto!?

My assignment for the *San Francisco Chronicle* started out routinely. Woody Allen has opened at a club called the hungry i, so I get over there, see his stand-up comedy routine, and do an interview with him. Simple enough, so I make the arrangements.

In April 1967, Woody Allen is still two years away from directing his first motion picture. He's still an up-and-coming comedian, who does stand-up, offering jokes about his Jewish heritage (he was born Allan Stewart Konigsberg in Brooklyn in 1935 to Yiddish-speaking parents) and always playing a troubled, neurotic soul, never failing to put himself down. One of his favorite lines bringing mama and papa into the limelight: "I don't think my parents liked me. They put a live teddy bear in my crib when I was a baby." But one has to admit, he has a way of self-depravation that sets him apart from other comedians.

In real life, he is seeing his psychiatrist as often as three times a week, so self-analysis is one of his repetitious shticks. He also has phobias, such as a fear of spiders, insects, dogs, high places, crowds, bodies of water, maybe even comedians that are funnier than him, and reporters from newspapers. Maybe they are the worst fear of all, as I am to find out!

In real life, he hates public bathrooms, always demanding his own personal bath whenever he stays at a hotel (meaning anyone with him cannot use his sinks or toilets!) All of these themes are played out in his comedy, and they are his funniest assets. Putting himself down is what makes him so popular on the nightclub circuits. The night I see his show, the gags are there.

"It's not that I'm afraid to die," he says during his act, "I just don't want to be there when it happens." . . . "If only God would give me some clear sign. Like making a large deposit in my name at a

This could have been the way Woody Allen looked shortly after he turned down doing an interview with me. I can see him rushing to sit down at his typewriter to create ... yeah, a Manifesto.

Swiss bank." . . . "I got on an empty elevator the other day and a voice suddenly said something anti-Semitic to me." . . . "Most of the time I don't have much fun. The rest of the time I don't have any fun at all." . . . "Warren Beatty once told me being a star is like being in a whorehouse with a credit card. But for me, it's like being in a whorehouse with an expired credit card."

I see the show and I laugh my head off, because I think he is the funniest! He's got a style and a technique all his own. I've never seen anything like it, anywhere.

Afterward, as I pull myself back to normal, I go over to the hungry i bar, where I am scheduled to meet him. I wait ten minutes.

He shouldn't show. I tell the maitre'd, who is also puzzled that Allen has not shown up. He rushes off to go backstage.

I wait a little longer. Finally, after a little more little longer, a meek Woody Allen steps up to the bar and bluntly, flat-out tells me he does not want to do an interview with me. He doesn't give a reason. I hastily assume it's one of his neurotic moments—he doesn't like meeting the press; it fills him with abject fear; his body shakes and trembles. My questions will do nothing but bring on bring new phobias. He will toss and turn in his bed all night long, hating each of my questions. Nothing is going to change his feelings, or his mind.

I know when I'm licked. When I have nowhere to go but to the nearest bar, which would be anywhere along Columbus Avenue. I say farewell and start to turn away when Allen suddenly tells me to stop. "Tell you what," Allen says, without smiling. "Come back tomorrow night. I'll have something special for you."

"Something....? What do you mean?" I ask, utterly puzzled. In all my years of doing celebrity interviews, I have never encountered a moment like this one—and with a leading comedy star of his day! Someone who has made me laugh everything but my heart away!

"I'll have my Manifesto for you," he says. "It will be written on paper so you'll have something to take back to your *Chronicle*."

Okay, so now I'm the one who tosses and turns all night, wondering just what the hell is going on. Like Woody Allen, I am neurotic all day long at work. I begin to develop a phobia about going to the hungry i nightclub. I go to a phone book and begin looking for the name of a good psychiatrist. I'll need some therapy to deal with this man, this Woody Allen.

Somehow I get through the night and the next morning. Then I have to deal with the afternoon. I can't eat lunch, so I have a couple of beers at Hanno's, a bar in the alley behind the *San Francisco Chronicle* building. Eventually comes the evening, and I know I have to go back to the hungry i and do my duty. I am faithful to my duty.

I see the Woody Allen stand-up comedy show for a second time, and am pleased to hear some new jokes. "Having sex is like playing bridge. If you don't have a good partner, you'd better have a good hand." . . . "There are worse things in life than death. Have you ever had to spend an evening with an insurance agent?" . . . "Not only is there no God, but have you tried to hire a plumber on the weekend?"

After his show, I'm at the bar again, right after the performance ends, waiting for another ten minutes, but this time—at the scheduled time—here comes Mr. Allen, loaded down with two sheets of paper, which he hands to me. "This is it," he explains. "This is my Manifesto. It tells what I would do if I ran for political office. Do with it what you will." He shrugs, turns his back on me and walks away. Gee, shaking hands with reporters must be another of his phobias.

The next morning, I tell my editor, David Kleinberg, the details of my two meetings with Allen. All he can do is shrug and tell me to go ahead and use the "Woody Allen Manifesto" as is. I decide to stick my tongue in my check in imitation of Allen.

Here is the story as it appears in the *San Francisco Chronicle* on Sunday, April 30, 1967.

"Man Oh Man, Here's a Feast: Oh, It's the Manifesto of Politician-to-Be Woody Allen

"To the people associated with the world of show business on a professional level, the name Woody Allen has come to mean many things. Unfortunately, none of those things can be printed in a family newspaper. To those around the periphery peering in, however, the name Woody Allen has become synonymous with film actor, film writer, playwright, Japanese film dubber, couch warmer for a famous psychiatrist, and nightclub comedian.

"But what most of these people do not realize is that Allen, like so many of his contemporary counterparts (Sonny Tufts, Herb Shriner, Andy Devine, Andy Clyde, Alfred E. Newman), is nurturing political ambitions. To him, as to the others, acting is only a logical step in the direction of the White House.

"Because he is currently appearing at the hungry i, Woody has decided to give the populace of the Bay Area first opportunity to hear the platform on which he has heaped his political ideologies.

Here then, for the first in any form, is the Manifesto of comedian Woody Allen:

'I, WOODY ALLEN, will first concentrate my political energy on getting some rest. I feel sleep is essential to rule those who live in a complex society. Also, I enjoy being unconscious. There's something subliminal about it.

'To achieve my ends I would operate under the slogan 'A World Without Herring.' For our country would definitely be in a better position without herring. Please, do not think I am in any way attaching a red connotation to herring. It just frightens me—chopped, pickled, creamed, marinated, barbecued. You see, I was frightened by herring in my formative years. In fact, my mother looked like Bismarck. I am also afraid of large quantities of cheese, though I have no fear of mice or Swiss in the least.

'Many have asked me what our biggest problem is today. Our biggest problem today, which many have asked me about, is that we, the people, are exhaling before inhaling, thus bringing about breathing inversion. We are sucking up oxygen and turning out carbon monoxide. This is clearly a problem of pollution. What, many have asked me, is the solution? Simply that everyone face in the other direction.

'If elected to office I would take a definite stand on Vietnam. I would first have all Vietnamese people stop what they are doing and march up and down in place. This would bring about national unity. I would harmonize them further with group participation exercises—such as spelling words like harpsichord and anachronism. As for our own government troops, I would assign them the construction of potato puppets—complete with skirts.

'Many times have I thought of my eventual political residence, and my site is set high. Already I intend to move it or renovate it. Should it come to remodeling, I would have it resemble the inside of a meat freezer. The sight of slabs of beef on hooks has always given me a sense of serenity. Every time I go into a butcher shop for a pound of hamburger, and the butcher goes into the freezer, I catch a glimpse of the interior of the locker room and it seems so very very peaceful.

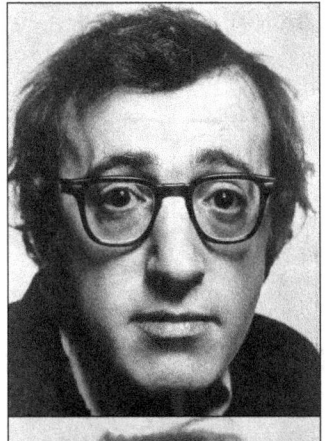

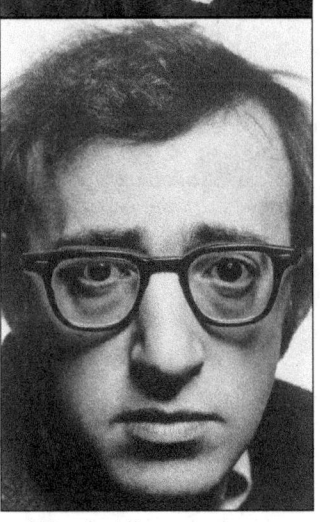

Woody Allen capturing a wide range of expressions in a trilogy of close-ups known as "Woody Allen in E-motion."

'I have meditated ponderously on my choice of close personal advisor, and despite all my big connections in Washington, I have decided on Jim Backus. I don't know him personally, yet I feel an instinctive trust in him that is generated from listening to his voice-overs in the *Mr. Magoo* cartoons."

'For other actors/writers/directors with political aspirations, let me advise them to collect as many cans of tuna fish as possible, for control of the government will one day go to him with the largest supply. You will note this is allied to the herring campaign. I have a recurring fish dream.

'To ensure that I go down in history as a great political leader, I intend to turn the USA into a central laundry service for all other nations, regardless of race, creed, color or clothing. We will starch, iron and spin dry at a very reasonable rate.

'As you can see, I am benevolent in nature. I want only to serve my country in the best of traditions as set down by my forefathers. I, Woody Allen, have spoken.'"

Given that Woody Allen might have begun his political career in San Francisco, call it coincidental that the Bay Area is where, two years after subjecting the American public to his Manifesto, he directed his first self-made film, *Take the Money and Run*. It was shot on seven major locations (including San Quentin Prison) and he was the star, portraying a criminal named Virgil Starkwell, who specialized in robbing banks.

Woody Allen has gone on to make one movie after the other, for a grand total of forty-five with the release of *Magic in the Moonlight* in 2014. Unfortunately, he never ran for political office, so his Manifesto has never been fulfilled. Thanks to all those who didn't collect cans of tuna fish!

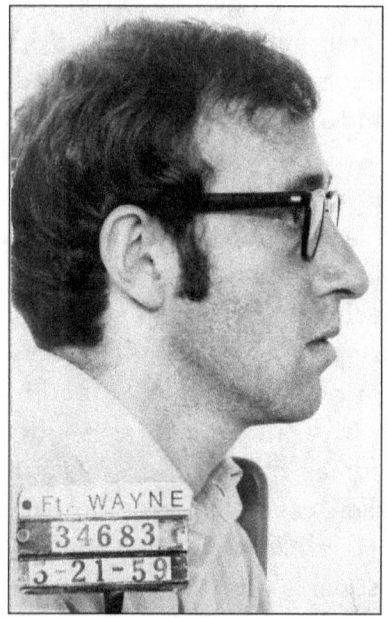
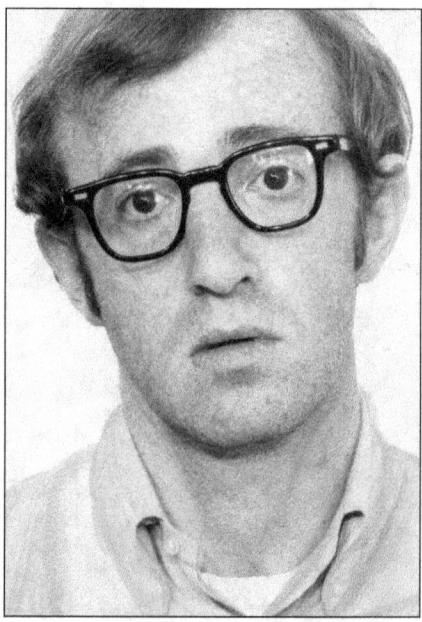

Here are the line-up shots of Woody Allen from his first feature film which he wrote, produced, and directed in the San Francisco Bay Area in 1969. In Take the Money and Run, he portrays bank robber Virgil Starkwell, styled as a pseudo-documentary, a genre that he would repeat in another comedy, Zelig (1983).

DONALD O'CONNOR
The Interview With a Song-and-Dance King That Never Quite Happened

The first time I meet Donald O'Connor is in the spring of 1962, when he is kicking up a storm at the age of thirty-six. He is performing in the South Shore Room at Harrah's Tahoe, located on the edge of Nevada's Lake Tahoe. Disappointingly, there is limited time that night for us to talk, for he is totally caught up in performing a mixture of music and comedy with a fellow comedian, Sidney Miller, and choreographer Louis Da Pron, with whom he has worked on *Patrick the Great* and other musical feature films.

It's a snappy 90-minute show ("This is the first time I've seen a crowd of people standing on people sitting on people knocked down") for which he had been receiving standing ovations every night. He and Miller, famous for their comedy bit in which two would-be song composers try out new tunes at a piano, all but steal the show. It is also still filled with the kind of vigorous dancing for which O'Connor will always be remembered. Then there are his parodies of personalities: Elizabeth (*Cleopatra*) Taylor: "I've been fiddling around in Rome too much." Kirk (*Spartacus*) Douglas: "My character certainly has its sticking points." Janet (*Psycho*) Leigh: "I'm never going to take a shower again." For the persona of President John F. Kennedy, O'Connor wears a busy wig, and for his caricature of Matt Dillon of *Gunsmoke*, he puts on a 20-gallon hat, described as "the funniest thing west of Dodge City."

Although there is little time for us to talk that memorable night, O'Connor will make up for it thirty years later when we meet again and converse for two straight hours. This time, I get answers to all the questions I couldn't ask him at Lake Tahoe.

Donald O'Connor did find time on the night of our initial meeting to sign this photo to my wife Erica. "Always the best of everything," he wrote. The date is 4/11/62.

The Aging Song-and-Dance King Who Danced All the Way to My Table

There could be something inherently sadistic in our curiosity about aging entertainers who have a long-standing show business history. When they take to the stage in their later years, we won-

On our second meeting, I insisted Donald O'Connor sign a photo to me. It reads: "To John, A Wonderful Friend Always."

der if they can still manage the marvelous feats for which they were once famous.

We ask endless questions, such as, "Will the voice hold up? Will the waistline be bulging? Will the luxuriant blond hair of yesteryear now be dull gray or pure white?" In the case of a once beautiful woman, can we expect her bosom to remain jutting on the same level? What about her once lovely waist and legs? Will we see a true facsimile of what we fondly remember from yesteryear, or only a wrinkled caricature?

As if to answer those questions in advance, which are flashing through my mind as I sit in San Francisco's Postrio Restaurant in

January 1992, Donald O'Connor dances his way playfully across the dining room to my luncheon table, humming the lyrics to Cole Porter's "You Can Bounce Right Back," which he first delivered in the 1956 film musical, *Anything Goes*.

He will turn sixty-seven in August, and he looks as if his facial features had been trapped in a time-warp fifteen years earlier and he hasn't aged a day since. The body is kept at a trim 160 pounds by exercising three times a week, and the blue eyes still have that comedy sparkle that he brought to his musical films and to TV's *The Colgate Comedy Hour* in the early 1950s. So, I think, the kid is aging pretty good. He's also right that you can dance half-way up a wall and bounce right back to the floor, standing upright!

Although O'Connor can honestly be described as a Hollywood legend that nostalgically evokes fond memories of Hollywood's musical era, his attitude is still that of an ageless, bubbly light-hearted song-dance-comedy personality. The comic child still lives excitedly within him.

"I know what you're thinking," O'Connor cries out to me with the adult voice of the inward child. "And the answer is yes. I can still leap over the furniture and dance on the wall. Well, sort of dance on the wall. Would you believe half way to the ceiling? And I can still recite 24 bars of that popular tongue-twister from *Singin' in the Rain*: 'Moses supposes his toeses are roses, /But Moses supposes erroneously. /Moses, he knowses his toeses are roses, /As Moses supposes his toeses to be.' Count 'em, 24 bars. The musical kind. Not the ones you get drunk in." He pauses to point to folks dining at nearby tables. "When I was checking in with the maitre'd, I could see I was recognized by some of the diners. That's why I danced to your table. Let 'em all see I still have what it takes."

O'Connor has come to the Bay Area to appear at the Paramount Theater in Oakland for a series of shows designed to please older audiences, the aging fifty-or-older crowd of men and women who will remember him from all those good old days—or sort of remember.

He explains he is going to replicate some of his acrobatics from the "Make 'Em Laugh" routine he performed so youthfully in *Singin' in the Rain*, the 1952 MGM musical that still stands as the ultimate

Flying through the air in Singin' in the Rain, *Donald O'Connor helped to make it one of the most memorable of MGM's large-scale musicals. O'Connor especially outdid himself in "Make 'em Laugh," a solo performance he completely choreographed himself.*

testament to his unique talents as a comedian-dancer with a lithe body that seemed, like Plastic Man's, to defy the common laws of gravity. (He won a Golden Globe for his role of Cosmo Brown.)

His upcoming appearances in Oakland no doubt will evoke some childhood memories, for playing on the stages of movie palaces began for him in show business (better known as Vaudeville in those days) at the age of three and a half.

Both his parents had started out as Ringling Bros. Barnum & Bailey circus performances, his father as an acrobat, his mother as a bareback rider, before they made a transition to Vaudeville.

"I didn't break in," O'Connor corrects me, "I was thrown in. As a member of a family act. You learned to be great really fast. You went out there and caught the audience's attention in the first twenty-five seconds or you ruined it for the whole family. If you heard laughter you knew it was working. If you didn't, you went into overdrive to be funny. That's how I learned. I was never taught. It all came naturally."

O'Connor is in his fourth decade as an entertainer. He was still wearing diapers the first time his parents—Vaudevillians trouping the country on three circuits—presented him on stage. By the time he was three, he was dancing to "Black Bottom," a popular dance of the Roaring Twenties, singing "Keep Your Sunny Side Up," and finally branching out into numerous acts with his mother and two brothers. At this very early age, he was dancing, singing, and cracking jokes, all without wearing diapers.

His alma mater, the Kitchen Sink School of Vaudeville, accounts for O'Connor's frenetic shotgun style and ability to do anything on a stage short of intense Shakespearean colloquies. This energetic dexterity, he says, has accounted for his survival over many decades. "I've always been able to fall back on one thing or another, including my butt, no matter how many times I've had to make a comeback, which probably now numbers at least eight or ten."

O'Connor, who describes himself as "a crooner with a musical-comedy voice," portrays what he calls "an illusionist—a trickster who quick-changes before your eyes. I capture your attention without giving you time to think about it. I move fast, I keep changing my hats. And the more pleased an audience is, the more energy I get from it and give back to the audience."

O'Connor refuses to "get mired in sentiment" when he performs nowadays. He appreciates the nostalgic bits of song, comedy, and patter his audiences expect of him, and throws in dollops of his yesteryears, "I keep my act as contemporary as I can. I prefer to be a 'today' person, a 'now' kind of guy."

Although O'Connor underwent a quadruple bypass a year and a half ago, he has not changed his outlook on his busy life. He still makes personal appearances many weeks a year. He also eagerly tells me, "Phoenix Video is releasing episodes of *Here Comes Donald*, a 1957 syndicated comedy series that was shot on film and preserved."

O'Connor's life has had its "peaks and valleys." He was less than a year old when his mother was pushing him in a baby buggy along a busy street in Hartford, Connecticut, with his seven-year-old sister, Arlene, walking beside them. Suddenly, an out of control car slammed into his carriage and threw him through a storefront's plate-glass window. Arlene was killed instantly. "For some miraculous reason, I wasn't hurt and survived with only a few scratches. So did mom." Yet a few days later, his overwrought father, believing that the show always had to go on no matter what, died of a heart attack at the age of forty-seven, dropping dead on the stage in the middle of a performance.

Donald was raised by his mother, a woman he describes as "domineering." Her life had never been easy: She had given birth to seven children, three of whom were stillborn. There was never a permanent home because the family was always on the circuits performing. Under their mother's guidance, Donald and his two brothers kept the act going for years after their father's sudden death.

"Mom raised me as the daughter she had lost in that accident," O'Connor explains, recalling how his clothing was often more suited for a girl than a boy. "I didn't know what it meant to be a child. When I'd meet other kids, I'd feel afraid."

Although he and his two brothers performed a musical specialty act in 1937's *Melody for Two*, his big break into films came in 1938, when he was in Hollywood at the Biltmore, doing a relief fund benefit. "Director Arthur Jacobson was casting a Bing Crosby picture then. He happened to see me performing, and, before I knew what was happening, I was signed with Paramount for a year, playing my first role as Bing Crosby's young brother in *Sing, You Sinners*.

He continued with adolescent roles in *Tom Sawyer-Detective*, *Beau Geste*, and *When Johnny Comes Marching Home*. While

Peggy Ryan dancing with Donald O'Connor in The Merry Monahans *(1944), one of several Universal lightweight musical comedies in which they costarred as a team.*

stationed at Universal Studios, O'Connor starred in a handful of low-budget musical-comedies, set in small-town America, opposite Peggy Ryan. Then came the fateful day he received his draft notice. The studio banged out more quickies with him and Ryan before he reported for military duty. While he served his country in World War II for the next three years, the film series thrived,

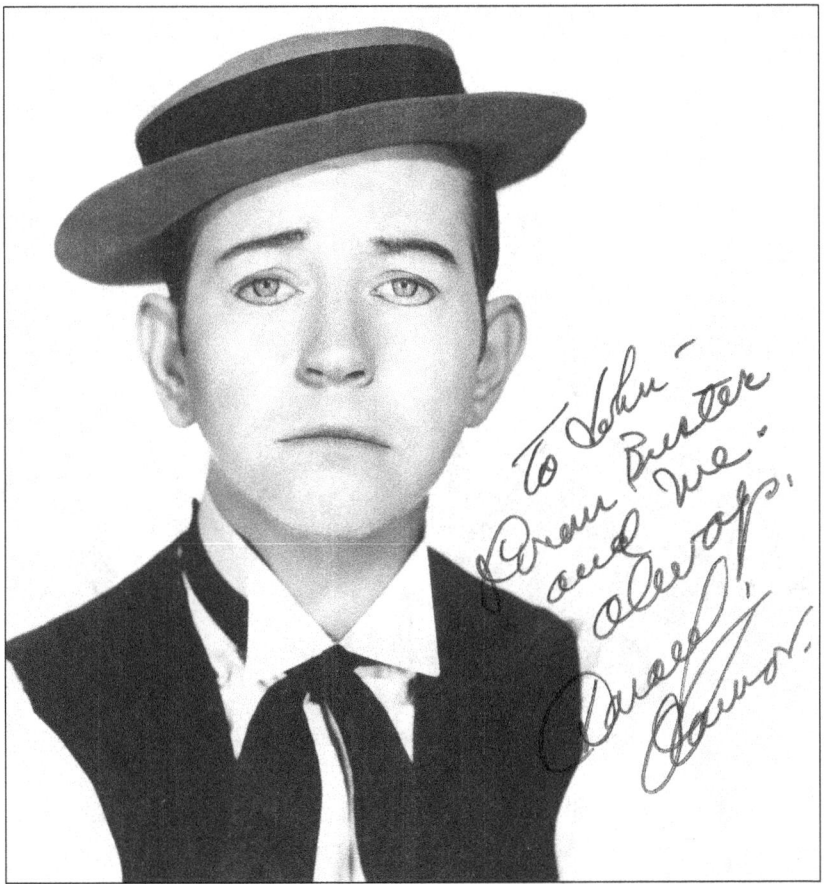

This photo signed by O'Connor is from one of his more unusual films, Paramount's 1957 The Buster Keaton Story, *in which he costarred with Ann Blyth and Rhonda Fleming. He signed it "To John, From Buster and me."*

keeping his reputation alive. But upon his return at the war's end, it was slow going. Universal had reorganized to become Universal-International, and he did not fit in as well as before.

So, he walked out of his contract, a decision that led to a few years of indecision and idleness. It wasn't until he returned to Universal in 1950 to make *Francis*, a comedy about a talking mule with the voice of Chill Wills, that things got good again.

Francis gave a swift kick to his career, which would now include the new medium of television, as he appeared as one of the hosts on *The Colgate Comedy Hour*. (He would receive an Emmy for best male TV performer in 1954.)

O'Connor and Marilyn Monroe in the 1954 classic musical There's No Business Like Show Business.

"After *Colgate*, I switched to a half-hour show, alternating weekly with Jimmy Durante. Before long, I was doing seven or eight shows with only three days' preparation time for each. So I finally bowed out."

Five more films with Francis the Talking Mule kept making money, even if O'Connor was always left holding the mule instead of the girl. (He did get a girl, Marilyn Monroe, in *There's No Business Like Show Business*, a lavish 1954 musical.)

O'Connor's first marriage ended in divorce, and he began drinking heavily when his work schedule in the mid-1950s became overwhelming. "I was doing nineteen one-hour shows a year, plus a constant stream of movies. And I was giving 100 per cent of myself, even when it was junk. Why? Because I'd been taught this tradition of always doing my best. I'd go and go until I was ready to drop, then I'd check into a hospital for six or eight weeks just to get some rest and have my meals served me. Finally, I just had to cut back."

What I call the postcard for the Francis the Talking Mule *Series. That's Donald O'Connor on the left dressed for his role as Lieutenant Peter Stirling. That's Francis on the right, also known by his enlistment serial number M52519 and by his unit, the 123rd Mule Attachment, which served its country gallantry during World War II.*

This scene is from the original Francis *(1950), in which Lt. Stirling (O'Connor) discovers that an Army mule can talk—voice provided by character actor Chill Wills.*

The joke goes that when he found out that "Francis was receiving more fan mail than I was, I decided to drop out of the series." Mickey Rooney took his place in the next one, *Francis in the Haunted House* (1956), but then the series died anyway. "I guess you could say the haunted house in that film had no spirit. I tried to restore some order into my chaotic life. I underwent therapy, and, thirteen years ago, took my last drink. Sobriety has been my savior. And now I work with hope, faith, and trust."

Yes, he admits, "I lived a crazy life back in those days, but I sustained by always going back to work and hearing the applause. It used to be an internal thing for me. But now when I hear applause, it's external. I feel it's for my abilities and what I do."

O'Connor was in Hollywood a few years ago, and decided to visit Universal-International and see Francis the mule. "It was a tragic sight: Francis was standing in his stall alone, almost forgotten. Only he was really a she named Molly. They'd denied the part to a male because of his ... well, you know the anatomy of a male mule.

"Poor Molly. The only recent part she'd played was a pack animal in a Western. She had become a has-been animal star, which just didn't seem right. And I apologized to my old co-star for the jokes I'd made about her over the years." (One wonders if Molly [aka Francis] kicked up her [his] heels in response.)

O'Connor laments the death of the American film musical, and expresses the fear that it is now a lost art, all the outstanding producers who once made them having died off. "Let's face it,"

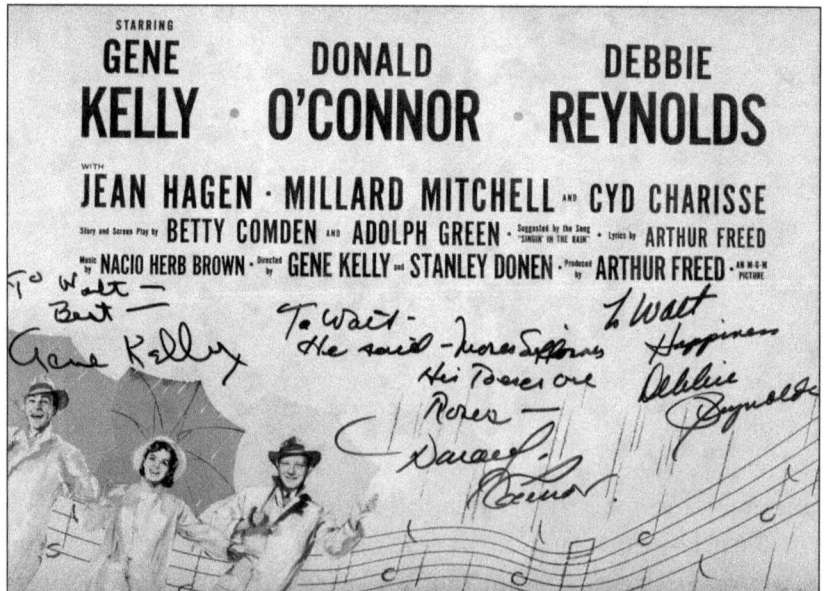

Here is that section of Walt Von Hauffe's Singin' in the Rain poster, signed (left to right) by Gene Kelly, Donald O'Connor (who has written "Moses Supposes His Toeses Are Roses") and Debbie Reynolds.

Donald O'Connor was kind enough, during our final meeting at the Paramount Theater in Oakland, to autograph another of his publicity photos to my son Russ. He signed it simply "Always, Donald O'Connor."

he adds, "the musical was always a calculated risk for the studios. They usually lost money. And the stories weren't always that good—usually bridges into production numbers.

"But the musicals of my era were important, I think, because of how they made us feel. They carried us away into another dimension, and we found a kind of truth in the musical. We saw that mankind could have a glow—that life could be singin' in the rain."

When I attend O'Connor's show at the Paramount Theater in Oakland two weeks later, I bring along an old friend, public relations man Walt Von Hauffe. He brings along a movie poster of *Singin' in the Rain*, being the film connoisseur and memorabilia collector that he is. Already, he tells me, the poster has been signed by Gene Kelly and Debbie Reynolds. What he needs, to make it complete, is Donald O'Connor's signature. So, after the show, we head backstage where O'Connor is in his dressing room, more than delighted to add his signature to the poster.

Bad health is to follow Donald for the next few years, and he barely survives an attack of pneumonia in 1998. Heart problems (remember he had undergone bypass surgery in 1990) continue to plague him until September 2003, when he dies of heart failure at the age of seventy-eight.

MAE WEST
Going Up to Visit With Hollywood's Bawdy, Naughty Courtesan . . . What a Bosom Buddy!

The invitation is in the Mae West tradition: "Come up and see her," but not totally accurate, since the original line from *She Done Him Wrong* (1933) was "Why don't you come up sometime and see *me.*" Nor is it followed by the line she fed Cary Grant in her follow-up film, *I'm No Angel* (1933): "Oh, you can be had!" No, this censored invitation is from CBS, which is preparing to televise a special in which Mae will be an unexpected guest. Unexpected because this is March 1976, at a time when she is eighty-two years

Mae West and her first movie co-star, George Raft, in *Night After Night (1932).*

Mae West in one of her more provocative poses from the 1930s, when she first established a reputation for herself as one of Hollywood's sauciest ladies. Unfortunately, the production code soon went into effect and she was never quite the same again. Still, she once said, "When I'm good, I'm good. When I'm bad, I'm better." Or, as she rephrased it later: "To err is human, but it feels divine."

of age, and she rarely agrees to any personal appearances anymore. Personal interviews on her docket, in recent years, have been all but nonexistent.

Suddenly, I am one of the lucky few invited to "come up and see her," and please, I am further told, bring your wife with you.

Mae loves meeting one's other half. As long as she isn't the jealous type, I cannot help but think to myself, *My Erica, jealous of Mae West? Come now.*

Erica and I waste little time in getting to Hollywood and to Mae's home, a penthouse in the Ravenswood Apartment complex at 570 North Rossmore Avenue. Beverly Hills it isn't, but it is a pleasant enough residential district of the movie capital, where Mae has resided since first coming to town in 1932 to make her initial feature film for Paramount, *Night After Night*, with tough guy George Raft as her rugged co-star.

Her luxurious Ravenswood unit has remained unchanged to her acquaintances, paramours, confidantes, journalists and assorted "gentlemen callers" over the years. It is certainly far removed from Beverly Hills and the rest of the glitter syndrome. Like so many other things that she has clutched to her ample bosom, Mae continues to cling to the roots of her personal and professional past, living the life of a once over-exposed, now under-exposed sex queen who has retained her original royal boudoir, allowing her general public only a glimpse now and again.

A ring of the bell brings a man to the door who introduces himself as Paul Novak. He does not have the appearance of a butler as he is wearing a common suit and tie. There is something about him very imposing: His coat is unbuttoned, allowing us to see that there is a holster attached to his belt containing a weapon that looks like a snub-nosed .38 pistol.

I cannot help but be reminded of Jack Webb's radio show of the 1940s, *Pat Novak for Hire*. Nothing big, this pistol, but it could put a fatal hole through a human body. Novak acts more like a confidante than an employee, and I have to assume that he is Mae's bodyguard. What a commodity he has to guard 24 hours a day, seven days a week, one assumes.

Novak gives us a sturdy once-over, as if to make sure we're not armed, then leads us into the main living room. "Please take a seat," he orders, in a gentle way. "Miss West will be with you in a moment." Nice guy, but there's no hint of nonsense, either.

Deposited to await the Eminent Presence, I am slightly disappointed. For it has been told (perhaps with apocryphal breath,

Here is the front room of Mae West's apartment, in which we sat and talked. That is a bear rug she is standing on.

on a legendary level) that Mae often greets visitors within her boudoir proper (or "improper," as she might have once preferred it). Reportedly, it is a boudoir enhanced by an oval bed with satin coverlet, canopy and down-stuffed pillows. It has been further described as reflecting a certain classy decadence with its ceiling of opulent wall-to-wall mirrors. A room with some view!

The less-erotic living room is of large size, furnished entirely in off-white, aging French Provencal trimmed in gold. The walls are a matching off-white. With some disappointment, I notice there is not a single mirror in the ceiling above us. One thing stands out, extremely: On the off-white piano that dominates the room rests a nude marble statue of Miss West. Decidedly, I decide, off-color too, but artistic nevertheless.

Cresting an off-white couch, slowly becoming decrepit since 1932 (one assumes), is a striking nude oil painting of Mae—she is sprawled on her bed with all the promiscuity of a beautiful courtesan awaiting her next lover, yet it is not nearly as exciting as the

This isn't quite the way Mae West made her grand entrance, but one can fantasize.

suggestiveness of her double entendres and Rabelaisian dialogue that she has made popular in her films and plays.

She was born in 1894 as Mary Jane West. She now wastes no time in making her Grand Entrance. She has retained her aura of Hollywood glamour and sophistication, not to mention constant sexual awareness. Her eyes wander up and down the bodies of those before her while her face holds a broad smile that is self-mocking. Perhaps this is intended to be a counterweight to her expressions of vulgarity for which she is world famous.

On this day, she is not overdressed or over-bejeweled, having poured herself into a clinging baby-blue pants suit without additional frills. Her blonde hair, which doesn't look entirely real, cascades down around her notorious bust, ending in babyish curls. Her face turns to stiffness and is a touch on the pasty side, but to criticize this still-reigning sex queen would be ungentlemanly.

The first thing Mae does is present my wife with a small container of perfume. To me she hands a pair of cufflinks encased in a small box. This is a tradition, Novak tells us, that Mae always carries out when she has house guests. It is a most pleasurable way to begin our encounter.

Her suggestion to relax takes on the same edge of innuendo that banned her from radio in 1937 when, on *The Chase & Sanborn Hour* with Don Ameche and ventriloquist Edgar Bergen, she invited Charlie McCarthy (a puppet) to play in her woodpile. With her first remarks, I cannot help but think that the husky sexiness of her voice is just beginning to be ravaged by age.

In this classic photo of Ms West, she is demonstrating there were days (or nights?) When she was underdressed but overly-bejeweled.

"Generally," she begins, "people pay to see me. And so I don't do much television. When I do appear, it's my way, not the network's. That's the way it's gonna be with Dick Cavett." She is referring to the fact that she will be appearing with John Wayne and other movie luminaries on CBS-TV's *Dick Cavett's Backlot U.S.A.* in the very near future. "I will be singing 'Frankie and Johnny' and 'After You're Gone,' but I'll be doing them *my way.*" (Frank Sinatra wouldn't have been happier.)

A publicity photo of Mae West tinkering with Charlie McCarthy, the guy with the wooden personality, who would bring about Ms West being censored from radio shows.

The reason she is making this rare appearance is "by popular demand. All that fan mail"—she makes cards and letters sound like breathing sex objects—"begging me to return. I get so much mail that I began to feel terrible about depriving all those people of seein' me. So here I am, at your ... complete ... disposal."

Movie fans who have felt deprived of Miss West will be delighted to learn, right from her own attractive lips, that her play, *Sextette*, first produced in 1961, will be made this very year into a motion picture starring ... take a wild guess. "It's the story of six men who're all—and I mean all—in love with the same woman. Of course, it's not the men in your life that's important. It's the life in your men that counts. Now, that's the kind of woman I play in *Sextette*. A golddigger with the biggest nuggets in hand. Right or wrong, when a woman goes wrong, men go right after her. This lady also happens to be a motion picture star. Hell, why hide the truth. She's me, Mae West!"

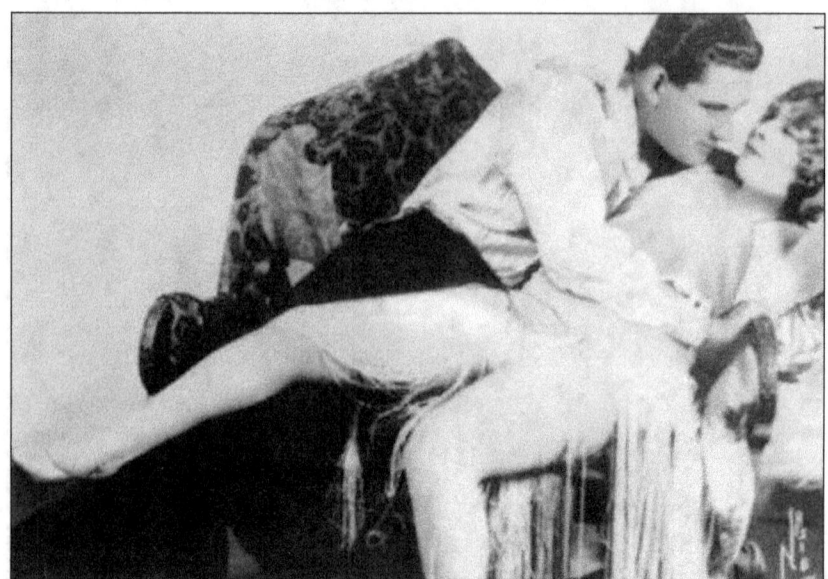

A provocative photo of Mae West with one of her leading men in her 1925-26 Broadway hit Sex, *for which she went to jail for a few days—and nights.*

There is a famous moment in her first film, *Night after Night,* in which a hat check woman in a nightclub sees West's jewelry and remarks, "Goodness! What beautiful diamonds!" And West replies, "Goodness had nothing to do with it, dearie." She took that gag and entitled her 1953 autobiography *Goodness Had Nothing to Do With It.* "I'm still writing books on my three favorite subjects: sex, ESP, and Mae West." (She does believe in flying saucers and extraterrestrial life forms, but only makes quick reference to them.)

Writing her own material would come to dominate her career, and very quickly she tells me she was born and raised in Brooklyn, and at the age of seven began to perform in amateur shows, displaying an unusual talent that enabled her to begin performing in Vaudeville at the age of fourteen. Early on, she became intrigued with female impersonators and was doing her first Broadway show at seventeen, singing and dancing in a way that was "snappy." Yes, she said, "they were loving me even then. Whether I knew it or not, I was already on a pathway to full sexuality. I had absolutely nothing to hide."

In her early twenties, Mae wrote-produced-directed and starred in her first play, simply and appropriately called *Sex.* It's

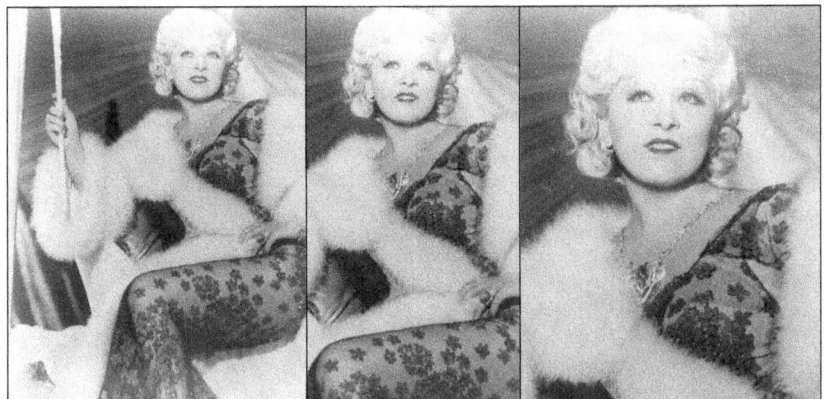

no surprise that that single word on the marquee attracted what she calls "an appreciative audience." But . . . "You won't believe what happened," she tells us. "We were selling a lot of tickets when suddenly the cops raided the theater and we all went to jail. Then it was prison for me for a week. On moral charges, can you believe that? Do I look immoral to you? Humph. And is it true that I wore silk undies in my cell? You tell me."

To this day, Mae feels that she was ahead of her time with her plays, such as *Diamond Lil* (1929). "They live on in my memory, those plays. Everybody talks about the gay set these days, but I was writing about it back in '27 in my play, *The Drag*. Yes, it was a 'drag' on the theatrical market. It hit home. I'd known a lot of homosexuals in my Vaudeville days, so it wasn't difficult writin' about them and their lifestyle. In the closet or out. We were sold out for months. What a 'drag.' Hah!"

With her next words, she switches from entertainment authoress to psychologist, but her smoldering voice remains the same. "A homo, of course, is a female soul trapped in a male body, while a Lesbian is a male soul trapped in a female body. I'm talkin' about the ones who were born that way. Not talkin' about all the rest—the ones who acquired the habit. Hell, with a little practice you can get good at anything."

Mae points to the painting, appropriately entitled "Sex," adorning her off-white living room wall. "I never did go in for nudity as such. Florence Kinzell painted that. It's insured by Lloyds of London, by the way. In 1934, Florence saw me backstage one night on Broadway

The train sequence in My Little Chickadee *(1940), in which Mae West tells W. C. Fields she's going to take him—and how!*

and said I had too gorgeous a body not to pose for posterity. I resisted at first, but finally gave in to her and posterity. Some people sit for a pose. I recline." She went on to claim that she had been offered $80,000 for the painting, but refused to sell it.

She points to the nearby piano. "That statue of me that was done back in '34. My measurements haven't changed, I'll have you know. I do weigh two pounds more today than I did back then. I exercise with weights. Of course, they're leather-bound so my hands won't get cold on that bare steel."

Has Mae changed her techniques with men as she has aged? She is startled by the question, but then smiles. "Thanks for asking. I haven't changed techniques, I'll have you know, but I have changed men. Never did have to look very hard for them. They just came around lookin' for me. Said they were protectin' me . . . from what? I never asked. I always kept a steady boyfriend for a rainy day . . . and one boyfriend for days when it wasn't raining."

Mae confesses that she doesn't think much of today's hardcore sex films. "They're not only without clothes . . . they're without good stories. You've got to have more than naked bodies . . .although I've got nothing against naked bodies, except maybe my own . . . but in show biz you need the material. In more ways than one, if you get the angle I'm coming from."

W. C. Fields, as far as Mae is concerned, "was a conniving little rapscallion who saw a good thing and tried to horn in on one of my screenplays. People are always talking about us workin' together, but the truth is, we did just that one picture, *My Little Chickadee*. All Fields contributed was one bar sequence with plenty of drinks going down. Just a few pages, yet he demanded his name be included in the credits as co-author. All for gallons of liquor."

I couldn't help but recall a scene in the film where Mae (portraying Flower Belle Lee) and Fields are on a train, and he proposes to her. "Will you take me?" he asks. She glances down at the suitcase full of money beside him, and replies. "I'll take you. And how!"

When Mae hit Hollywood, she was all of forty. That was a little old for an up-and-coming star, but because of her excellence with sexual innuendos and provocative costuming, she was a well-accepted face in such hits as *She Done Him Wrong* (the film version of her play, *Diamond Lil*), and *I'm No Angel*, her biggest hit at the box office, in which she again co-starred with Cary Grant. Then came the morality code, the Hays Office, which began censoring sexual themes that would restrict her from portraying her characters so blatantly, and eliminate the double entendres that had made her so popular. Even the title of one of her films-to-be, *It Ain't No Sin*, was changed to *Belle of the Nineties*.

"I made all of twelve pictures," she says, "before I quit Hollywood in 1943. I'd saturated the market with all I had. If you get my drift. The theater owners were still clamoring for my stuff. I decided there was no use givin' them the chance to get sick of me." For a moment, she singled out George Raft. "After we made *Night After Night* together, he said that I'd stole everything but the camera." Well, he kept making movies. Hundreds of them. Not many, at that rate, could've been very good."

Mae turned to TV guest appearances, and even did an episode of the talking horse series, *Mister Ed*. She also did a show in Las

Mae West as she appeared in Myra Breckinridge.

Vegas involving body-builders. She refused to make another film until 1969's *Myra Breckinridge*. It turned out to be an unhappy experience for everyone, even though she was titled "The Queen of Trash" for participating in a movie about sex-change. "There was all that hoopla about me and Raquel Welch not gettin' along, but that was only publicity. We had only one scene together, so how could we hate each other? She struck me. I mean, she struck me as being a nice, sweet girl." Mae added: "I wrote my own scenes in *Myra*. And I came out of it the only surviving rose in a bed of wilted flowers. But then, I always did know my way around a bed."

She sums up her career thusly: "My biggest problem was censorship, which was due to my highly volatile personality. I was never censored for an overt act; it was for what I was suggestin' down

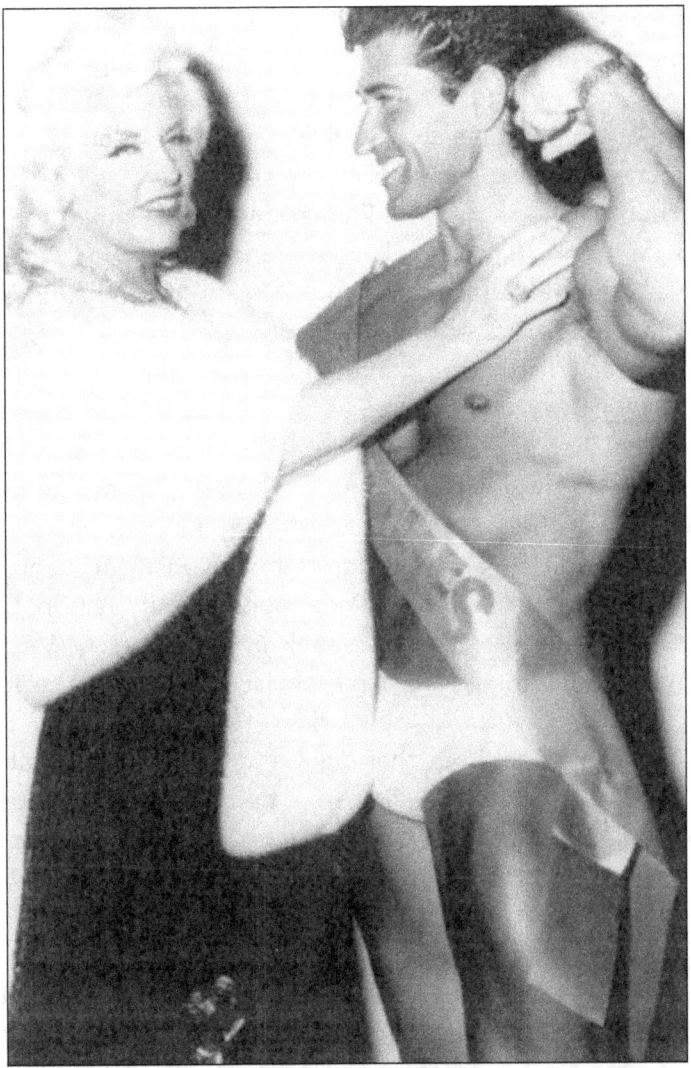

Mae West posing with her bodyguard-to-be, Paul Novak, whom she met during her smokin' 1954 Las Vegas bodybuilders show. Novak, the guy who met my wife and I at Mae's front door packing a .38 pistol, became famous for punching out fellow he-man Mickey Hargitay, lover and eventually husband of actress Jayne Mansfield.

underneath. I've always known what I wanted from life, since I started singin' at the age of seven. And permanent romance never fit into my plans. Of course, I managed to squeeze a lot of fellas in on a temporary basis. The institution of marriage might be right for some people, but I was too busy with show biz."

Because Mae is beginning to show signs of tiredness, Paul Novak suggests that our interview be concluded. Mae offers a pliant hand and floats from the room. I sit for a moment, boggled by the thought that at her age she is still a legend in on-screen ribaldry, in off-screen finesse and double meaning. She has lost none of her touches. She is still a monumental spokeswoman for Hollywood glamour . . . its unchallenged, longest-surviving archetypal sex symbol. As Mae might have put it herself, "I'm the kind of girl who climbed the ladder of success wrong by wrong."

Years later, I discovered that the man who met us at Mae's front door, Paul Novak, whom I had assumed was a hired bodyguard, was really Chester Rybinski (1923-1999), a one-time wrestler and Mr. California title holder. He had first met Mae during her Las Vegas show in the 1950s and had remained her central lover for the rest of her life, living with her in the Ravenswood penthouse.

As for Mae, I would see her one more time in person, but we did not have an opportunity to speak. In November 1978, she was driven from Los Angeles to San Francisco for a premiere screening of the film, *Sextette*, at the Warfield Theater on Market Street. The theater was sold out that night and a huge crowd gathered outside, hoping to catch a glimpse of her when she arrived. I was in the audience with Erica, anticipating a pre-screening interview that was to be presented on the theater's stage. We watched as Mae entered and took her seat.

However, by then she was in failing health, something that had been subtly suggested by Paul Novak when he brought our meeting to a rapid close. Making *Sextette* with director Ken Hughes a short time after our interview, she had difficulty walking and seeing. So it was that Mae, at the last minute, did not have the energy to walk to the stage. And so the planned interview had to be cancelled.

Things did not get better. Mae suffered from a stroke in August 1980 and went to hospital, where she underwent another stroke. Finally, she was allowed to return home even though the doctors knew the end was near. Maybe the docs were remembering one of her most famous lines: "Marriage is a great institution, but I'm

Mae West in her final film role as Marlo Manners in Sextette.

not ready for an institution." On November 22, 1980, she died at the age of eighty-seven.

But wow! Sex has never been funnier!

JIMMY DURANTE
Stop duh Music! It's Time to Meet duh Most Famous Schnoz Ever to Extend Into Show Biz

Top to bottom, it measures 77 millimeters, or just a little over three inches. From side to side, its range is four inches. Scientifically there is a name for such a vast acreage of human skin: platyrrhine-leptorrhine-messorhine, which means simply it got busted up one night in a street quarrel on the Lower East Side of New York when its owner was still a kid growing up in an Italian immigrant family.

One cannot study Jimmy Durante, a unique radio, TV and motion picture comedian, without focusing on *The Schnozzle*. Or, as Gene Fowler called it in the title of his biography of Durante: *The Schnozzola,* a humorous take on the Yiddish word for nose, schnoz. Durante himself merely addresses his bulging unit as, "You cute little moneymaker, you," stroking it affectionately on occasion, and studying it whenever he stares into his bathroom mirror. "Dat's my proboscis," he would sometimes remark to himself. Or to others within earshot.

If not the most famous nose in history (there is still a faction that holds the nose of Cyrano de Bergerac in greater reverence), it is certainly the most talked about in terms of American show business. It has been Durante's "landmark" for decades, from the days and nights when he was a ragtime pianist on Coney Island. It has also been responsible for at least one recorded lawsuit, and for some years now a mold of it has been on display at the Smithsonian Institution. (Just ask for the nose department to find it.)

While one could go on examining the nose at greater length (ahem . . . .), there are other Durante "talents" of a far-more "sophisticated" nature. He's great at the piano with ridiculous lyrics, the most famous being "Inka Dinka Doo." I will also always remember the way he and his piano sank into a large swimming pool

Jimmy Durante, schnoz to you.

in the 1947 Esther Williams musical, *This Time for Keeps*. With that powerful voice of his, Durante knew how to bring extra strength to his portrayals in such movies as *Joe Palooka* (1934), in which he all but stole the show as Palooka's manager, Knobby Walsh. Then there was his teeming teaming with Frank Sinatra in *It Happened in Brooklyn* (1947), so that eventually Sinatra fell to his knees to do an impression of a singing Durante.

Holding his hat into the sky was always a trademark of Jimmy Durante whenever he made an appearance. Inka dinka doo to you, too.

Then came television, with *The Jimmy Durante Show* running from 1954-1957. Most of the programs were set in a small nightclub called the Club Durant. With him appeared Eddie Jackson, long-time friend and partner from Vaudeville, Jules Buffano on piano, and Jack Roth on drums. Behind him was a chorus line of beauties

Frank Sinatra and Durante teamed up to do It Happened in Brooklyn, *with Sinatra doing his impression of Durante in one of their musical numbers.*

called The Durante Girls. All these shows were done live, many of them from Las Vegas where it was convenient to grab the casino stars and showcase them at his side.

Those things are in his past. Now it is April 15, 1967, a chilly evening outside the Nugget Casino. The seventy-four-year-old Schnozzola pauses to observe the winking lights of the neon signs which hail him as the current attraction in the Circus Room, along with his omnipresent partners: the aforementioned Mr. Jackson and Sonny King, another long-time collaborator within his live shows. He releases a sigh of satisfaction and turns to face the street. There is a sign of hunger written into his eyes. It's even possible he can smell food aromas coming out of the hotel's kitchen, possibly even restaurants within sniffing range.

Durante is bundled in an overcoat and ancient rumpled felt hat that forever adorned his nearly-hairless head. Finished with his first performance of songs, piano playing, and joke flinging of the evening, and with two hours to kill before his second show, his destination is Trader Dick's, just across the street from John Ascuaga's busy casino-hotel, for a "few bites" of dinner. I can hear a melody rummaging through my head: *Chompa Chompa Cruncha Doo!*

He strides briskly for his age, his hands buried in the deep pockets of the hardly-new coat. He speaks in that curious Durante vocabulary, a mixture of mispronunciations and slurred words delivered in the familiar sandpapery voice. "So yuh liked the show I just did with duh boys. My pals Eddie 'n Sonny. Glad tuh hear it. We was makin' mosta it up as we went along, me 'n duh boys. Dat's why we got so much fun with dis show." Durante pauses in the middle of the boulevard that runs through the center of Sparks, oblivious to approaching traffic, to make note of minute snowflakes which have begun to fall from the night sky. "How duh yuh like that," he roars, slapping his hands against the overcoat. "I no sooner steps outside den it begins to pre-cipi-cipi-cipi-tash."

A verbal warning of oncoming traffic brings Durante quickly to the sidewalk, where he pauses to stare into the plate glass window of a hardware store. "Dese places got so many things for a guy tuh see. Have yuh ever noticed how much fun can be had in a joint like dis?" He goes a few feet farther, this time stopping to peer into a grocery store. "I'm always buyin' too many foods in dese places. Der goes my money."

Durante leads the way into the Polynesian decor and atmosphere of Trader Dick's. He is soon seated at a table, ordering baked chicken ("dis time whichout the bone"), rice, pea pods, and non-Oriental tea. It turns out that conversation with Jimmy Durante is a series of sudden bursts of laughter and excitement, his hand often flying out and clutching the nearest arm (mine!) to emphasize his enthusiasm. At times, he gropes for a memory, cannot find it, but continues on unfazed, offering up an anecdote or comment even if it is unrelated to the topic at hand. "You're probably wonderin' where I picked up dis misprenunciation business. Well, it twas an accident, believe me. I always tried tuh prenunce words in duh proper manner, but there was dis name of a ship—I can't even remember how tuh prenunce it right now.

"Anyways, I'm standin' on the stage 'n I can't get it tuh come out right. Everybody's laughin' and pretty soon I figure maybe it's a good thing tuh keep in duh act. Duh whole thing is one big catastra-stroke."

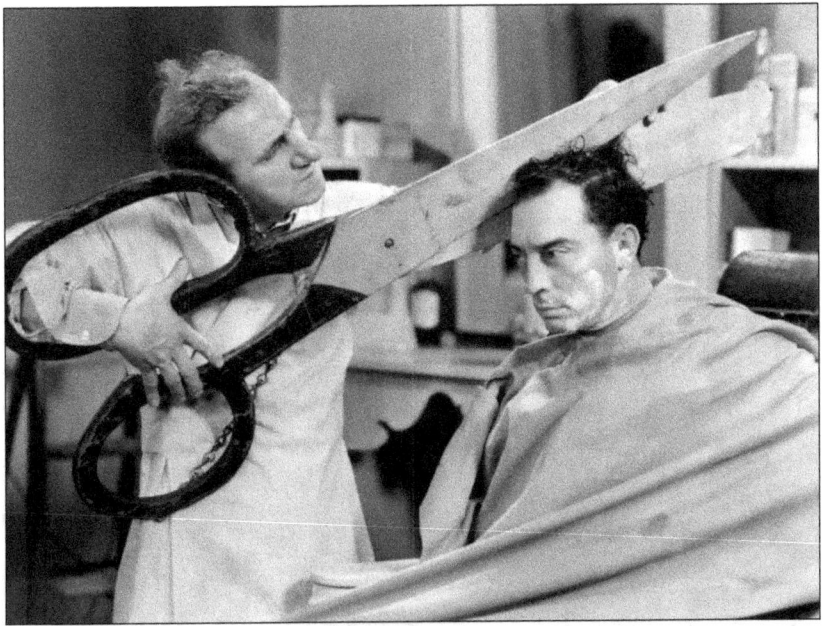

Obviously Jimmy Durante was on the cutting edge of show biz when he gave a haircut to silent film star Buster Keaton in Speak Easily.

What does he attribute his continuing success to? "Holy . . . ." Durante leans far back in his chair, his hands raised as though he had become a prisoner of war. "Nobody knows dat! Holy . . . I think of all duh breaks I've had since 1910 when I was playin' Coney Island. Who knows what makes success? But I'll tell yuh the three biggest thrills in my life. One was playin' duh Palace on Broadway, the second was bein' signed by Ziegfeld, and duh thoid was bein' asked a few years ago tuh play in Billy Rose's movie *Jumbo* [1962] after I'd played it on duh Hippodrome stage way back in '36 . . . Stop the music! I almost forgot to tell yuh about Buster Keaton. We did this movie together, *Speak Easily*, back in '32. Dat I loved.

"Listen," continues Durante, his hands tightly gripping the edges of the table, "yuh know what it is dat's so great about dis business? People come over tuh me and say: 'Jimmy, I got no need for an entertainer, but I wanna shake your hand 'cause I like yuh as a poison. I hope yuh live to be a hundred.' That's why I keep on goin' in dis business. People respect yuh. I'd quit tomorrow if I stopped havin' any fun. I don't know if I'm the last of my kind er

Durante always considered himself behind the eight ball, as he decided to show us literally in this publicity photo.

not, but nobody could kid 'round on the stage like us guys 'n get away which it."

How do today's audiences differ, Mr. Durante, from—?

"Wait uh minute! Hold everything! Stop duh music! I jest taught uh somethin'. You're from duh press. 'N dat reminds me uh duh time I give this press party in London, see. Well, I took a train tuh Italy next thing. Italy's where they got all these towns, one after 'nother. Well, I picks up dis newspaper and suddenly I see duh word Durante in every column. I figure, the party I gave paid off. Sos I take the scissors I use tuh cut duh ends of my soggy cigar butts 'n start clippin' out duh stories which got my name in dem. Den I decide I gotta go tuh duh men's room.

"When I get there, I notice my name's on a sign on duh toilet seat. I figure everybody's tryin' tuh get into duh act 'n I start askin' round. I come tuh find out, Durante in Italian is duh word for, like, 'Don't flush too much.' Dat's what the toilet was tryin' tuh tell me. No wonder my name was poppin' up in all dem newspaper stories dat guys like you write."

Why, Mr. Durante, have you devoted so many years to show business when you could have retired comfortably a number of years ago? "Geeesss...." A slapping of his thighs. "Stop duh music. Retune up duh piano! Stop everythin'. I'd deprepitate. Maybe even rot away. Tank God I'm in good health 'n can keep workin' four or five months of duh year. I even been makin' dem TV commercials." He might have also told me that, despite his age, he is still very busy doing voice-overs, such as Humpty Dumpty in *Alice Through the Looking Glass*.

Does he have a single piece of advice for show business beginners? "Stop duh music again. Go no fodder. Anybody goin' intah this busines–dis thing show business–has got tuh love dat followin'. Too many folks nowadays don't like what they're doin'. Dey wake up in duh mornin' which a grudge. If a guy's got talent, he can't hide it. Sooner or later, it's gonna crop out. Myself, I couldn't wait tuh get intah duh thick uh it when I was a kid being' raised on duh East Side uh New York. 'Ragtime Jimmy, King uh Harlem,' dat was yours truly. We all gotta take our ups 'n downs in dah business."

"Also," he continues, "we all gotta learn some tricks. Not many. Lookah me. How many tricks does I really know? Three or four, maybe, dat's it. Slappin' my sides, sayin' 'I gotta million of 'em,' singin' 'Inka Dinka Doo,' biddin' good night to Mrs. Calabash, wherever she is. Or sayin' 'Everybody's tryin' to get into duh act!' Dem things is all part uh me. Lotsa things I can't do. Just ain't my forty."

His dinner is almost completely eaten up, and it's time to get back across the street to the Circus Room. My last question: "Any additional advice for my readers?"

> *The letter I received from Jimmy Durante shortly after our interview. When I first read it, I waved it around the editorial office and shouted "Stop the music! I just had a catasta-stroke!"*

Jimmy Durante
511 North Beverly Drive
Beverly Hills, California 90210

May 4, 1967

Mr. John Stanley
San Francisco Examiner
San Francisco, Calif.

Dear John:

Thanks a million for the write-up you gave me in the Sunday issue of the Examiner. I received many copies from my fans and friends and believe me I got a big kick out of it.

Very best wishes.

Sincerely

Jimmy Durante

Jimmy Durante

JD/lt

"Don't get intah duh racket unless yuh loves it. If yuh got ambition, yuh'll make it. Just keep wokin' hard. And be yourself." To make his point, Durante pounds the table with both fists. "Too many guys dese days're tryin' tuh project my image."

Almost immediately after our interview, I receive a letter from Jimmy Durante, dated May 4, 1967. He identifies my newspaper as *The Examiner*, an easy mistake to make, since in 1965, the two papers had merged into a single business unit, with *The San Francisco Chronicle* publishing in the morning and *The San Francisco Examiner* in the afternoon. The Sunday edition was also a joint effort, and hence Jimmy's misunderstanding.

Durante would continue to live a full, busy life until 1972, when he suffered a stroke and had to remain in a wheelchair from then on. Before his death in 1980 from pneumonia at the age of eighty-six, it was revealed that the closing line from his radio and TV days, "Good night, Mrs. Calabash, wherever you are," was in reference to his first wife Jeanne, who had died back in 1943. The name "Calabash" had come from Calabasas, the California community where the couple had lived during the final years of Jeanne's life. How duh ya like dat one?

Good night, Mrs. Calabash, wherever you are.

LIBERACE
Candlelight, Comedy and Musical Classics at the Piano of The Glitter Man

The first impression of Wladziu Valentino Liberace, better known as just plain "Lee" to friends and associates, is that of a well-groomed dresser with a mild manner and gentle touch. He strides across the spacious terminal of the Reno-Tahoe International Airport, conspicuously clad in a flashy red sports coat and sleek black trousers. On hand to greet him and his small entourage is Don Barnett, publicity man for John Ascuaga's Nugget Casino Resort, where "Lee" (okay, Liberace to you) is to begin a three-week engagement this very night.

For a moment, the forty-seven-year-old entertainer, who has established a reputation for excellent piano music combined with a style of self-put down comedy and the ever present candelabra, stands beside a sign promoting his upcoming engagement while a photographer snaps a few pictures. Despite a pressing rehearsal schedule, Liberace pauses at the luggage counter to shake hands with admirers and to speak to a Black woman holding an infant in her arms. There are introductions all around, but at this close range there is no hint of the heavily-scented cologne and toilet waters that so many critics have accused Liberace of drowning himself in.

On the way to a waiting limousine, Liberace explains he has just arrived from Las Vegas, where the night before he enjoyed an exuberant dinner at Caesar's Palace. (By now, everyone knew he had earned millions of dollars working in Las Vegas and other major venues throughout America). Then he, his luggage, and entourage are off in the limo, headed for nearby Sparks, a suburb of Reno, Nevada.

Six hours and ten minutes later Liberace is standing on the stage of the Nugget's Circus Room, this time living up to his widespread reputation as an effeminate, prissy man. His body is cloaked in a

When I met Liberace at the Reno airport, he paused in the lobby to have photos taken as he stood beside a poster advertising the show he would begin performing that very evening.

light-blue sequined jacket, tailored trousers and white bucks with jeweled buckles.

"I don't dress like this to go unnoticed," he tells the audience. "Of course, I'd never wear these things on the street. I'd get picked up in a minute." He also flashes his candelabrum-shaped ring and piano-shaped wrist watch. "My diamonds aren't large, but then I don't have to do anything to earn them."

Comparing himself to a pallbearer at a butterfly funeral, and indicating his shorts often bunch up when he is seated at his elongated Baldwin piano (which was made especially for him with a plexiglass top for $15,000), he finally settles down before that very piano to offer a medley of show business tunes in a style that is fast and contemporarily jazzy. Next comes "Exodus," "More," and "Alley Cat"—and then he hurries offstage "to slip into something more spectacular."

He soon reappears looking like a circus ringmaster. He's now wearing a sparkling gray suit with more sequins than the first. Later, he dons a Count Dracula-style cape and vest. (It brings to mind the wild assortment of ostrich feathers, capes, and mink coats he often adorned himself with over the years.) Finally, he winds up his performance with tunes from *My Fair Lady* (Karen Wessler singing), *Hello, Dolly!,* Liszt's "Second Hungarian Rhapsody," and "I'll Be Seeing You."

The Glitter Man (another way he is often identified) receives a standing ovation for his two hours of performing, thirty minutes more than the Nugget management had wanted or expected, but nobody is going to argue with a man who has won six Gold Album awards, two Emmy Awards, and has two stars on Hollywood's Walk of Fame.

What kind of man is *Mr. Showmanship*, really? That question leads me to seek out associates of the unusual entertainer, born in Wisconsin to Italian-Polish parents, who themselves had a background in music. I talk with Larry Deutsch, who has served as one of his lawyers for six years. Deutsch calls "Lee" a "fabulously true gentleman," while his personal manager for sixteen years, Seymour Heller, is a bit more profound. "At first, Lee was just a talent without flair, but now he's grown into a polished showman. He uses the same basic ingredients he used in the beginning, but he's polished them, given them a genuine sense of humor and flamboyance. He's a unique mixture of comedy and music."

Liberace's musical arranger, Gordon Robbins, admits he is too prejudiced to be profound, but still insists that the pianist-comedian "has been understanding and easy to get along with during our fifteen-year association."

Liberace at his Grand Piano during a special visit to the Muppets' TV show. At right is the most famous Liberace prop of all, the candelabra.

An hour after the opening show, Liberace is enjoying a gin and tonic in his dressing room. He is alone, which seems unusual, since stars of his magnitude are usually surrounded by managers, agents, etc. For the moment, he is dressed comfortably in black pants and a green pullover sweater. His manner has returned to that which he demonstrated at the airport: responsive, unpretentious, pleasant. Nor is he hesitant to answer touchy questions.

Why, for example, does he try to convey such a foppish image on stage? "One has to develop an individuality in order to survive in show business," he tells me. "And in my case, I am merely going along with what people have assumed about me. It has made me one-of-a-kind, as Sinatra, Presley, and The Beatles are one-of-a-kind. And that, I think, has perpetuated my career. You find yourself in heavy demand. I go everywhere. For the music. For the laughs. Mix them the right way and you win."

While Liberace does not resent the jokes about his sexuality which have circulated about him for many years, he has twice taken defensive (and often admired) stands against these attacks—once in the case of *Confidential* magazine (which explicitly implied there was "a man" in Liberace's life), and once against Cassandra, the columnist in the *London Daily Mirror*, who lambasted the pianist as being "fruit flavored," a "mincing, ice-covered heap of mother love" while he was touring England in 1959.

The latter assault forced Liberace to press a libel suit on grounds the article had implied he was homosexual. "To belittle an entertainer is one thing," Liberace tells me, "and that is to be expected. But when the attack becomes personal, aimed at an individual's way-of-life and living habits, it becomes defamation of character. And when slander is involved, you've got to fight back. If you don't, you leave the door open to constant ridicule.

"I, therefore, became a tool that opened the sores of British journalism that stood up as an example for all the others who hadn't stood up after being downgraded by the press. I won my suit, and as a result, English libel laws were heavily revised and more clearly defined. I like to feel that I have made a contribution that goes beyond the stage."

Liberace enjoyed more years of fame, touring the world with his piano and his entourage, but the times were changing, and while "Lee" would always deny any claims that he was homosexual, the truth finally began to emerge in 1982 when he separated from Scott Thorson, who had accompanied him on his journey of success as chauffeur and live-in lover. Thorson sued for $113 million in 1982, but four years later, after visiting Liberace one final time when he learned that he was ill, settled for only $75,000. The full story of their love and final hatred was recounted in Thorson's autobiography, *Behind the Candelabra: My Life With Liberace*, which was brought to life by HBO in a 2014 drama starring Michael Douglas as Liberace and Matt Damon as Thorson.) After Liberace died in 1987 at the age of sixty-seven, an autopsy revealed that he had contracted AIDS.

PETER SELLERS
He Played a British Goon, He Played a French Fool,
And Kept the World Laughing All the While

What an invitation! In the summer of 1978, I have been asked by United Artists to attend the world premiere of *Revenge of the Pink Panther*. Not a premiere in Hollywood, like most premieres, but a premiere in the Hawaiian Islands. I feel as if I am a major part of movie history. To travel so far to meet possibly the funniest detective of all time, the incredible Jacque Clousea! The French Surete will never be the same again!

I fly to Oahu, and then I'm transported with other members of the American press to the windward side of the island, to the exquisite Kuilimia Hotel. It's a gala gathering that includes all the key contributors to this, the fifth comedy in the *Pink Panther* series. Waiting at the hotel for our arrival is producer-director Blake Edwards, with composer Henry Mancini standing at his side, along with key members of the cast. Most key of all, naturally, is Peter Sellers, known the world over by now for his portrayal of Chief Inspector Jacques Clouseau. With him are Herbert Lom (also famed by now for his Inspector Charles Dreyfus, also trapped within the French Surete, who is always being driven around the bend by Clouseau's incompetency), Burt Kwouk, portrayer of Cato Fong (Clouseau's karate-happy man servant), and Dyan Cannon, (who will provide what little romantic interest the film offers.)

The *Pink Panther* franchise has been a gem in the career of Peter Sellers. Four times during the past fourteen years, the British actor has made a laughing stock of the Surete of Paris with his portrayal of the bumbling French detective Clouseau, proving with a cash flow of more than a half million dollars that there's always a market for slapstick comedy in the Laurel and Hardy tradition.

Peter Sellers in the role of Inspector Jacques Clouseau, a thoroughly inept French detective who will stop at nothing to be incompetent in Revenge of the Pink Panther. *This particular production shot was signed by Sellers on the day we met, but his signature, spread across his left raincoat lapel, has faded with time so badly that it's almost unreadable.*

In this fifth offering in the series, Clouseau is in pursuit of the French Connection, an underworld kingpin running dope through Hong Kong, and Sellers characteristically rollicks through his role, posing as a one-legged Swedish pirate, a Chinese mandarin, a street walker, Henri de Toulouse-Lautrec, and as the Godfather.

In Revenge of the Pink Panther, *Peter Sellers as Clouseau seeks a drug dealer known as the French Connection.*

The worldwide popularity of these *Panther* films should not be underestimated because of their basic inanity. The Pink Panther (originally a flawed diamond that was always being stolen by The Phantom) is no longer part of the story lines. The image of the cartoon-like animated panther has come to symbolize Clouseau's misadventures and maladroit detective work and is now available on greeting cards, posters, coffee mugs, skateboards, skis, toothbrush holders, and women's lingerie. In Japan alone there are 300 different Pink Panther products.

When I meet Sellers, I wonder about his health. I know he suffered a series of heart attacks in 1964 while making *Kiss Me, Stupid* in Hollywood, a film he was unable to finish. In March 1977, he had suffered another heart attack and now wore a pacemaker. There were also many stories in circulation about his problems with alcohol and cocaine. Nevertheless, he looks well-tanned and in the best of humor, offering samples of his many dialects and voices, frequently holding the hand of his young wife (British actress Lynne Frederick, whom he had married a year earlier) and flashing her an infatuated smile.

Blake Edwards, director of Revenge of the Pink Panther, *who sat next to Peter Sellers during our interview.*

"Heart attacks?" he says, echoing my question. "I tried to give them up. I'm down to two a day now. In fact," he adds, glancing at his watch, "I'm due for one any moment." His face becomes cloudy with solemnity. "I really shouldn't joke about my heart this way. You really can't ignore such an experience; it's very traumatic. Fortunately, it doesn't interfere with my work to any degree and I don't think too much about it."

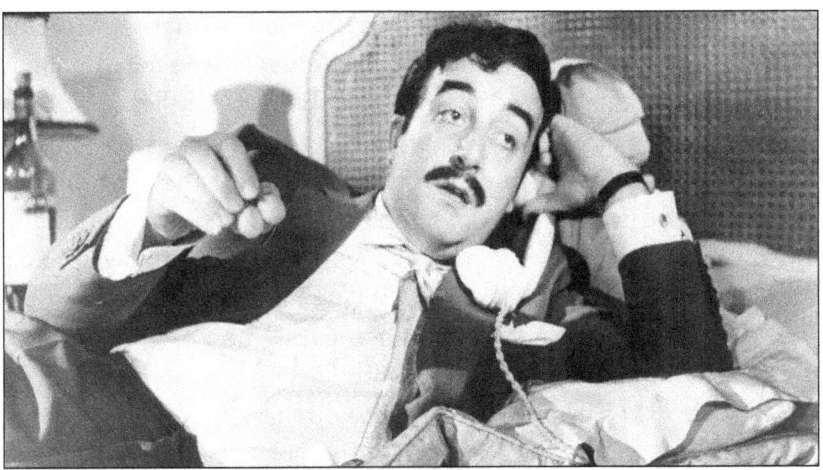
Peter Sellers as the Prime Minister of the Spanish island of Gaillardia in the 1959 British comedy, The Man in the Cocked Hat.

"The only thing I worry about," interjects Blake Edwards, who is in attendance with his wife Julie Andrews, "is having to give him mouth-to-mouth resuscitation on the set."

Sellers resumes. "This is our fifth in the series and it well may be true that we won't make any more Panther films. Five is my lucky number and it might be a good number to bow out on. We've had a lot of success and we've done very well and we've been very lucky. I've had a long and varied career since *The Lady Killers* in 1956 and I've played all kinds of roles. I enjoyed playing in such films as *Casino Royale* and *The Man in the Cocked Hat*. They were all challenging in their own special way, and I shall go on from Clouseau to do other things."

"Ask about a sixth film," interjects Edwards again, "after we've seen the grosses on this one."

"Well, there you are," says Sellers, "that's always the bottom line in this business, isn't it? Of course, there are other ways of gauging the success of the films—by the number of people who write letters, and by the people who come up to speak with you. Unfortunately, a lot of people seem to think I have this panther suit with a long tail and ears, and I go around wearing it. That's one false impression I'm trying to dispel."

Sellers eagerly discusses the creation of Clouseau and the metamorphosis of the character. "Blake and I were riding in a taxi from the Rome airport when we formulated the character. It was done all very quickly. In the first film, Clouseau spoke with a less exaggerated accent. Before we made the second film, *A Shot in the Dark* (1964), I was staying in a Paris hotel and there was a concierge there who tried to emulate some of the language of American tourists. It gave me the idea to begin experimenting with certain words. Every language, you know, has its own music, and I've tried to deal with the music of French in a special way. Now Clouseau will say 'bem' for bomb, or "men-ky" for monkey. Words are stretched and played with."

Sellers brushes away invisible flies with his hands. "I don't want to make it sound as though the Panther films are more than we intend. These films don't demand anything. They're very easy to do. I always live the characters I play, except Clouseau, whom I know so well anyway.

"Actually, Clouseau is a very serious man. He doesn't know he's a loser, he doesn't know he's accident prone and certainly he won't admit it. When an accident does happen of some proportion, he will say, 'What is that you said?' He imagines that perhaps someone has made an unkind remark. He's very dignified within his limits.

"I think it's important that Clouseau is basically a kind man. People take easily to someone who can't really pull it off. Just as long as he's not arrogant. If I made Clouseau arrogant, audiences wouldn't like him. He wants to be one up on people all the time. Someone will say there is a call for him, and he will reply, 'Ah, that would be for me.'"

Sellers is asked to discuss Clouseau's disguises. "You surely understand that Clouseau's disguises are not meant to be flavor. They're terribly bad. You see, Clouseau goes to the shop of Dr. August Ball, a get-rich-quick character in Nice who's seen Clouseau coming for years. Clouseau honestly believes he can go undetected in crowds, or move freely within the criminal world. Ball cashes in on that. He offers the worst make-up, such as noses with strings attached. Clouseau often looks like he came off the back of a Kellog's Cornflakes box."

Sellers reveals that Blake Edwards "allows us a great deal of improvisation. In fact, about 60 per cent of our broad comedy is improvised. But you must understand that once the improvisation has been accepted, it goes through many rehearsals until it becomes an intricate part of the picture. On the other hand, there will be times when Blake will say 'Let's rehearse this once on film—you never know what you'll get.'

"Stanley Kubrick is another director who allows improvisation. The period I worked with him making *Dr. Strangelove* is the most exciting in my career, next to the Goon radio shows I did with Spike Milligan and Harry Secombe. With Kubrick, words are not golden until they fit your tongue. I remember during *Strangelove* that Stanley suggested I wear black gloves for the role of the German scientist. Maybe, he said, your hand was mutilated in some sexual nuclear experiment. Now in the screenplay there was no reference to the right hand acting in a bizarre fashion. But suddenly, when the camera rolled, my hand became rebellious, leaping at my own throat and doing all those other crazy things. And if you'll watch the actors around me closely, you'll see them breaking up. They were totally taken by surprise. So I consider improvisation a very important part of acting—but it must be kept under control.

Sellers announces that he and his wife will be costarring in a few weeks in a remake of *The Prisoner of Zenda*. He would also like to go back to do a play in London, but for a short run, no more than three months. "More than that and I get terribly bored. I was recently asked to revive a play called *Bruhaha* by George Caburi, which might do well with things in the world as they are."

Once again, Sellers glances longingly at his wife Lynne, clutching her hand and making it clear he has other things on his mind than continuing the interview. The proceedings come to an immediate close.

Peter Sellers had only two more years to live after our Oahu encounter. In addition to failing health, he was plagued by mental issues which he refused to do anything about. His one remaining film achievement was *Being There* (1979), for which he was nominated for an Academy Award as Best Actor. Although he didn't win

Peter Sellers as Chauncer Gardner in Being There, *an eccentric "black comedy" about an obsessed gardener-TV watcher that walks through life without showing any emotions.*

the Oscar, he did win four other film awards and some critics felt it was his most unusual role. He was planning to attend a reunion in London of *Goon Show* cast members in July 1980, when he was stricken by another heart attack and died at the age of fifty-four.

HENRY MANCINI
Mancini—The Coolest of the Cool Among Hollywood Film Composers

As the interview with Peter Sellers ends, I notice that sitting alone, on the far side of the room, is composer Henry Mancini. Not a single other reporter pays any attention to him. I think, *There sits the forgotten genius who created the memorably comedic music for the Pink Panther films and animated TV series.* I immediately seek out a United Artists publicist and ask for a meeting with Mancini. The high-energy promoter returns in a short time to say that Mancini would be delighted to have breakfast with me the next morning, an exclusive, one on one encounter.

Few composers have been more instrumental in changing the sound of film music in the past twenty years than Henry Mancini. In 1958, Mancini created a jazz-oriented score for Blake Edwards' *Peter Gunn* TV series. It was a cool, low-key sound, unique in that it eschewed the traditional symphonic treatment and came closer to a dance band arrangement: blues, jam sessions, brass and saxophone ensembles augmented by strings.

The "Peter Gunn Theme" earned Mancini an Emmy and two Grammys, selling more than a million copies, and suggesting to producers that perhaps the shortage of film music on the record market had been a gross oversight all those years. Almost overnight, film music packaging became a new art, with producers releasing anything on a record that might have a "pop" or jazz quality.

Within two years, Mancini won an Oscar for his *Breakfast at Tiffany's* score, with the main theme song, "Moon River," (first presented over the main titles), becoming a national hit. His score for *Days of Wine and Roses* was another Oscar winner a year later. Mancini's name became synonymous with pop hits, and one of his albums proclaimed: "The place—Paris. The movie—great. The music—Mancini."

Henry Mancini, at the peak of his career in 1978.

    Continuing to work off and on under his mentor Blake Edwards, Mancini's most lasting theme became the humorous main title arrangement for *The Pink Panther*.

    Now, during breakfast at the Kuilimina, Mancini tells me all the things I didn't know. "In the case of the Panther films," he opens up, "each score is brand new—only the theme music used behind the animated titles and over the closing titles is repeated. I look upon each film as a new challenge, because Blake is constantly coming up with new concepts for Clouseau. Some of the things

I had fun with are a chase through Hong Kong and a sequence where Clouseau is disguised as a Norwegian sailor with a peg leg and an inflated parrot on his shoulder. As usual, there is a popular song, 'Move 'Em Out,' just in case the public wants to grab at it."

I ask Mancini about his work habits. "A composer normally has a Moviola right next to his bed, or a tape player that runs a copy of the film back and forth. I don't like to work that way. I prefer to go into the studio projection room and see a film as many as eight times."

This is always after the film has been fine cut. "There's no use looking at a film any earlier because changes are constantly being made. In the case of the *Panther* movies, there are always large chunks that never get used. Blake has to keep trimming the reels down to a workable, compact size. He keeps whittling away until he develops a rhythm. Anyway, each time I see the final cut I get a clearer idea about what kind of music is needed. Then I sit down with Blake and we discuss where the music should go. Usually, we agree on about an hour's worth of music.

"After I've written the score, which takes from two to three weeks, we go into the recording studio for six three-hour sessions. Writing music is a funny proposition—until you put something together you never know for sure how it's going to work. And if it doesn't work, we can take out the music in the final mix. In some movies, the music means nothing. It just lies there; it's the nature of the picture. Even some of my own ... in the case of *Man's Favorite Sport*. In the final analysis, the music didn't serve a strong role."

Born in Cleveland, Ohio, on April 16, 1924, Mancini was introduced to music by his steelworker father, who taught him to play the piccolo. Next came the piano and the flute. He attended the Juilliard School of Music for only one year before being offered a job by Benny Goodman, but that step forward was interrupted by World War II. Mancini served with the U.S. Infantry for the duration. After the war, he became pianist/arranger for the return of The Glenn Miller Orchestra under the guidance of Tex Beneke, who had been with Miller's band from its inception in 1938 as leading saxophone player (and who became famous when he sang "Chattanooga Choo Choo" in the 1941 musical *Sun Valley Serenade*).

"Here's where things began to change," says Mancini, finishing his breakfast and pushing his empty plate away. "When Universal-International asked Beneke who was the best choice to do the arrangements for the upcoming Jimmy Stewart movie, *The Glenn Miller Story*, Tex told Joseph Gershenson, head of the studio's music department, there was only one man who could do it. That was me. Next thing I knew, Gershenson hired me to do the film's arrangements. It was the opportunity of a lifetime.

"I had just finished up, and was packing up my briefcase, when I was asked to report immediately to Gershenson's office. Oh oh, I thought. I've written something he doesn't like. Sheepishly I walked over to his office, figuring my career as an arranger was over.

"But no! Gershenson said he loved my arrangements and asked me if I'd like to join his studio staff of composers and write music for films. I couldn't believe it! A dream come true! I asked him what my first assignment might be. He looked at a list of titles and said, *Bonzo Goes to College*. I sucked in my breath and asked what my second assignment might be. Gershenson glanced at the list again and said *Ma and Pa Kettle at the Fair*. I held my breath again. Not quite what I had hoped for, but I accepted the job. It's a good thing I did. At the time, Universal would have several of us writing music for the same film so it could be finished quickly, and I wrote pieces for countless movies without credit. I started out with *Has Anybody Seen My Gal?* and *Meet Me at the Fair*. But there were different genres. Westerns, like *War Arrow* and *Stand at Apache River*. Adventure: *Yankee Pasha*. Horror: *Creature From the Black Lagoon*, *Revenge of the Creature*. Science fiction: *This Island Earth*. Finally, Orson Welles' *Touch of Evil* gave me my first full solo screen credit." (He had also been nominated for an Oscar for those arrangements he initially did for *The Glenn Miller Story*.)

Somewhere along the way, he met Blake Edwards, who was a struggling TV and screenwriter after a career in radio. "What's important to know is that Blake had written and directed radio episodes of *Richard Diamond, Private Detective*, starring Dick

Powell. Powell was a lover of jazz, who had a huge collection of records, and through him Blake developed an interest in jazz. Powell gave him the chance to direct episodes of *Four-Star Playhouse*, and Blake finally started directing films in 1955 with *Bring Your Smile Along*. One day, he came to me and said he had an idea for a variation on the Richard Diamond private eye character. Each episode would feature a private eye going to a jazz club because the lead singer is his girlfriend, and she's really sexy. What Blake felt was needed was a kind of jazz theme, tinged with romance.

"And so I left Universal-International, and in 1958, we started making *Peter Gunn*, and next thing I knew I had won an Emmy and two Grammys. It was my first freelance job. By no means was it the first jazz score. I was preceded by Alex North's *A Streetcar Named Desire* and Elmer Bernstein's *The Man With the Golden Arm*. But *Gunn* was the first score of its kind that hit the masses week after week; that had a chance to grow on everybody."

Mancini ranks John Wayne's adventure-comedy, *Hatari*, among his personal favorites. "It was purely fun. Howard Hawks, the director, was having trouble with the sequence where the elephants walk through stores. After he cut it together, he realized that it definitely needed some very amusing music behind it. It was an example of music saving the day—or adding the final crowning touch. Creating musical sounds that have an amusing twist to them, that is a challenge I love."

Mancini feels his most difficult score was in 1974 for *The White Dawn*, a film about whalers stranded with Eskimos in Alaska. "It was almost impossible to find anything ethnic to give the film a theme. Finally, I used the chant of an old Eskimo woman, which actually turned out to be an attractive melodic piece. Unfortunately, too few people saw the picture."

Mancini ranks Edwards as his favorite director (as well he should), with Stanley Donen taking a close second (Mancini scored *Charade* and *Arabesque* for him) and George Roy Hill next. "When I was writing a score for *The Great Waldo Pepper*, I found George to be very knowledgeable about music; he even plays the piano better than I do."

Contemporaries he admires are Elmer Bernstein and the young composers Billy Goldenberg, Pat Williams, and David Shire. Members of the old school who had an early influence on him include Victor Young, Alfred Newman, and Dimitri Tiomkin. "Newman used to call and tell me if he liked a particular score of mine. Max Steiner, of course, was the prototype of Hollywood composers. Technically, he and Newman made several important contributions to synch scoring."

The only time Mancini wrote a score and it was rejected was for Alfred Hitchcock's 1972 thriller, *Frenzy*. "To this day, I don't know exactly what happened. Hitchcock's never spoken to me about it; he simply passed the word down the line. He was there during the whole recording session in London and never said a negative word. I consider myself flexible. I'm capable of making changes on the spot. But nobody ever said anything to me. Sure, it was tough on my ego, but those things happen. In fact, the very same thing happened once to Bernard Herrmann when he did a score for Hitchcock."

Upcoming scores by Mancini will include *Nightwing* (a supernatural thriller) and *Someone Is Killing the Great Chefs of Europe* (a satirical whodunit). "I no longer worry about whether a film is going to be a success or not. Not any more. I must be getting mellow in my old age. Films are like streetcars; they keep coming and going. You do what you can; you do your best on every film. That's all you can be concerned about."

Henry Mancini stayed incredibly busy for the remaining sixteen years of his life, writing music for TV series: *Remington Steel* (83 episodes), *Hotel* (115 episodes), *Newhart* (184 episodes). He died of pancreatic cancer in June 1994 while still working on a score for a Broadway musical version of *Victor/Victoria*. The following year, he was awarded posthumously with a Grammy Lifetime Achievement Award. During his lifetime, he had turned out ninety music albums and had won four Oscars, twenty Grammy Awards, and one Golden Globe.

Finally, the American Film Institute ranked his music for *The Pink Panther* as #20 among the great film scores of all time.

Henry Mancini, behind the instrument he loved the most.

MOE HOWARD (THE THREE STOOGES)
"Nyuk! Nyuk! Nyuk!" – Bonk! Thunk! . . . And Now "Spread Out!"

In an era of political correctness, is it not sacrilegious to poke your finger into someone's eye? To slam a lemon meringue pie into another's face? To label an associate "Moron!" and, wham, drop a mallet atop his skull? To request a ham on rye after a presiding judge has pounded his gavel and demanded "Order in the court!"?

My, how times have changed since the slap-happy days of The Three Stooges. Back then, who really wanted their comedians to be proper or prim or profound when it came to tomfoolery and mischievous mayhem? With the snickering sound of "Nyuk! Nyuk! Nyuk!" as a starter, the buffoon trio's two-reeler nonsense of dialogue and sound effects included *Boink!* . . . "Eh Eh Eh" . . . *Splat!* . . . *Thunk!* . . . "Idiot!" . . . *Squish!* . . . *Plop!* . . . "Yah Yah Yah" . . . *Whop!* . . . "Imbecile!" . . . "Ummm" . . . *Ka-pop!* . . . *Crunch!* . . . *Ka-pow!* . . . "You turkey head!" . . . *Bonk!* . . . "Numbskull!" . . . *Plunk!* "Rowlf! Rowlf! Rowlf!"

The boss in charge of this threesome—the one who always gave the order "Spread out!"—also spread out his brain to study classic art and music. Call him the Head Stooge. That would be Moses Harry Horwitz—better known to millions of fans as Moe Howard.

As for his fellow Stooges, two were from his own family. There was brother Curly (aka Jerome Lester Horwitz or Curly Howard) and brother Shemp (aka Samuel Horwitz or Shemp Howard). The third original Stooge was not family, a guy named Larry Fine (aka Louis Feinberg). As things changed over the years, generations of fans were also exposed to Joe Besser (for just two years, 1957-1958) and Joe DeRita (aka Joseph Wardell, billed as "Curly Joe" because of his resemblance to Curly).

In the summer of 1965, a motion picture composer named Paul Dunlap, whom I have met through a friendship with writer-producer-director Samuel Fuller, has suggested I should interview

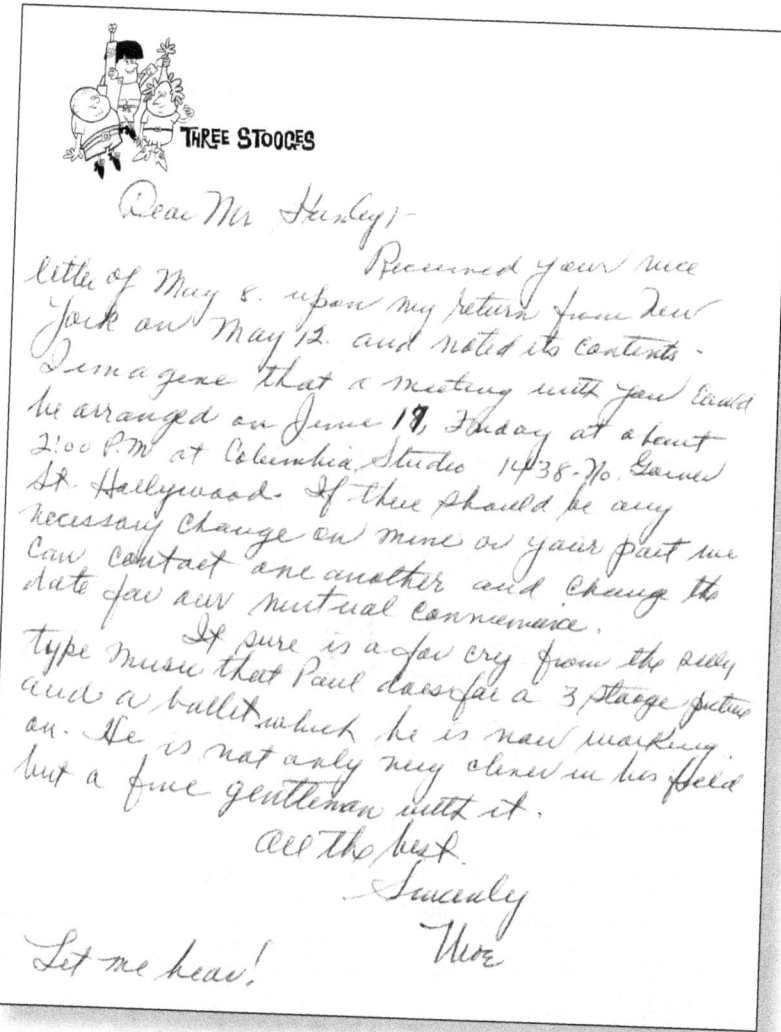

Here is the letter Moe Howard sent me to officially invite me to Columbia Studios to meet him.

Moe Howard. (Dunlap, who had written the music tracks for four of the team's recent motion pictures, including *The Three Stooges Meet Hercules*, must have been thinking it would elevate my IQ level.) I have been invited to Columbia Studios in Hollywood to meet and speak with Moe.

He wrote me a letter to officially invite me to meet him:

"Dear Mr. Stanley: Received your nice letter of May 8 upon my return from New York on May 12 and noted its contents. I imagine that a meeting with you could be arranged on June 17, Friday at about 2 p.m. at Columbia Studio 1438 No. Gower St. in Hollywood. If there should be any necessary change on mine or your part we can contact one another and change the date for our mutual convenience. It sure is a far cry from the silly type music that Paul [Dunlap] does for a 3 Stooge picture and a ballet which he is now working on. He is not only my [unreadable] in his field but a fine gentleman with it. All the best, Sincerely Moe." [P.S. without the P.S.] Let me hear!"

Don't turn your back on Moses Harry Horwitz or he might put a finger into each of your eyeball sockets. You see, Horwitz is the alias for Moe Howard, gang leader of the Three Stooges. This is precisely the face that confronted me but with a much more pleasant look.

Leaving my political correctness at the door on the appointed day and hour, I step into an executive's office at Columbia Studios and soon learn how to conduct myself when meeting an intellectual Stooge.

Moe is nobody's stooge. By playing the boss nitwit in a wacky trio known as The Three Stooges, he has proven by the age of sixty-eight to be a most durable and affluent performer. After scores of short subjects and feature films, he remains the senior of his partners in pranksterism, mayhem, and physical squishing/squashing. He's still raking in so much money that one executive at Columbia, the team's home studio since the 1930s, has suggested that Moe might really own the studio and just hasn't bothered to tell everyone working there.

To speak to a journalist, Moe is willing to break away from a story conference with his contemporary co-duffers, Larry Fine and Joe DeRita. They are preparing to do voice-over work for a new TV project subtly entitled *The New Three Stooges*, an animated series also featuring freshly-filmed footage of the three slam-bam-wham actors.

For the next hour, without a sign of fatigue, Moe subtly discusses the thirty-one-year history of the indefatigable comedy team. On first meeting, Moe is conspicuously missing the bowler-cut wig he has always worn in his pictures and is disappointingly straightforward, apparently eschewing his gawky screen image for that of a gentleman with a sedate, pleasant manner. Not once does he try to stick a finger into one of my eyes nor does he label me a "witless idiot." Not once does he scream, "You nitwit! Remind me to kill you tomorrow!"

More fitting to his Stooge tradition, however, is his physical appearance: He is a surprisingly short man, less than five feet tall, with delightfully huge baggy eyes. After I've been around him for a while, I begin to feel that he is eyeing me with a cool malevolence, as one sizing up a target for a juicy lemon meringue. Maybe, I think, *that poke in the eye is rummaging around in the back of Moe's mind. "Take this, you birdbrain!" Thuck!*

"Show business began for me doing small roles in silent movies as far back as 1909, but then things got better on the Mississippi

Here they are, The Three Stooges in all their glory. Left to right: Larry Fine ("Why, I oughta...."), Moe Howard ("Oh, wise guy, huh?"), and Curly Howard ("Rowf! Rowf! Rowf!")

River," says Moe. "I was performing in melodramas. Those were the days when you sincerely hissed the villain. Later, my older brother, Shemp, and I worked our way into Vaudeville with a Black-face routine, and it was then we became associated with Larry Fine. One of our first acts together was with Ted Healy as 'The Three Country Gentlemen.' Later, we became 'Ted Healy and the Stooges' when we did short films with him. But Ted started drinking heavily, and we decided it'd be better to slip away to get loaded in a different way—with dough."

Soon after, in the early 1930s, Shemp left the group to play Knobby in the *Joe Palooka* movie series, and Moe's other brother, Curly, became part of the film trio for the next ten years. When Curly fell ill in 1946, Shemp returned to resume his earlier deadhead role.

I ask Moe to talk about his favorite shorts from the "Golden Age of Stooge Two-Reelers." "You don't mean the shorts in my bedroom drawer?" Moe replies, keeping a straight face. He begins telling me about *Men in Black* (1934), in which the boys become medical students who "cut up" during surgery classes, "needle" the interns, and "raise the temperatures" of the nurses. "We got

Shemp Howard, who replaced Curly in the mid-1940s.

nominated for an Oscar, the only time it ever happened. But we lost. So I called the boys and told them 'We didn't win, you imbeciles! You're both knuckleheads!' "

You Nazty Spy! (1940), according to Moe, was the first Hollywood film to spoof Adolf Hitler, even preceding Charlie Chaplin's feature film lampoon classic *The Great Dictator*. "Me, I did my take-off on Adolf. Larry, he gobbled up the screen doing an im-

You Nazty Spy! *starred Moe Howard as Der Fuhrer, Curly Howard as Hermann Goering, and Larry Fine as Josef Goebbels—one of their most memorable shorts.*

Joe Besser performed in fifteen shorts, replacing Curly.

pression of the Minister of Propaganda [Josef Goebbels]. Curly, he was goring the audience as Hitler's field marshal [Herman Goering]. This thing went over very well, so we made a two-reeler sequel, *I'll Never Heil Again*. It was something 'right in the Fuhrer's face,' and we all wished it was more than a damn pie."

Speaking of pastries, Moe also mentions *In the Sweet Pie and Pie* (1941), which ended with a pastry-throwing marathon like no other. "It was impossible to count the number of splats," he says. "One critic called it *Custard's Last Stand*.'" Moe's final words to his pals: "Didn't I warn you imbeciles to duck? You're both knuckleheads!"

Joe DeRita, replacement for Shemp, remained with the group to its end.

The iceman who cometh in *An Ache in Every Stake* (1941) led to a marathon involving two giant birthday cakes. "What a mess that was," remembers Moe, and he releases a puff of air as if blowing out candles on a . . . cake maybe? Among Stooge classics remain a double-bill of 3-D shorts, *Spooks* and *Pardon My Backfire* (both 1953). Into the camera, just for starters, come flying pies, a long hypodermic needle, and a water hose going full blast. *Bo-iiing!!*

Today both of his brothers are dead. Curly suffered a stroke in 1946, but because of mental deterioration, never made a screen comeback before his death in 1952. Shemp died suddenly of a heart attack in 1955. Beginning in 1946, Joe Besser served in fifteen film comedies, and Joe DeRita, who bears a startling resemblance to Curly, joined the act in 1958 and has two years to go under his present contract. Things, Moe says, look promising.

Things looked good for a good reason: The Stooges have been enjoying a revival ("a slam-bang resurgence," Moe calls it) of popularity since Columbia released seventy-eight of their short comedies to TV in the late 1950s. On the strength of renewed enthusiasm from U.S. and foreign juveniles (and, I suspect, adults), The Stooges began making modest, full-length motion pictures for Columbia. Many critics went into immediate convulsions. However, the films—bearing such titles as *Have Rocket, Will Travel*—were greeted abroad as if they were part of the Foreign Aid program. So, guess who's been laughing all the way to the bank ever since.

Their newest full-length feature film, *The Outlaws Is Coming*, directed by one-time comic book artist and editor Norman Maurer, is a travesty on the West, poking harshly at TV commercials (the "coo-coo" razor blade, for one) and includes a most unusual portrayal of Billy the Kid by Johnny Ginger.

At the present time, The Stooges are eagerly putting together a new syndicated TV package of 156 five-and-a-half minute cartoon shows, each featuring "live" footage of the Stooges for lead-ins and closings. (The series is set for fifty stations across the country.)

The Stooges have always engaged in an elementary bashing form of humor. Says Moe, "We lay awake nights dreaming up new punishments and more grotesque sound effects." One thing, though, The Stooges have given up since exposure on television is eye-gouging, as parents complained of their children practicing imitations on fellow playmates.

In all these fracases, accidents do happen. Moe has sustained broken ribs and has been knocked unconscious when the timing went askew. Larry has had at least two teeth knocked down his throat, and a sharp-pointed fountain pen once lodged into Curly's forehead, drawing great quantities of blood. Nobody has bothered yet to total up all the welts, bruises, and broken bones.

"Get one thing straight," says the Brooklyn-born Moe. "We don't do slapstick. That's a circus word to describe two barrel staves with an exploding torpedo between them. The only barrel we're involved with is a barrel of laughs. What we do on the screen is pure farce—the kind that's been purely popular since Grecian and Roman days, since the kings had court jesters. And the laugh was on royalty.

"Our formula," he continues, "is a simple one: the upsetting of dignity. You can't throw a pie at a poor man and get away with it. But throw a pie at a millionaire, get his spats and vest all gooey, destroy the carnation in his lapel, and the people love to laugh. They love to see the dignified man brought down to size. And our Stooge-like behavior is excusable because we usually pose as common working men who don't know any better, who unintentionally cause all the trouble. In short, we're Innocents, who enjoy making a laughing stock of those who take themselves a little too seriously."

As the interview ends, and as Larry Fine and Joe DeRita enter the room demanding that Moe return with them to the meeting, Moe sums it all up. "The trouble, as you have seen for a few decades now, always leads to total chaos, without which we, The Three Stooges, could not survive."

If only Moe had had a peach cobbler in hand, he would have thrown it directly into my face, and the spirit of Shemp would have declared "Nyut! Nyut! Nyut! Nyut!"

By the time I ended my interview with Moe, his career in the entertainment industry was also coming to an end. The cartoon series would actually be the final project for the Stooges. There

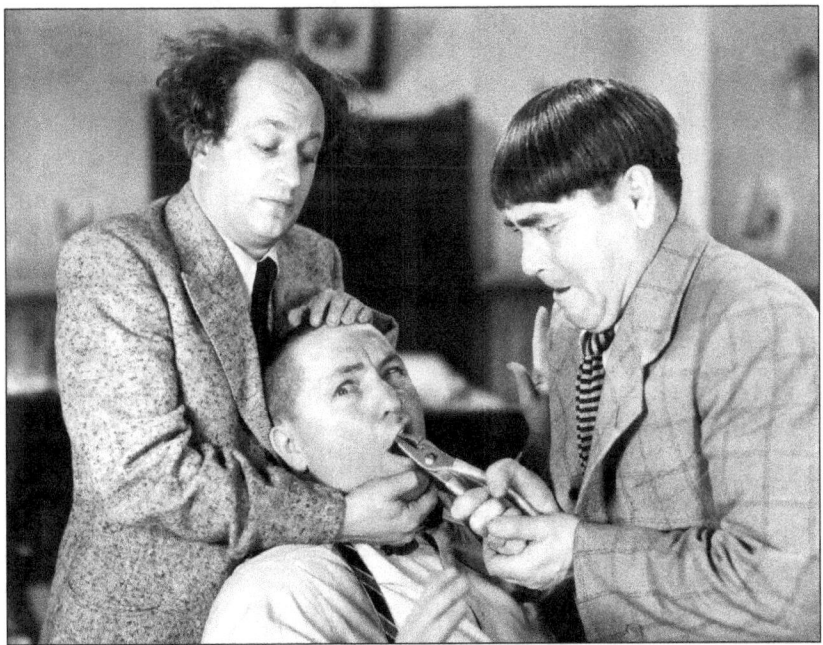

There isn't any kind of visual mayhem The Three Stooges didn't indulge in. This is obviously an example of Moe Howard showing that he had a lot of pull in Hollywood.

Here the boys try to find out of one of their partners had a real head on his shoulders. Or are they just trying to see if he measures up to their standards?

were 156 animated shorts, but, for some odd reason (probably to save money), only forty live-action segments involving Moe Howard, Joe DeRita, and Larry Fine were filmed that summer of 1965.

"Years later," according to DeRita, "after they ran the whole forty episodes, they'd just start over by using the same introductions for the next 116 episodes. [All new stuff, with no repeats.] This turned out to be misleading because viewers would say, 'Oh, I've seen this one before,' and they'd turn off the television. They didn't know it was a new cartoon." (In fact, the series would continue in re-runs through 1973 and must have still made Columbia a ton of money.)

By this time, the boys had aged to the point they could no longer take the risk of face slaps, body falls, or leaps off high ledges. Moe was afraid he wouldn't be able to duck a pie flying toward his head, or a sledgehammer coming down from above. So, to avoid all that physical danger, Moe told Columbia to "Nyut! Nyut! Nyut!" off. He turned to selling real estate for a while, then began writing his autobiography, *I Stooged to Conquer*.

In January 1970, Larry Fine died of a stroke. Moe passed away in 1975 at the age of seventy-seven. Joe DeRita lived to be "The Last Stooge," succumbing to pneumonia in 1993.

Two years after his death, Moe's book was finally published under a new title, *Moe Howard and the Three Stooges*. My guess is that Moe would have hated that colorless choice. Every Stooge short subject had some kind of word play in its title. I can hear Moe telling the publisher, "Here's mud in your eye, imbecile!"

WALLY COX
A Square Set Loose On San Francisco Streets Has Us Running in Circles

Having grown up in the early 1950s watching *Mr. Peepers*, a super-popular comedy series, I was all too eager to respond to a request that I cover a comedy documentary being produced in San Francisco starring Wally Cox, Mr. Peepers himself. My face must have lit up, remembering the fun I'd once had watching that show. I must have looked full of surprise, just like I remember Wally Cox's face in close-up, vivid detail. It was July 1968, and here is what happened:

Wally Cox as he appeared as a somewhat meek school teacher in his 1950s series Mr. Peepers.

Inside Fergoda's Motorcycle Shop, where Valencia intersects with Market Street, one of the employees is wailing and mad. "I bet I've lost five deals this afternoon! It's impossible to show the merchandise to customers!"

It's impossible to show merchandise because the showroom and adjacent outside lot have been taken over by a crowd that can only be described as strange. There's a hippie sprawled casually across the fender of a used car. Not far away, a Hell's Angel-type, his face smudged with charcoal, keeps shambling back to the Coke machine with the attitude of an addict.

There is a publicity man wearing sandals, and there is a Little Old Lady in lavender who keeps tugging at the sleeve of the PR guy, asking "Why hasn't Wally arrived yet? I want to meet Wally. I'm an old fan." Everyone is drinking Coke and growing restless because it's getting hot and "Wally" and the others are now two hours overdue. The Little Old Lady sighs and says, "I do hope everything turns out all right. I do so much want to meet Mr. Peepers."

All this activity is over a half-hour TV special entitled *What Gap?* or *What's It All About, Wally?*, depending on which title producer David Yarnell decides on when things calm down. Thirty-eight-year-old Yarnell has just spent two years producing *Firing Line*, a political debate series starring William F. Buckley. Now he has become best known as a purveyor of pseudo-documentaries: *The Miniskirt Rebellion, Hit the Surf* and *The Great Mating Game*. With this new one, he is satirically probing the Now Generation and how a square might react when exposed to it.

In this case, the square is Wally Cox. He, Yarnell, director Gary (*Get Smart*) Nelson, and a small camera crew are spending a week in San Francisco, using sundry and familiar backgrounds for Wally's "initiation."

There will be scenes of Wall skydiving, being introduced to hippiedom, riding motorcycles, and doing other things that will, in the final analysis, comprise one lengthy sight gag. Fergoda's Motorcycle Shop will serve an important part of the story, for it is here that Cox and Ann Prentiss (all-knowing guide to where the action is) are to buy a means of transportation. Already the old sign outside has been supplanted with a new one: Big Daddy's Motorcycles.

By six o'clock there's still no Wally Cox. An assistant director, whose main job is to select decent luncheon sites for cast and crew, glances nervously toward the sun, which is sinking lower and lower. Time, obviously, is running out.

The Little Old Lady, it turns out, is a seventy-seven-year-old resident of San Francisco, Miss Fanny Lubritsky, who has yearned to act since she made her debut at three on a London stage. A one-time ingénue, Fanny recently appeared in a number of productions by the American Conservatory Theater (one of San Francis-

This would be Mr. Peepers (Wally Cox) having a session with a fellow teacher in his popular comedy series. Could it be they are discussing the history of the birds and the bees?

co's major stage groups) and got this role through the Ann Brebner Casting Agency after telling Yarnell she looked good in a miniskirt.

"I do have good legs," she insists, "but they wouldn't let me wear a miniskirt. They felt it would be too much exposure." She begins to explain that in the pseudo-documentary she plays a Sweet Oldster out buying love beads for her wheelchair-bound husband, when she is suddenly interrupted by a white Cadillac pulling to a stop in front of Fergoda's and the production crew scrambles into action. The Cadillac, I conclude, must contain Wally Cox. It does. Yarnell quickly climbs out and hurries away. Cox remains, at least for the moment, forgotten in the back seat. This is the time, I decide, to interview Cox before he gets busy again.

Being 5' 6" with a framework best described as "slight," Cox appears to be half-sunken into the cushiony red upholstery. His tie is all askew, his brown suit is limp, like one that has been washed but not ironed. Strands of disheveled hair droop left and right atop his head. He peers blandly out from behind dark-rimmed glasses. When he speaks his voice is so faint, it is almost lost to the roar of traffic along Market Street.

It is often said of Wally Cox that he has yet to live down the image he created for *Mr. Peepers*, a half-hour sitcom that aired on NBC from 1952-56. He portrayed Robinson J. Peepers, a junior high school science teacher, timid in manner with a voice high-pitched. En toto, a slow-paced, shy-mannered fellow always getting himself into embarrassing situations with faculty members and students.

I ask him why he continues to accept parts that in some way reflect the Peepers persona.

Cox's thin lips finally part. "I try not to bother my head about image and all that. After almost twenty years, you begin to look upon this whole thing as just a living. I'm doing this particular show, I guess, because hopefully it'll give encouragement to others to find out what's new in today's world. Perhaps."

I must lean toward the rear of the car so my words are not drowned out, and I ask Cox if he enjoyed playing a comedy character who became the talk of America during the 1950s, and gave him a prominent place in the world of comedy. "There's no nostalgia connected with playing Peepers. It was a confusing time for me. A time of frustrations, of irritations. Peepers is not my best thing. It's the role I do least well, if you want to know the truth. I originally did nightclub stand-up comedy. Little monologues about dead-end kid Dufo. Or the small-town Kansas banker. Or the PFC in charge of a barracks in an Army hospital. What I liked better was my Hiram Holliday role, which was a mixture of the intellect of Peepers and the physical prowess of Errol Flynn."

Wally Cox conferring with a woman involved in foreign intrigue in his spy spoof series, The Adventures of Hiram Holliday.

Cox is referring to *The Adventures of Hiram Holliday* (1956-1957), a follow-up NBC sitcom that came in the wake of *Mr. Peepers'* success. Holliday was a one-time newspaper proofreader who was now on a trip around the world with the power to track down foreign spies and solve assorted mysteries, often with physical force–the very thing that Mr. Peepers always failed at.

"TV," Cox tells me, "is too much a throwaway medium. I never put my energy into a TV show because the artistic return is nil. There just isn't enough time to work it out."

Ann Prentiss, Wally Cox's partner the day we met, was the sister of Paula Prentiss.

Nor is there enough time to finish the interview, given the questions left to ask. Yarnell prances back to inform Wally all is in readiness for the scene in which he and Ann Prentiss pull up in front of Big Daddy's in a white 1959 Edsel convertible and proceed to purchase a motorcycle, on which they will then drive away into the streets of San Francisco.

Cox climbs behind the Edsel's wheel. "Who looks more right than Cox to be driving an Edsel?" shouts Yarnell from the sidelines, while a make-up woman combs out the flowing brown hair of the lovely Ann Prentiss (younger sister of actress Paula Prentiss) and straightens out her golden blouse. "Okay," shouts director Nelson. "Action!"

As Cox pulls the Edsel up to the curb, some high school kids join the crowd of gathering onlookers. "Who's that funny looking guy?" queries one of the boys.

A middle-aged spectator informs him: "That's Wally Cox."

Responds the youth: "Has he ever done anything?"

Yarnell, who is standing behind the high school students, smiles knowingly. "Talk about the Generation Gap," he mutters. A second take is called for as Fanny, the Little Old Lady, rushes up in a ratty-looking stole and silly-looking hat. "Hey, I'm supposed to drive that over there." She points proudly to a Land-Rover parked nearby, then scurries off again.

Before the second take begins, an assistant director places a red flower in the antenna of the Edsel. Now all is ready. Cox pulls the car in again, but director Nelson shakes his head.

Shadows are falling on the Hermann Safe Company across Market Street—the light is failing fast. Too many deepening shadows are destroying the effect he wants. Yarnell confers with Nelson, returns to tell Cox that it looks like they'll have to reschedule this sequence for later in the week.

Fanny rushes to Yarnell's side. "You mean all this was for nothing today?" Yarnell reluctantly nods. Dejectedly, Fanny returns to the Land-Rover and sits on the hood, swinging one leg back and forth. Too bad they hadn't given her that miniskirt, I think.

As the crew starts packing up, Wally Cox stands off to one side, his hands knotted behind his back, watching with curiosity those who are watching him. Among the high school boys, enlightenment has spread. A newly arrived student peers out between jostling shoulders, unable to resist asking who the celebrity is. "That," says the boy who only minutes before had never heard of Wally Cox in his life, "is Mr. Peepers."

I have no memory of ever seeing the "psuedo-documentary" starring Wally Cox, nor can I find any Internet listing to confirm it was ever played on network or syndicated TV. Wally had also told me about the making of a film called *The Toy Grabbers*, which was going to be the first of three movies made through his own production company. "I play a sloppy guy with a total disregard for social niceties. It's low comedy." There is nothing like it in his credits, and I must assume the company folded and the film was shelved.

On the other hand, Wally Cox continued to have guest appearances in many TV series, and continued to be the upper left-hand square on the TV game show, *The Hollywood Squares*, through 1973, the year he died at the age of forty-eight. Newspaper accounts accredited his death to an overdose of sedatives, which would sound reasonable given his age. However, his close personal friend Marlon Brando would later claim he died of a heart attack. You can take your pick. Whatever the cause of death, I'll always remember watching those early episodes of *Mr. Peepers*, and I will treasure those few moments we had together in the back seat of that Cadillac as it was parked just off Market Street.

GREG GARRISON (DEAN MARTIN'S PRODUCER)
The Martin Clinic: Where Mutual Trust Is Golden

I never had the pleasure of meeting a man who, in retrospect, I considered to be one of the funniest of Hollywood's comedy legends. He was also a great singer, and there were times when he would superimpose his sense of comedy atop the song, and it would be as funny as if he were doing a stand-up routine. His name was Dean Martin.

Although there were years when he teamed with zany Jerry Lewis to create one of the most beloved comedy teams of all time, I think his funniest image emerged when he became a member of the Rat Pack, that small group of entertainers that included Frank Sinatra, Sammy Davis Jr., Peter Lawford, and Joey Bishop. He proved he could stand alone without Jerry Lewis, that he could do comedy monologues, usually holding a whiskey glass and speaking as if he was half loaded. He could sing songs dramatically, as the writers had intended, or comically, as he intended with his sense of humor. He could also be part of the larger group, wisecracking and fitting in like butter spreads on bread.

While our paths never crossed, I did get lucky in November 1968, and I did get to meet the producer of *The Dean Martin Show*, a classic one-hour series that ran on Thursday nights for nine seasons (1965-1974), always with the theme song "Everybody Loves Somebody Sometime" voiced by Martin. That producer was Greg Garrison.

NBC's press unit invited me to the studio where they were preparing the next show. I was told, "When Dean Martin was first approached to do a weekly show, he flat out rejected the idea. Said he didn't want to spend an entire week, which was what most stars needed, to prepare. Garrison came up with the idea to have Dean for just one day a week, and the production team would

Dean Martin, as he appeared during his Rat Pack years.

spend the rest of the time blocking everything out, so all Dean had to do was walk through it once, then do it that same evening. Garrison makes the show work without ever being underhanded or furtive or tyrannical. He understands people and knows how to manipulate them to his needs—and Dean's needs. Think of him as a psychologist."

The corridor outside Greg Garrison's office is narrow and antiseptic, conforming to the clinical atmosphere of a mundane one-story building that squats ungraciously on a busy street in Burbank, just a few convenient blocks from the NBC-TV Studios.

Perhaps a clinical look is appropriate, since it is here that a gang of specialists labor weekly to prepare the next installment of *The Dean Martin Show*.

Garrison, the head specialist, is to be found at the far end of the hallway. On the way there, creative residue is visible in now-empty conference rooms on both sides of the passage. Elongated

Dean Martin and his producer Greg Garrison. They say Martin had a better relationship working with Garrison than he had had with his long-running partner Jerry Lewis.

tables, from which chairs have been carelessly pushed back, hold coffee cups, some overturned, others still half-filled. The liquid turned cold long ago. Crumpled balls of paper that represent crumpled ideas have been discarded on the floor in every direction.

Mort Viner, personal manager of Dean Martin, comes out of Garrison's office, discussing with the producer a plan to put The Golddigers on their own NBC series. (The Golddiggers, a group of twelve lady singers/dancers, are the property of Garrison and first joined the series a year earlier as replacements.) Garrison tells Viner that they'll talk more about this later. He'll call Viner. Just hang loose.

Garrison has just returned from the funeral of a friend and there is a discernible strain on his face. However, he doesn't in any way seem melancholy as he welcomes me into his "inner sanctum" and removes his black overcoat and pushes up the sleeves of his shirt. It's time to get back to work, and by the way, here's some Pepsi to keep you from dying of thirst.

Dean Martin

If you study the photographs of Garrison at work, casualness is what he would seem to thrive on. Always in short-sleeved shirts, slacks, loafers, white wool socks, never any ties, fancy shirts, or silk scarves. Always a boyish smile on his face, perhaps even a laugh now and then. The country boy from Libertyville, Illinois, has made the big-time as a producer-director, but he's still the country boy, easy-going and casual despite the pressures of his job.

For Garrison, this has been a normal day—excessively active. Morning consisted of conferences, ringing phones, appointments, and a light lunch. At 1:30 p.m. he made an important decision, walking to a huge board on the wall (which has a breakdown on who will guest star on each show) and switching Buddy Ebsen's card to an earlier taping. He made the necessary phone calls to clear the change. Between calls, he sang to himself.

A little later, Garrison got on the phone to discuss his TV production of *Guys and Dolls*, which he plans to produce in late March with Orson Welles directing and Jackie Gleason starring. As the afternoon dragged on, Garrison repeatedly told his joke for the day: That Dino was working for just union scale.

Turning from that, he read a few gags that had been submitted for "The Closet Door Sequence," a recurring spot on each show as Dean goes from the piano of Ken Lane (a regular in the series) to a nearby door. Dean always pauses to open that door—and always behind that door is a new surprise. Sometimes it's Frank Sinatra. Sometimes it's Johnny Carson. Once it was a twenty-six-piece high school band.

Among the day's entries: "Dean opens the door and a line of wet clothing comes out, moving across the stage. Underwear and lingerie do a wild dance." . . . "As Dean opens the door, a pair of shoes with no one in them dances across the stage."

Garrison then put aside this idea, slipped into his black suit coat, and went to the funeral of his close friend.

Back in his office, with the work day almost over, Garrison sinks gratefully into a chair. For a few minutes, he talks about Orson Welles, James Stewart, and Dom De Luise, all frequent guest stars and, by now, close friends. And Dean. What about Dean?

At first, what he says about Dean seems flattering, perhaps even a little saccharin, but then he becomes frank, delivering his opinions in a soft meticulous voice. "Dean is in a class by himself. Not because he's a successful star but because of the kind of man he really is. There isn't anyone who comes within fifty feet of him who doesn't feel his presence in an overwhelming way."

Some interesting facts come to light. Dean and Garrison function completely on trust. Garrison trusts Dean to come in at the last minute and bring off the show; Dean trusts Garrison to have everything ready when he arrives.

Here's the way it works. Dean is only available to Garrison half a day a week—the Sunday afternoon of the taping. Martin strolls into the studio around noon and begins to study the material in a carefully prepared script version. Skits, songs to be sung, and guest star patter. Then, he quickly rehearses (or just walks through) each segment. At 7:30 p.m. the taping begins before a live audience and usually is wrapped up by 8:30 p.m. or sooner. No dress rehearsals, no retakes. You get what you get.

Then Dean Martin vanishes, presumably to carry on the other aspects of his day-to-day life, such as going directly home to watch a Western film on TV—oaters make up his favorite movie genre; such as playing golf (well, not until the next morning anyway). Maybe he heads for home to read the latest Matt Helm private eye movie script. Maybe he just stumbles drunkenly across his front lawn. (That's a joke.)

Monday morning, Garrison and his staff are back putting elements for the next show together, and life goes week to week, month to month, year to year.

Mental labor is how Garrison got his start in TV in 1947—as the janitor in a TV station. The story goes that within nine days he had been hired as a director. He thought the height of power had arrived when he was earning $35 a week to produce *Super Circus* with Mary Hartline.

At the age of twenty-two, Garrison was directing *Your Show of Shows* with Sid Caesar and Imogene Coca. They were calling him "the boy genius." He remained cool, unshaken by his behind-the-scenes popularity. Nobody can recall that he ever lost his temper. Milton Berle, who lured Garrison away from Caesar for his 1953 comedy series, claimed he had lost his mind to "hire that kid to direct," but it meant more shows for Garrison; it meant greater success.

"Are you successful," I ask Garrison, "because you have an easy-going style that meshes with Martin's?"

The question seems to delight Garrison. His eyes flash and he gives me that broad smile of his. "That, perhaps." His voice drops in pitch, in its own way emphasizing his next words. "But there is a secret to the show's success. The secret is: it's called *The Dean Martin Show*. That's why people tune in. They want to see Dean. Period. And, the folks want to see how he's going to react to other performers. He's always got a surprise reaction. We just cater to the crowd. We know what the crowd wants."

Suddenly Garrison pretends he's a viewer living somewhere in the Midwest, reading *TV Guide*'s thumbnail capsule of a show. "'Juliet Prowse is the guest, huh? She's cute. Maybe she'll dance with Dean and he'll hug her and make funny comments about her legs and fanny. And Lorne Greene—last time the horses kept whinnying, wouldn't stand still. Maybe that *Bonanza* guy and Dean will sing a little ballad, do a little Western spoof.'" He becomes Garrison again. "That's all we do here; we cater to the crowd."

Are there any strains working with Martin? "The only strain will be the day Dean quits TV and I'll have to work with somebody

As Greg Garrison left the office at 5 p.m., I couldn't help but think it was the cocktail hour. Wherever Dean Martin was that day, he would just be sitting down to his favorite mixture in a glass.

else. My crew knows me better than I know me. They do things before I ask them. We all understand each other. This is purely a labor of love."

Surely, though, Dean must rehearse the comedy routines during that short time he's in the studio. "I try to keep him away from the comedy as much as possible because I want that freshness. When people see his spontaneity, I want them to laugh. I want the viewer to say: 'Damn, he's doing that ad lib for the first time. It wasn't rehearsed.' We want to be honest with the audience. We don't lie to them."

At five o'clock, Garrison's voice drifts from the hallway, "Let's go home." He prepares to leave. Switch off show biz and switch on an evening with his wife. "I'm a reasonable man," he says on his way out the door. "I'm not a big deal. I remember yesterday, which is why I'm not so much of a helluva big shot today. I've had my bad times, too. And maybe things won't be so good tomorrow. So, I behave myself today."

And Garrison gently closes the door to the office behind him.

The Dean Martin Show will thrive through 1974, for a total of 264 episodes. About the time the series ends, Garrison takes over *The Dean Martin Celebrity Roast* series, working with almost every comic and superstar in the business. (He also oversees the digital remastering of all the old shows for new DVDs, which are now on the market.)

Greg Garrison lived to the age of eighty-one, dying of pneumonia in 2005.

FRANK GORSHIN
The Deranged Cackling of The Riddler —Just One Side to a Master of Voices

The thing I remember most about Frank Gorshin: his sense of humor. He was great at ad libbing and revealing an inner character that saw the humorous side to almost anything you said to him.

It all starts in July 1979, when he is my guest on my Bay Area TV show, *Creature Features,* which I have been hosting for only a few weeks. Each Friday, I taped a series of segments at Channel 2, KTVU, located in Jack London Square in Oakland. These were intercut with a full-length feature (horror, sci-fi, or fantasy) and sponsors' ads. The final results ran the next night in the 11:30 p.m. time slot. I had gone out of my way to find celebrity guests, and my ratings had been pretty good. Usually, a guest would appear in only one segment, but I have decided to devote the entire show to Gorshin's career and have him in each of my four major on-camera appearances.

My adventure with Gorshin (call it a comedy moment, given his amusing nature) begins in the backseat of a limousine (rented for the occasion by KTVU) after we have picked him up in front of the Fairmont Hotel, where he is appearing in the Venetian Room for the next two weeks. (He had agreed to do the show because he knew it would be good hype for his engagement, given that *Creature Features* had been popular for eight years.) On the way across the San Francisco-Bay Bridge, I tell him the entire show will be devoted to him, and I have some surprises in store. Gorshin is constantly smoking a cigarette during our trip, and he often fumbles with it like a comedy prop. "This show of yours," he says, imitating the voice of a gangster type, "I gotta see with my own eyes. People don't mess with me without payin' for it." If anybody, I think, he's imitating George Raft.

On my shows the two previous weeks, I had announced that I would soon be presenting "The Sinister, Terrifying Guest." So, in my opening segment, the camera is focused on a large piece of

This is one of several photos taken of me and Frank Gorshin during our time on the Creature Features *set. The following week, I sent it over to the Fairmont where he was still performing, and he signed it with, "John! Thanks for your time. Enjoyed it. Frank Gorshin."*

cardboard with a giant question mark on it. I ask that "The Human Hand" remove the cardboard to reveal what is behind it. The hand of one of my "stage hands" comes into view, pulling away the question mark to reveal a huge portrait of Gorshin as The Riddler, a role he had played on the *Batman* TV series back in 1966. Totally ad libbing, Gorshin instantly begins cackling madly in the style of the masked character, and I feel great. He is already contributing his comedy to the presentation, and I have yet to introduce him. Now . . . .

"And here he is, The Sinister, Terrifying Guest," I cry out. "None other than . . . Frank Gorshin, world-famous impressionist, motion picture actor, song-and-dance man, and currently at the Fairmont Hotel with one of his best shows."

"How good was it, Stanley?" Gorshin queries, bursting out with more of the deranged cackling that his Riddler has become famous for. I can't help but think that this voiced madness has been

Frank Gorshin as Basil the bass player serenading Connie Francis before he falls into a fish tank in the 1960 comedy, Where the Boys Are.

inspired by Richard Widmark's criminal character Tommy Udo in the classic 1947 Film Noir, *Kiss of Death*. Time to kid Udo . . . I mean Gorshin. "Frank," I say, "you don't look very sinister to me."

"I've never been very terrifying, either."

The station's art department has drawn up a book cover that reads "INSIDE FRANK GORSHIN," which I hold upward so one of my cameras can capture a close-up.

Gorshin beams with pride, seeing his image on the book cover for the first time.

"Frank, you were born and raised in Pittsburgh, Pa."

"I loved my home town. City of Angels."

"What kind of youngster were you? In front of a mirror doing impressions?"

"No, no," he responds, "I was never the class clown. I was a quiet kid. But I spent a lot of time at the movies. I worked in those early days as an usher. So, I would see the same movie over and over again. And I'd start to imitate the voices of the stars. If a gangster picture was playing, I'd turn to a pair of customers and say [in an Edward G. Robinson-styled voice] 'All right, the three of us are goin' down this aisle and only one is comin' back. See? Get it? Yah yah yah.'"

I continue to feel great because Gorshin is wonderfully ad libbing his comedy to the moment, and it is making the show unique.

The dark side to Frank Gorshin's performance talents are exposed in the crime thriller, Portland Express *(1957).*

This is followed by a series of still photographs I have picked of Gorshin's early movies. First up: Frank Gorshin as Basil, the bass player, serenading Connie Francis before he falls into a fish tank in *Where the Boys Are* (1960). This was followed by a photo from *Hot Rod Girls* (1956).

"Hey, that's me with Lori Nelson," he says. "That was one of my earliest, right after I'd served in the Army Special Services. We shot that exploitationer at the old ZIV Studios, where they made

Highway Patrol, Science Fiction Theater, and *Silent Service,* that old submarine series...."

I tell my audience that I have dug up a photo of Gorshin from *Invasion of the Saucer Men* (1957), but at the last minute I decide to spare him the embarrassment. Gorshin responds by fiddling around with his half-smoked cigarette. More strange sounds imitating aliens invading Earth.

Portland Express... "Yeah, a good noir."

I then show a photo from *Where the Boys Are,* depicting Gorshin wearing thick-rimmed glasses, as if he were a nerd, and holding a bass guitar.

"Hey, Dolores Hart was with me in that one, and she became a nun not long after."

Then, *The DuPont Show of the Week.* "That's me in '64 as Jeremy Rabbit, public avenger."

Then, *The Kopy Kats.* "That was a TV series I did with Shecky Greene and various voice comics."

Then, *The High Chaparral.* "Yeah, I played Patrick 'Stinky' Flanagan, a guy who owned this camel."

My next surprise: I have sequences from his 1956 war thriller, *Between Heaven and Hell,* in which he portrays a bodyguard to officer Broderick Crawford and is slapped around by Robert Wagner.

Gorshin is loving it, seeing these old scenes brought to new life for my audience. He begins talking about Crawford. "Yeah, the old Ten-Four [a radio code Crawford always used on his TV series *Highway Patrol*]. "He was an amazing actor. He'd show up in the morning and you knew he'd been drinking the night before. He'd carry a script, but you could see he hadn't studied it at all. No markings on the pages, no folds. But just before a scene, he'd scan it, then throw the script down, and do the entire scene rapid-fire, like a machine-gun. He'd capture the full essence of the scene."

Then, I tell Frank I am going to show the sequence in which he gets blown up by a mortar blast when the Japanese shell the soldiers' position. "Oh, I can't wait to see me go to pieces again."

"Ten-Four for you, Frank," I tell him.

This exchange is soon followed by something Gorshin loves even better: his portrayal of The Riddler in a series of scenes

Frank Gorshin as The Riddler, a memorable criminal characterization from the Batman series that starred Adam West. While still on the Creature Features set with me, he signed this photo to my son Russ and daughter Trista with "Good Wishes to Ya."

from a 1966 episode of *Batman,* in which his henchmen tie Batman and Robin (Adam West and Burt Ward) to rotating cylinders.

Afterward, I ask Gorshin how he landed the role of The Riddler. "I'd worked for William Dozier, the producer of a series called *Empire,* with Richard Egan, which didn't last too long. I had done a

Gorshin as the humanoid alien Bele, in a well-remembered episode of Star Trek *from 1969.*

guest starring role. Later, when he became the *Batman* producer, he called me and said he wanted me to play The Riddler. I really did have fun."

"You gave that character a zany, uninhibited style."

"What a job, working with some kind of regularity. I did ten half-hour episodes."

Next I show a sequence from "Let That Be Your Last Battlefield," his 1969 episode of *Star Trek*, which featured him as Bele, a humanoid alien with half his face painted black, the other half white. Again, Gorshin shows his pleasure as the scene unfolds before his very eyes.

It is time to close the show, so I ask Gorshin to do an impression of Burt Lancaster. He jumps right in. "My first meeting with Burt

This is the publicity card for the show Frank Gorshin was doing when we met for the second time in November, 1980.

was eight years ago at the Fairmont. He was in town doing a play with Kirk Douglas. He came into the New Orleans Lounge and saw me and said [in his Lancaster voice]: 'Hi, I'm Burt Lancaster. I wanted to tell you my family saw your show and I'm going to try and see it tonight.' Then I said [still using the Lancaster voice], 'What're you trying to do? Make fun of me?'"

This photo of Frank Gorshin was taken in 1979, when he was my guest on Creature Features. I brought it with me to the Fairmont on the day of our second interview and he signed it "Good Luck with Your Book," in reference to the first edition in my Creature Features Movie Guide *series I was then planning to publish.*

The *Creature Features* show is over, but my meetings with Gorshin are only beginning, and a friendship will grow that takes us one year into the future to 1980, when Gorshin is once again performing at the Fairmont Hotel, and I will do an exclusive interview with him for the *San Francisco Chronicle*.

Yocking it up with Frank Gorshin, a cool, impressionistic Kopy Kat, begins when the man answers the door. He has dancing blue eyes that vaguely look like Burt Lancaster's. Around the jaw, even though there's no dimple, is a resemblance to Kirk Douglas. He reminds you a touch of Jack Nicholson when he cocks his head in a questioning manner, and there's a faint similarity to Rod Steiger in his voice when he clears his throat. His fingers curl around his cigarette with the intensity of Lee J. Cobb, and his eyes blaze with the passion of Edward G. Robinson.

A man who looks like that must have an identity crisis. Is Frank Gorshin Frank Gorshin, or is he an amalgamation of all the actors he's seen and loved since ushering in a neighborhood theater in Pittsburgh, Pa.?

"I'm just lovable me," says Gorshin, stepping back from the entrance to his suite at the Fairmont Hotel. He looks sharp in a snow-white sailing jacket (with a patch that reads "Chris-Craft Commander"), gray slacks, and shiny black shoes with golden chains. He's of slight build with brown hair that is showing signs of receding. "Come on in and make yourself homey in the presence of famous men. Or if you prefer, just come in and make yourself homely."

Among famous impressionists, Gorshin, now forty-seven, has held his own for nearly twenty years, surpassed only by Rich Little because Little is always expanding his mimicking horizons while Gorshin, in recent years, has not. "Maybe I'm too complacent," he says, settling for a pot of coffee in the company of a harder drinking journalist. "But the truth is, I don't feel I'm in competition with other impressionists. Let's see, I got down Telly Savalas and Dustin Hoffmann . . . I guess the last actor I added to my repertory was Jack Nicholson, and that was after *One Flew Over the Cuckoo's Nest*. I just haven't seen any new stars that I've wanted to mimic."

One of his best moments during the Venetian Room show is a visit to Heaven, where we hear the voices of John Wayne and other major stars that have passed on in recent times. It's funny as hell, but it's also nostalgic and just a touch sad to think that all those talents are now gone.

He continues. "People always think I'm doing new impressions, but really all I'm doing is putting the same characters in new comedy situations. People even come up to me and think they remember a voice I did, and I never did that." Gorshin denies there is a secret formula for his mimicking bits. "It was just something I did as a kid going to high school and later as an usher when I would see the same movies over and over. It worked for me when I got into show business. I never really worked at it like some people. Either it came to me or it didn't. It's a gift. It's just a thing I do."

Perhaps so, but impressions are what gave Gorshin a vast following in the early 1960s after his performance as impressionist Harry Simmons on "The Hundred Lives of Harry Simmons" an episode of *The Defenders*. It was then that he became a hot nightclub commodity. Then came The Riddler on *Batman*. Gorshin was so hot after that he threatened to crash through the top of a thermometer. Things were only cooling slightly when he co-hosted *The Kopy Kats*, ABC's excellent series featuring a collection of mimics. Then came Gorshin's Glacial Period. Ice Age Period.

"I've never been hot like that since," he confesses. "The opportunities dissipated. Suddenly, I wasn't in such a good position to pick and choose. I wasn't calling my shots like I had been. Outside of my cult of fans, there was no longer a demand. The people with the acting vehicles became unaware of me as a talent.

"Even today, they still think of me as The Riddler or a guy who does impressions. It's nobody's fault, that's the way the business turns. Now I need an effective vehicle where I can be seen by everyone."

Gorshin's dissatisfaction with his career is further reflected by the fact that he recently fired his old manager ("imagine three years of non-progress") and hired a new one. If better things are in the offing for Gorshin, they will no doubt be in the acting field.

[Author's Note: The above paragraph will come back to haunt me, but in a positive way. Hang on, that part of the story will come later. Right now, let's continue the interview.]

What Frank Gorshin really wants more than anything else is to act. In movies, TV shows, plays. He just wants to act. "I want to diversify as an actor, expand all the horizons in directions away from nightclubs. On the other hand, I may know what I enjoy doing but that doesn't mean that's what I should be doing. I might think of myself as a great actor but that doesn't make me one.

"Maybe I'm not a great actor. Maybe I don't have the magic or the charisma. Maybe what I should do is be obstinate and say, 'I'm going to be an actor and nothing else,' and deny myself everything else and work hard at it and starve if I must. But I've never done that." An actor, he continues, "must be endorsed by the people. If you don't have that demand, a career can be very difficult."

Gorshin turns down most comedy-variety shows on TV—they do nothing but perpetuate an image he would eventually like to leave behind him—and he rarely turns up in a dramatic series. As for feature films, Gorshin has not been making many lately. Last spring, he finished *Underground Aces*, a comedy about parking attendants at a luxury hotel and what happens to all those expensive cars once they're out of the owners' sight. He thinks he will have better pickings next January when he will open a seven-week run in Chicago's Drury Lane Theater in the comedy *Man With the Plastic Sandwich*. Although Gorshin has done theater before, including major Broadway productions, he admits he is "scared but excited" about doing a previously unproduced work. New plays, he points out, are closing every night of the week.

Gorshin says there was nothing complicated about his childhood. His father was a railroad worker, who was a good provider through the good and the rough years. He recalls how he started with the voices of James Cagney, Al Jolson, Edward G. Robinson, Boris Karloff, and Peter Lorre. He had that incredible ability not only to sound like a famous actor but to look like him too. "I guess you could call me uncanny."

At Carnegie Tech, he dreamt of being an actor, a dream he began to fulfill as a PFC with Special Forces. He was just about to be mustered out when he heard they needed background players for *The Proud and the Profane* (1956) and he found himself in the Virgin Islands working with William Holden. He couldn't wait to get his discharge papers and head directly for Hollywood.

When Gorshin arrived, he had arrived. He was the kind of kid low-budget producers were looking for. He had the look, he had diversity, he could be cute (*Where the Boys Are*), he could be menacing (*Between Heaven and Hell*), and he could do all those crazy voices. His ultimate role would be The Riddler, for he obviously enjoyed going stark raving bananas as he made the strangest kind of laughter imaginable.

The best years came and went. Gorshin, bored with the "sameness" of Hollywood living, sold his home and moved to Greenwich, Connecticut with his wife, Christina, a former waitress he had met at the L.A. Purple Onion, and their son, Mitch. This past year, they sold that house to Diana Ross and bought a new place in Westport, Connecticut. It puts Gorshin closer to the ski slopes of Stowe, Vermont, where he would eventually like to buy a chalet. "Skiing," he says, "is the one time I can completely put aside my problems and really unwind."

End of interview. End of story? No, not quite. Only one day after my story runs in the Sunday *Datebook* section of the *San Francisco Chronicle*, I receive a phone call from Richard Chase, who runs Baytide Films, a Bay Area-based film production company. (Three months earlier, I had written a story for the *San Francisco Chronicle* about Chase and his pending projects.) Chase says he has read my Gorshin piece and very much needs to talk to him about the possibilities of starring in a film that will soon go into production. "We've got a project we think he'd be suited for. In your story, he talked about wanting to make movies again. Well, maybe this is his chance." He goes on to explain that the project is a crime film entitled *The Uppercrust* and is to be directed by Austrian director Peter Patzak, famed in Europe for a series of TV movies about a police detective named Kottan. "Elliott Gould had been signed to play the leading role," explains Chase, "but suddenly he backed down and now refuses to fulfill the contract."

I immediately call the Fairmont and contact Gorshin. "So what kind of movie are these guys talking about?" he asks me.

"Not sure," I say. "It's about a gangster. Part of it would be shot in Europe, probably Austria. That's where the director is from. And part of it would be shot here in San Francisco."

"I'll give them a call," says Gorshin. "And hey, thanks for putting me in touch."

"Good luck," I tell him. "I hope it's the kind of project you're looking for."

It was.

I get one more call from Gorshin.

"Well, they offered me the leading role, but I'm still not sure. Like you said, a good part of it will be filmed in Austria, which means I'll be out of the country for a few weeks. And I've read the script, and frankly I don't completely understand it. Whatta you think?"

"Hey Frank," I tell him, "the Austrians serve some of the best sauerbraten in all of Europe. And don't forget the Sacher Hotel serves the best chocolate cake in the world, the sacher-torte. If nothing else, you'll get some great food while you're there."

Here is Frank Gorshin as hit man Harry Werner, preparing to fire his weapon from a hotel window in Vienna in the crime thriller, The Uppercrust, *directed by Peter Patzak.*

"I like sauerbraten," Gorshin says. "And chocolate, you say? Yeah, you may have something there."

Within a few weeks of signing the deal that Elliott Gould had reneged on, *The Uppercrust* is in production in San Francisco and producer Richard Chase has invited me to tag along. I spend a day following the production unit from location to location in December 1980. Strangely enough, Gorshin's costar from *Between Heaven and Hell*, Broderick Crawford, had also been cast in what appears to be an oddball thriller. I figure Crawford has been brought into the casting because of Gorshin's impressions of him—an inside joke.

The movie was about a bureaucrat's hit man and "Ten-Four" for one memorable former TV highway cop, but Gorshin, who had the guts to admit to me weeks earlier that he didn't know what the hell the story of *The Uppercrust* was all about, is now the star of that film. Seated in the back seat of a car, he points a .45 automatic pistol at the man in the front seat. As if to remind me of that moment when he made that confession about not understanding the screenplay, he says, "Look, there've been plenty of movie scripts that I read and thought I understood and thought would be big hits, and they fell flat on their asses. So, what do I really know about scripts?"

He presses the barrel of the .45 pistol against the bare neck of that man in front of him, Broderick Crawford. " Pardon me, Brod, is that too much pressure? Want me to pull back a little? Or should I press harder?"

Crawford, pulling his checkered overcoat tighter to his bulky neck, shakes his head and lights up another Kool cigarette. He's an old pro with the patience of Job. Gorshin scratches the end of his nose with the barrel of the .45. "Where was I? Oh, yeah. I play the young assassin, Harry Werner. Also known as Nash when things get too hot. I hit a coupla guys, take 'em out. I got faith in the director and the project. I want to make pictures. Movies. That's the bottom line. And look at me now. I'm working."

Now, in the back seat of an International Travelall 1010 station wagon parked in a lot beneath the Embarcadero Freeway at the foot of Broadway, Gorshin and Crawford are enacting a game of life and death. Crawford, portraying Mike Carrady, a retired gangster who knows too much, has just been shot in the back of the neck by Gorshin and is slumped slightly forward. The camera isn't turning so he looks more asleep than dead. Suddenly, he returns from the dead to make a comment. "The producer, Richard Chase, has a movie lover's sense of humor. A little while ago, we were up on the Embarcadero Freeway, and this Highway Patrol car pulls up alongside. Richard had rigged it that way. He wanted to pay homage to my old TV series, *Highway Patrol,* by having me and the cop car in the same shot. And now he's got Gorshin, who's always mouthing off with my Ten-Four routine in his nightclub act, shooting me in the neck. Life is full of twists and surprises."

Gorshin leans above Crawford to slide the .45 into the coat pocket of the "corpse." Outside the car, the Viennese director, Peter Patzak, is chain smoking like a fiend and trying to catch up on his shooting schedule, delayed earlier that morning by a tie-up on the freeway. Patzak has just wrapped seven weeks of continuous filming in Vienna and is exhausted. He's eager to see his single week of San Francisco location shooting completed as quickly as possible, so he can return to Vienna to begin editing. Or maybe he misses those chocolate cakes from the Socher Hotel.

I get out of the car and stand at Patzak's side for a few minutes, learning that he had never heard of Frank Gorshin until Chase had signed him up. "The first thing I did," Patzak tells me in his thick Viennese accent, "was run to the nearest bank, stop the first American tourist I saw, and ask him if he had ever heard of a comedian named Frank Gorshin. The tourist, thank God for my bank account, praised Gorshin to high heaven. Called him the funniest comedian in America. So I had no choice. I had to call Chase back and tell him that Gorshin had the part."

When I climb back into the car, sliding into the back seat next to Gorshin, he grabs my arm. "Hey, buddy, you were right."

"Right about what?"

"The food in Vienna. It was great." He continues with a thick German-style accent: "Every day, sauerbraten. And I got over to the Sacher Hotel, quick. Schnell. Chocolate cake up the gazoo. Sacher-torte. Covered with apricot jam."

"I told you, Frank," I said, trying to imitate Frank Gorshin's German-like voice. "Javowl, der ist nothing like it in der world."

"Stanley, you're the worst voice imitator I've ever met."

The Uppercrust didn't do much for Gorshin's career, even though some critics singled him out for an excellent performance. Unfortunately, it was barely shown in America. When I visited Peter Patzak in Vienna in 1985, actually helping him edit a TV movie

This was taken in a gymnasium the day I spent with Frank Gorshin as he made The Uppercrust. *Left to right: Me, actor Joey Forman (also in the cast), and Broderick Crawford, with Gorshin sitting above him in the bleachers.*

he was working on at that time, he told me that the film had done well in Europe but had never given much of a chance in America.

As for Gorshin, he kept on smoking an average of five packs of cigarettes a day, and he kept on working in movies and TV shows. In fact, he became a regular on the soap opera, *The Edge of Night*, using his talent to impersonate other members of the cast. Perhaps his most popular role was in a one-man show on Broadway, *Say Goodnight, Gracie*, in which he impersonated comedian George Burns. (The play was nominated for a Tony Award.) In fact, in 1995, Gorshin had just finished a performance in Memphis, and was flying back to Hollywood, when he had trouble breathing and required an oxygen mask. He was admitted into a hospital, but soon died at the age of seventy-two. Cause of death: lung cancer, emphysema, pneumonia. Upon hearing of his death, I couldn't help but remember how he smoked one cigarette after another, often fumbling around with a butt as if it were a comic prop.

Frank Gorshin is one character I will never forget.

Although he never told me that he had ambitions to be an artist, this early photo of Frank Gorshin shows him doing a drawing. Often that would include caricatures of famous actors.

RICH LITTLE
The Little Man With a Big Voice
... Maybe Not a Thousand, But Would You Believe at Least 200?

The words of Rich Little are terribly frustrating to record. As a matter of fact, it's downright impossible. It would require capturing the mannerisms and vocal characteristics of John Wayne, Jack Benny, Jack Paar, George Burns, Jack Lemmon, Gregory Peck, Kirk Douglas, Fred MacMurray, and countless other celebrities with familiar voices.

Is it possible that Rich Little is America's leading voice impersonator? In only a few years in the world of show business, he has, in the opinion of many critics, surpassed Frank Gorshin, Will Jordan, and other leading impressionists, not only in style but in the ability to do voices of the famous that others have not attempted.

Now a new phase of show biz has opened up for Little. He has been signed to play a secondary role on a new TV sitcom, *Love on a Rooftop*, as a would-be joke writer who lives with his wife (Barbara Bostock) next door to the main protagonists (Peter Duel and Julie Hammond).

Little, based on a sample episode I see, is constantly turning up at the worst possible moment to spout aloud his latest gag and make the lives of his neighbors as miserable as possible. I can only hope that Little, with his wonderful sense of timing and the frequent use of one of his voices, will save the series.

I have been asked by the *San Francisco Chronicle*'s chief TV critic, Terrence O'Flaherty, to visit Little in Los Angeles and learn what I can about the new series. It is the summer of 1966, and what I really want to find out from Little is a lot about his voice work. The TV show seems of minimal interest to me.

"Learning voices," he tells me, when we're finally seated face to face, "is a technique of hearing yourself. I guess you could call it the inner ear. In a way, you serve as your own tape recorder. If you can't

When I went searching for a signed photo of Rich Little, all I could find was this one, which he had autographed to my son Russ. What does that kid have that I don't?

bear yourself, then you'd better forget about being a voice mime. You'll never know when you're ready to deliver a new character."

Little is a native of Ottawa, Canada, and he began by imitating his school teachers in Halifax. By the time he was all of seventeen, he and another voice specialist, Geoff Scott, were imitating the voices of Canadian politicians in nightclubs. After working in little theater, he landed a job as a disc jockey and tried out many of his voices on radio. In 1963, he came to the United States to appear on *The Judy Garland Show*, doing among others an impression of James Mason from the film *A Star Is Born*.

Little is bubbling with anecdotes. Like the time he called George Burns on the telephone. In Burns' voice, Little told the famed comedian that he did an impression of him. With typical aplomb, Burns told him he would like to hear it some day—and hung up. Or the time he auditioned for a flower commercial, using the voice of Frank Fontaine, once a regular on *The Jackie Gleason Show*. So, who got the job? Frank Fontaine!

James Cagney, Jimmy Stewart, Louis Armstrong, Cary Grant—these, says Little, ". . . are the kind of impressions a professional avoids. They'd kill my act faster than laryngitis. For one thing, there's always some two-bit comic who can do those voices. For another, the cliché voices have a way of cheapening your act and your art. As you can hear, I go in for the unusual, the offbeat, such as Lloyd Bridges, Batman and Robin, Sean Connery, anybody who is currently popular. Right now, I'm trying to decide between Governor Brown and Ronald Reagan.

How does he feel about jumping into a situation comedy the likes of *Love on a Rooftop*? "There's always a danger of going into a series. Even if you're great, you still run the danger of the show flopping in the ratings. Frankly, I believe TV hit an all-time low about a year ago. Maybe I'm too close to *Roof* to see the light of day, but I think the show's pretty well-written and will give me an opportunity to learn."

I was right about how I felt that *Love on a Rooftop* was just another sitcom that would come and go. It lasted one season, but Little kept appearing here and there in one-shot character roles, and would eventually work his way onto *The Tonight Show* with Johnny Carson, adding the late-night host's voice to his list, as well as the voice of Richard Nixon, which he would do repeatedly over the next two decades. He became a regular on *The Julie Andrews Show*. She once said to him, "With Bob Hope doing my walk and you doing my voice, I can be a star and do nothing." Little would join such other voice impersonators as Frank Gorshin, George Kirby, Joe Baker, and Charlie Callas on *The Kopy Kats*.

Check out his website (www.richlittle.com) and you will see that he is still appearing around the country, still yocking it up with all those voices. Some forms of comedy never die.

ELLIOTT GOULD (M*A*S*H)
The Ad Libbing Surgeon
Cutting Up on the Set of
"M*A*S*H": A Slice of Strife

A snatch of dialogue on a soundstage at 20th Century Fox exemplifies the manner and style of exchange one is apt to overhear in Hollywood circa 1969.

First Technician: "When are we gonna film the nude scene for this flick?"

Second Technician: "What makes you think they're gonna have a nude scene?"

First Technician: "Are you kiddin'?"

Yes, 1969, the very year when Hollywood has finally thrown away its morality code (called "The Hays Office," "The Motion Picture Production Code," just plain "Movie Censorship," or "Sorry, Viewer, No Sex, No Violence Anymore of any Extreme Nature"). Scenes of raw nudity and consensual sex are now permitted. Because of that, boy, are some producers gonna go hog-wild in depicting the true nature of man and woman coming together, fulfilling their most primitive, flesh-driven desires—something forbidden since 1934, when the Code took full affect and dominated movie content for decades, angering producers and directors who wanted to portray things in a more realistic fashion. Censorship definitely went to an extreme, and now it's headed for another.

Just twenty feet away, in a teahouse set, kimono-clad Elliott Gould, more commonly known in recent gossip columns as "the estranged husband of Barbra Streisand," is puffing a cigar and twisting the ends of his elongated mustache in the style of Oil Can Harry. No, he is not filming a Popeye cartoon. This is the film version of *M*A*S*H* and it's going to make cinema history as a comedy classic, with Gould portraying Captain John Francis Xavier "Trapper John" McIntyre. Forget all that and just remember "Trapper John," the name that's going to stick to his character.

Donald Sutherland and Elliott Gould goofing around on a golf course in the feature film version of M*A*S*H. A new kind of Laurel and Hardy? A variation on Abbott and Costello or Two Stooges?

Not just when the film comes out, but in years to come. Not just on the big screen but on the little one. For eleven seasons (1972-1983), a network television series version of *M*A*S*H* will thrive, but who knew when it was just a feature film?

DONALD SUTHERLAND (M*A*S*H)

*Donald Sutherland, relaxing on the set of M*A*S*H.*

Curled up next to Gould, dressed similarly in kimono, is Donald Sutherland in the role of Captain Benjamin Franklin "Hawkeye" Pierce. All you really have to remember is "Hawkeye," the name that is going to stick to his character. Not just when the film comes out, but in years to come. If, in 1969, I could only see into the future of CBS television . . . .

Both Sutherland and Gould's legs are tucked together, Japanese-style, and for a moment they stare questioningly into steaming bowls of rice and meat set before them by a curvaceous Geisha Girl, she of finest visual quality. There is something ludicrous about Gould's chemistry of cigar, mustache, and kimono, and everything he says, even in total seriousness, adds to that satiric effect. So it is at 20th Century Fox in 1969, and so is the situation for Scene 81 George, Take One, for *M*A*S*H*.

M*A*S*H? A military abbreviation for the 4077th Mobile Army Surgical Hospital, a fictional outfit that serves as a catalyst for misadventures for this Korean War comedy based on a somewhat irreverent novel by a wartime doctor who has chosen to remain hidden behind the pseudonym of Richard Hooker. The full title of Hooker's novel: *M*A*S*H: A Novel About Three Army Doctors*.

The word "comedy" is used loosely, for comedy, in the usual sense, *M*A*S*H* is not. Most of the film is ad libbed, made under the direction of Robert Altman, a director still trying to climb up the ladder of success. The performers take the basic script by Ring Lardner Jr. and work freely and wildly with it, no matter what Lardner Jr. might say in reaction to such destructive alterations to his original writings. In each retake of 81, dialogue and character movements may vary, yet the essence of the scene is unaffected.

Standing behind the camera, his hands shoved into his pockets, his ears trying to hear every attitude and reaction on the set, is director Altman. In close up, he seems to loom above everything and everybody, staring intently through dark glasses and stalking the set with absolute assuredness about what he expects others to do or not do. He is allowing ad libbing and voices crossing over each other, for he feels it is all closer to reality, to the way people actually behave. People have disrespect or indifference toward others, so what's to worry about? Don't argue too much

Director Robert Altman, whose career rose to the top in Hollywood after the success of M*A*S*H.

with Altman. He is notorious for giving you a piece of his mind if he disagrees with you.

"This is a film about behavior," Altman explains, as if he can read my mind, his eyes riveted on Gould and Sutherland. "We're more concerned here with response than plot. In fact, it's not a plot film in the usual sense. We have twenty-two running characters, and it's taken a blueprint to keep them straight in our minds." Each character, incidentally, has been given a nickname. An unusual twist for a movie about war, in which doctors and nurses fall back on their senses of humor to survive all the horrors they must endure while living on the edges of the frontlines.

Altman is still staring intensely at me as he says, "As far as humor goes, if the joke relies on a lie, we throw it out. And as far as sex goes, it's an integral part of how men behave, especially men on the fringe of the lunacy of war, as these doctors are."

Altman, age forty-four, directs M*A*S*H fully aware of the "lunacy of war," having flown fifty combat missions aboard a B-24 Liberator while serving with the 307th Bomb Group during World War II. He was all of nineteen in 1944 when fulfilling his role as crew member. After making many industrial films and documentaries, he finally crashed Hollywood in the late 1950s for a career in B movies and episodic TV shows. He also wanted to make major movies.

Despite a thinning head of hair, Altman is looked upon by the film community as young blood, a fresh newcomer, who works in an independent fashion, eschewing the Hollywood stereotype, fighting with those who disagree with him. He and his producer, Ingo Preminger (brother of director Otto Preminger), have worked at 20th Century Fox without interference from the Darryl F. Zanuck hierarchy, and it is Altman's intention to remain aloof, in this and future pictures, from the superimposition of others' values on his work.

Altman is enthusiastic about forthcoming projects but has little to say about his 1968 film, *Countdown*, in which James Caan and Robert Duvall played U.S. astronauts trying to be the first to reach the moon. He does tell me, "It was a failure. Warner Bros. and I had differences of opinion, and Warner won." He does not mention that he was fired from the project after refusing to edit footage down to a length acceptable for theatrical showings. He is more ecstatic about *That Cold Day in the Park*, a psycho-thriller in which Sandy Dennis traps a young man (Michael Burns) in her apartment. That film had bombed at the box office and received little praise from film critics.

Suddenly, Altman's calm, slow-speaking demeanor is interrupted by an exchange of banter between Gould and Sutherland, who next begin singing in harmony: *"Hello, I love ya. Those are the words that I say to the sky. Hello, I love ya. Don't make a sour face, lady."*

"Before this film," the Unit Publicist whispers to me between lyrics, "Elliott and Don had never met, but right away they became another Bob and Ray. I've never seen anything like this on a movie set before."

(The pair of actors told one interviewer who came to the set before me that they were working on a system to mine Kryptonite, and the reporter, unfamiliar with the origin of Superman, and perhaps comic books in general, accepted it as a straight-faced fact and reported it in his article that way. On another occasion, according to the Unit Publicist, Gould and Sutherland led a studio guard on a merry chase through the Fox parking lot, posing as interlopers.)

Due to lighting complications, a break is called. Gould and Sutherland wander from the teahouse set and make themselves available for an interview, each speaking briefly, allowing the other to follow. Short phrases, back and forth. Each adjusting to what the other has just said. Interview? Well, it vaguely resembles an interview. Sort of. Kinda like. And so it begins:

Gould: "This is Elliott Gould."

Sutherland: "And this is Donald Sutherland. We're here at the center of mass making—"

Gould: "—a motion picture set at the turn of the century about a widow and her streak of grief."

Sutherland: "Say the Secret Word and the duck will fly down."

Gould: "The duck?"

Sutherland: "Duck, you sucker. The duck from overhead, it pays a hundred dollars if you say the Secret Word. Groucho Marx, remember?"

Gould: "That's American trivia."

Sutherland: "From a trivial!"

Gould: "Do you know who we are? He's Harry Ritz and I'm Harry Richman."

Sutherland: "I'm Dr. Crankenbush and he's Doctor Cronkite."

Gould: "This is a motion picture dedicated."

Sutherland: "A serious motion picture dedicated."

Gould: "Very serious."

Sutherland: "Anti-war."

Gould: "Very real comment on that."

Sutherland: "We represent disorientation of the American."

Gould: "I demonstrate a total lack of sexual prowess."

Sutherland: "I represent sodomy . . . and a little Gomorrah . . . but I babble."

Gould: "With religious overtones."

Sutherland: "Yes, religious. I just hope I can get an aspirin from my doctor next time I have a cold."

Gould: "This picture is related to just about everything. Even my grandmother."

Sutherland: "My grandmother makes the best potato pancakes."

Gould: "My grandmother smokes grass."

Sutherland: "One day, Elliott and I intend to become actors."

Gould: "As soon as I finish this ridiculous interview, I'm going to become an actor."

Sutherland: "Now, back to the film . . . ."

Gould: "Yes, the film. Back to the sexual aspects."

Sutherland: "Sophomoric and juvenile."

Gould: (Deep baritone) "When sophisticated men, crackerjack surgeons, highly educated, come into a situation where they live like animals in a violent, immoral, lascivious, grotesque, horrifying . . . ."

Sutherland: (Deep baritone) "And so, these honorable men, so that they might continue to function in the operating room, do asinine, fatuous, inane, ridiculous . . . ."

Gould: "If this picture turns out right, it could be moving—."

Sutherland: "—to another theater."

Gould: "It's not a war picture, M*A*S*H isn't."

Sutherland: "Just try to pronounce those ridiculous things between the letters."

Gould: "But it's motivated by war."
Sutherland: "We are motivated by more amoral aspects."
Gould: "Back to the sex."

But no, sex has to be dropped, and so does the interview, if you want to call it that. It's time to get back to the teahouse set because director Altman is finally ready with the lighting. On the first run-through of 81 George, everything goes perfectly. He calls for a print, then waves his hands through the air, for it is time for sex to return. "And now," he says bluntly, "we shoot the last scene of the picture. The nude scene."

A technician suddenly clicks on a Klieg light and coughs so everyone can hear him. Another technician waves at him, as if to say, "Didn't I tell you so?"

Except for a camera crew of minimum size, the sound stage must be cleared. As the superfluous file out, Ingo Preminger, Gould, and Sutherland are standing near the exit door, beaming with pleasure, suggesting they can't wait for the "nude scene" to begin. As I pass them, heading for the exit, they turn to face me:

Gould: "I'm Dr. Zarkoff."
Sutherland: "And I'm Dr. Malone."
Gould: "And do we like nude scenes—"
Sutherland: "—of the most licentious order!"

That's when I walk off the sound stage, back into the real world, wondering what kind of movie is M*A*S*H,* really. How could all that silliness amount to anything?

If only I could have foreseen the impact this movie would have on the American public, earning over $80 million at the box office, I might have realized soon after its release that those moments I spent on the Fox sound stage were going to become memorable. I had inspired an ad libbed comedy piece I doubt any other reporter had seen and heard. Then there was the impact the film had on the movie industry, which gave Lardner Jr. an Oscar for best screenplay, and which nominated Altman, editor Danford Greene, and Sally Kellerman for her performance as Margaret "Hot Lips" Houlihan.

Almost immediately, the Fox execs must have heard Bugs Bunny whispering in their ears: "What's Up? Doc?" Realizing that the prospects for a TV sitcom were enormous, given the traumatic and sometimes zany twists doctors and nurses had to bring to their profession while tending to the wounded of war.

ALAN ALDA
Hawkeye Without a Musket: Doctoring the Art of Warfare In the Alan Alda Style

Would you believe it? They're going to do it to *M*A*S*H*. They're going to take that box office smash, that critically acclaimed hit film, and turn it into another situation comedy.

So it was in the summer of 1972 that Terrence O'Flaherty, TV critic for the *San Francisco Chronicle*, asked me to journey to Los Angeles to talk with Alan Alda, who had been signed as one of the leading stars of the CBS upcoming series, *M*A*S*H*. My meeting with Alda would be only the first in a series of interviews with the headliners.

All those characters we came to love—Hotlips Houlihan, Spearchucker, Hawkeye, the 12th Disciple—Father John, Trapper John, Lieutenant Dish—are to be turned into TV stumblers and bumblers. The climate it right, as the anti-war flavor that is ultimately projected fits in nicely for a majority of the American public tired of the current war in Vietnam. It has never been a popular war and it would appear that a TV *M*A*S*H* will serve its purpose.

The things those characters did on the screen had much to do with the cynicism of doctors attached to the 4077th Mobile Army Surgical Hospital behind the lines during the Korean War (1950-1953). This cynicism was directed at hundreds of casualty cases pouring in from the front lines and at their own private search for an escape from the boredom and grimness of war. What made it seem meaningful, or just downright grotesquely funny, was its use of uncompromising language (of a kind that was being allowed for the first in movies since the imposition of the Hollywood Morality Code of 1934) and great quantities of spurting blood all over those operating rooms.

Unfortunately, none of these things, or the characters as originally conceived, would CBS dare to present on its forthcoming

Alan Alda as Captain Pierce, combat surgeon, on the TV version of M*A*S*H.

M*A*S*H series in quite the same light. It's known as The Watering Down Process. Designed to protect you and me and the rest of the American Public from the Unspeakable. Certainly our eyes and ears would be destroyed forever.

So the question is: Why bother at all, CBS? The answer to that significant question is answered personally by Alan Alda, who will portray Hawkeye aka Captain Benjamin Franklin Pierce, combat surgeon, taking over the film role of Donald Sutherland.

Open your ears wide, reporter. Here it comes from Alda. "When you've got a winner at the box office, you play off the name and the fame all you can. Okay, okay, we won't have any of the blood, but the original intent of the gore will be carried in the way we handle the patients. And while the attitudes of the surgeons are about the same, they'll have to be a little less abrasive. We can't have any swearing, either." Just to emphasis that point, Alda swears a couple of phrases at me.

Let's see, I reply to Alda, no blood, no abrasiveness, no cursing. Damn it. Well, that leaves plenty of room for sex! Right?

"Wrong," responds Alda, shaking his head. "On television? Are you kidding me? Yeah, you look like a kidder. Look, I think we'll still be getting across pretty much the same impressions that the movie made."

Good luck, Alan, I think. Good luck, CBS.

Alda is seated in the commissary at 20th Century Fox at the height of the luncheon hour. He describes the blinding headaches he's been getting since filming began. "When you do TV, you have no chance to relax. The pressures build and build, and there never seems to be an outlet. *M*A*S*H* is especially hard because the entire cast is responding in a dedicated fashion. We're trying our best to make some difficult things work. This requires a great deal of creativity. Too often in film work, things don't work out. Actors get yelled at. Actors get turned off. So all you end up giving is a day's work and then you go home. But with this series we're trying to be as sincere as possible. Never letting it become mechanical, or just another comedy series."

The biographers say Alda once wanted to be a doctor, which sounds good for *M*A*S*H* publicity.

"No, no," insists Alda, shaking a finger at me, "that's a genuine fact. My dad's idea, originally, so I followed through with pre-med. But I slept through most of the classes, and made it crystal clear that I wasn't cut out to be a doctor by getting a score of 10 out of 100.

"I never had a great thing about doctors because I suffered from polio when I was seven years old. They used the Sister Kenny treatment on me. Wrapped me every few hours in steaming, hot blankets. Lots of physical therapy, manipulating of the muscles.

It's kept me limber all these years, but it turned me off to the world of medicine."

Alda stares out across the commissary for a moment. "Strange," he says, "how I've never dug doctors, now that I think about it. Yet I'm willing to give away part of my soul to play one in a TV comedy. Figure that one out."

Alda portrayed Hawkeye in all 251 episodes that ran on CBS through 1983. Portraying a doctor would ironically haunt him in future years, when he played Dr. Gabriel Lawrence on *ER* (1999) and Dr. Atticus Sherman on *The Big C* (2011-13). When not doctoring, he got into politics on *The West Wing* portraying Senator Arnold Vinick.

LORETTA SWIT
Time to Meet the Gal Known for Her Hot Lips . . . Or Is It Loretta's Intellect That Men Seek?

She begins by saying, "Hello, I'm a walking dream factory and I'm here to blow you a kiss." Not a bad way for a thirty-five-year-old woman with shapely charms to introduce herself, especially in a secluded bedroom setting.

Too bad (for me, anyway) that Loretta Swit is just teasing. On the other hand, she is a great kidder, but what isn't kidding, even when she's being funny, is her earthy vitality and a smoldering kind of sexiness that is enhanced by a deep-throated Lauren Bacall effect.

Not so funny, especially to her, is a case of the sniffles she just picked up on a junket to Atlanta and Chicago to promote her TV series, M*A*S*H, which will soon begin its third season.

Here's the picture as I see it in the summer of 1973: Loretta Swit, all very sexy and fiery, in a bedroom suite at the Sheraton-Universal Hotel, dressed in a black safari jacket (with gleaming silver belt) and white pants, moving sensuously around the room. On each wrist is a silver bracelet (to match that shining belt) and they flash in the reflection of the sun pouring through the window of her room overlooking the Hollywood Freeway.

Loretta is eager now. Not about me, she's eager to talk about Hot Lips Houlihan. You know, Major Margaret—you put Hot Lips into parentheses—Houlihan, that M*A*S*H nurse who indulges in devilment and trickery so that certain Korean War surgeons assigned to the 4077th won't go off the deep end.

Loretta talks about the art of acting at great length, first about not being too self-conscious when she performs for TV, then about her constant use of humor in her day-to-day existence. Next, she admits somewhat flatly, that she is "basically shy."

So all this chatter . . . just a cover-up for her insecurities and inner weaknesses. She's a woman in hiding, is Loretta Swit, hiding in

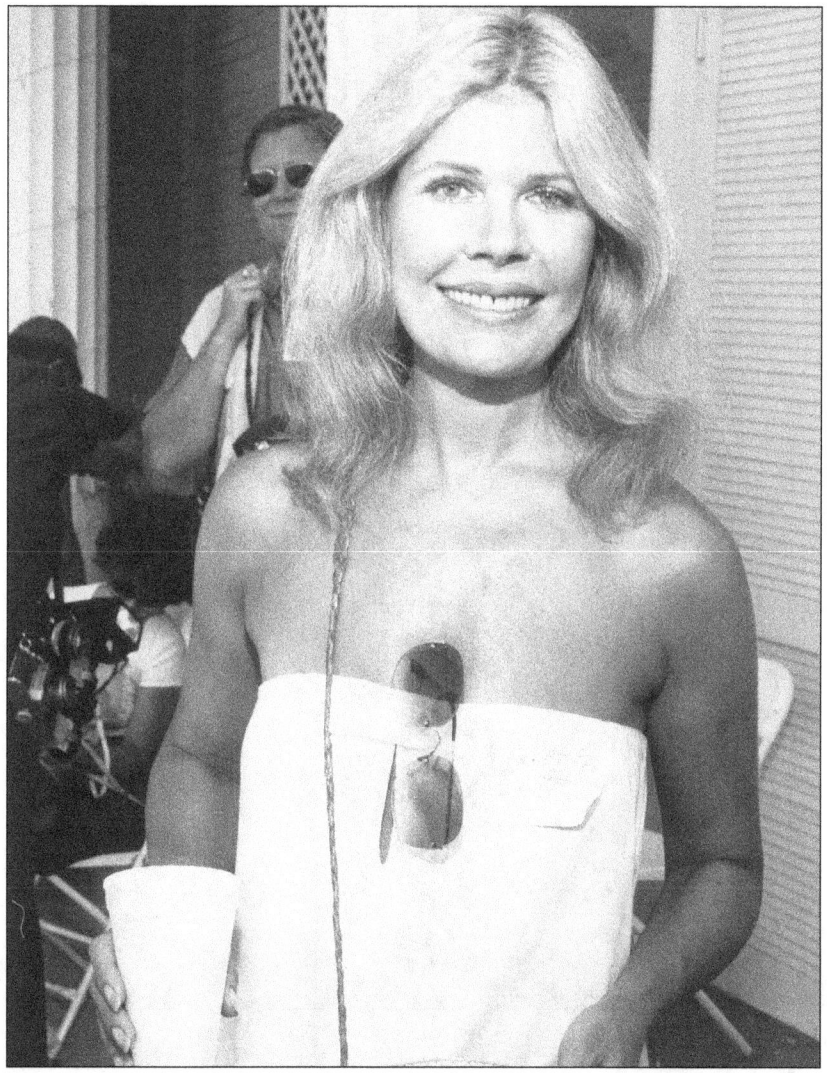
Loretta Swit in her role as "Hot Lips" Houlihan.

real life behind that humor and chatter, hiding on TV behind the name and character of Hot Lips. That's the way it is.

Because, she explains nonstop, "I'm basically a person. Just a human being. And that takes in a lot of territory. I'm very capable. I'm very vulnerable. We all like to cling to familiar things. I find most things impossible to give up. I'm too secure with those things."

Loretta Swit in her role as "Hot Lips" Houlihan.

To Loretta, acting is a business. Very black and white. Very tangible. "I guess it's the only profession I've ever been in that has given me security, even though I'm still an insecure person as I've described. Yet I thrive on pressure, and TV is pressure. I even create my own pressures and deadlines. Nobody forces them on me; I create these demands myself. On the weekends, sometimes, I miss the hectic schedule of shooting M*A*S*H. I don't like vacations. I go away from my securities, and I don't like that."

Loretta Swit was in San Francisco recently to portray the wife of a hijacker in *Freebie and the Bean*, a film about two San Francisco detectives played by James Caan and Alan Arkin. However, she says she cannot discuss the character she plays for fear of giving away the plot. "She was this woman, but I can't tell you more. Your city, San Francisco, it was good. Pink and white. Parfey. Blum's. Flowers on street corners. [At Market and Powell, where the streetcars meet?] The food was excellent. You have wonderful restaurants."

She also had a role last year (1972) in *Stand Up and Be Counted*, in which she played the wife of an advertising man (Steve Lawrence,) who ends up being offered a high-paying magazine job while he's unemployed. Loretta doesn't want to talk about it. 'I was just a person."

Don't think that Loretta is being evasive. It's the only way she knows how to describe the women she plays. "You just can't always talk about people with words."

Loretta steps over to a nearby mirror to comb her hair. "Almost time," she tells me, "to get back on the Hollywood Freeway and return home to Beverly Hills." New scripts for the fall season of *M*A*S*H*, now that the Writers' Guild of America strike is over after a four-month delay, will be coming off the assembly line soon. Got to be ready to read those lines as only Hot Lips can read them. She turns from the mirror. "How do I look, baby?" she asks, assuming a Houlihan pose and tossing her head defiantly, her hair waving about her.

So there you have it. Loretta Swit. Ooops, I mean Hot Lips Houlihan—very earthy, very sensual, very sexy—even when she has the sniffles.

Loretta will remain with her "Hot Lips" for eleven seasons, completing 240 episodes. She'll continue with many TV roles and also become politically active in the protection of wildlife, actually refusing to appear at a Bay Area amusement park because she heard that the animals there were being mistreated. I remember this vividly because I had interviewed her about that appearance, only to receive a phone call a short time later telling me to bury the story—she wouldn't be going near that park anytime soon. I could only imagine her breath was as hot as her lips when she made that call to me.

HARRY MORGAN / MIKE FARRELL
The Combat Team of Harry & Mike: Even Without Their Boots On, They're Kicking Up a Comedy Storm

Even when Harry Morgan and Mike Farrell take off their combat boots, they cannot stop living the roles of men assigned to the 4077th Mobile Army Surgical Hospital. That would be *M*A*S*H* to you, TV viewer, in October 1975.

The two-man squad of Morgan and Farrell delight in sardonic quips that reflect the comedic defense against misery and death that *M*A*S*H* personnel build up in time of war, and which actors build up in time of film production to defend themselves against infiltrating reporters from far-flung newspapers across America.

Harry Morgan signed this photo "To John, Erica and George, With My Very Best Wishes, Harry Morgan." But I gotta ask: Who the hell is George?

This Harry Morgan photo was signed just to Erica.

Their caps and combat boots are removed because the luncheon is taking place in a posh Beverly Hills Japanese restaurant, a weird coincidence when I think back to that moment in 1969 when I was covering the making of the feature film version of M*A*S*H at 20th Century Fox. I wandered onto a Japanese restaurant set, where Donald Sutherland and Elliott Gould paused in a middle of a sushi meal to create a two-man monologue you can read in the opening segment of this coverage of M*A*S*H.

Mike Farrell in his M*A*S*H role as Captain Hunnicutt. He signed: "Thanks for writing all those nice things. Peace! Mike Farrell"

I first met Morgan when he was costarring with Jack Webb in the 1967-1970 rebirth of Dragnet, portraying Officer Bill Gannon. In the third season of *M*A*S*H*, he had appeared in the episode, "The General Flipped at Dawn," as a weirdo officer, Major General Bartford Hamilton Steele. Now, as the fourth season begins, he has been newly assigned to portray Colonel Sherman Potter, an old Army dogface, who still wears his World War I campaign hat, often reminisces about the battle in the Argonnes woods, and has been around long enough to know that "doughboys" are not bakers' assistants.

Farrell, meanwhile, portrays Captain B. J. Hunnicutt, a wacky "cut-up" of a character whose bizarre surgical activities during the Korean War tears at the Colonel's pride. Military etiquette is shattered, irreparably. The Colonel revels in past glories, trying to shut out the "horrors" of modern warfare. (As if the trenches along the Somme weren't bad enough in 1917.)

Morgan and Farrell are "repple depple replacements" for McLean Stevenson and Wayne Rogers, who allegedly "asked for transfers out of this chicken s - - t outfit" because of differences of opinion with Alan Alda, the star of the series (as Captain Benjamin Franklin "Hawkeye" Pierce) who reportedly has his own code of Stanard Operational Procedure and can be downright mean and adamant, revealing not an ounce of mercy toward his co-stars.

"We'd like to give you all the dirt," says Morgan, "but we came along after the fact. It's already been swept away so there are no remnants left to discuss." (In truth, McLean Stevenson had left the series to star in his own TV comedy, *The McLean Stevenson Show*. It lasted only twelve episodes and he would later admit leaving had been a major misstep in his career.)

"Harry," says Farrell, "is always after the fact—ever since he was Jack Webb's partner on 'Dragnet.'"

In response, Morgan tells me, "Farrell spends most of his time on the set playing Scrabble, always getting the letters mixed up. Me, I don't waste my time playing Scrabble."

"That's true," agrees Farrell. "Harry plays Perquacky. A word-dice game."

As for explaining why Wayne Rogers had abandoned his role as Captain "Trapper John" McIntyre after the third season, Farrell says, "I think he was jealous of Alan Alda getting the best lines. But who knows for sure?"

How does Morgan's role differ from Stevenson's? "I'm playing him older and shorter in height," replies Morgan, who has also played older and shorter characters in such series as *December Bride, Pete and Gladys, Kentucky Jones*, and *Hec Ramsey*. What nuances and character subtleties will he give to Potter? "All of them," he says, smiling.

What of Farrell's Hunnicutt? Farrell smiles his boyish smile. "I'm a gentle, quiet type." He says it quietly and gently, spilling not a drop of his egg noodle soup. Farrell has played quiet, gentle types in two previous series: *The Interns* opposite Broderick Crawford and *The Man and the City* opposite Anthony Quinn.

"Neither was a long-running hit," interjects Morgan.

"Neither was *Kentucky Jones*," interjects Farrell.

Okay, so why is *M*A*S*H* such a major hit?

"The writing," claims Morgan. "It's in the scripts. I used to watch the show before I became a regular because it was so well-written, and it's seldom that I watch TV."

"Harry's near-sighted," says Farrell. "He doesn't know anything about writing." He digs into a mixture of beef and vegetables. "Seriously, though," and he shifts his tone of voice to indicate he is serious, "*M*A*S*H* clicks because of its tremendous gallery of characters. And the man I'm sitting with should have his picture in a gallery—a shooting gallery."

Morgan nods. "Your photo is already up in the gallery, and it's full of holes, right where your brain is."

Both actors break out laughing, and so do I. Then Morgan picks up things, his voice matching Farrell's for its—ahem—deeper meaning. "Ah, it's the writers. They've taken an idea with substance and they've made it work by remaining true to concept. No jokes just for the sake of a bunch of jokes."

"Yeah, no shtick," picks up Farrell. "Everyone stays in character. This is a show you can respect, because it respects the viewers' intelligence."

"Too bad," says Morgan between bites of food, "that you can't say the same about all the other members of the cast. Me and Mike, we're exceptions."

Farrell laughs, his head turning toward Morgan. "Hey, I'm one lucky guy to be working in this series."

"You're lucky just to be working," replies Morgan.

The pair finishes eating and put their combat boots back on. They square away their caps. "Sorry, but we got to go back to work," says Morgan.

"Yeah," agrees Farrell, standing upright. "We got scenes to do."

"My scenes," says Morgan, "are gonna be better than his."

"We'll see," says Farrell.

Off they go, the team of Morgan and Farrell, a two-man Korean War squad leaving the Japanese restaurant, returning to the 38th Parallel, to the wacky world of medicine mayhem at nearby 20th Century Fox, where *M*A*S*H* plays itself out.

The time has come to return to war, Scrabble and Perquacky.

Morgan completed 180 episodes of *M*A*S*H* and was nominated nine times as Best Actor, winning only once in 1980. He also starred in the post-*M*A*S*H* series, *After M*A*S*H*, replaying his role of Colonel Potter. He lived until the age of ninety-six, dying in 2011 of pneumonia.

Farrell completed 179 episodes of *M*A*S*H*. He always praised Morgan as a close friend, one who had such a remarkable talent for humor that he was always cracking up other cast members. "We had great fun doing the show; and much of it was laughing at some silly gag that one of us had pulled on the others." He lives on as actor, producer, director, and writer, and has a reputation for being active in liberal politics.

LARRY LINVILLE
M*A*S*H Doctor Who Winged It Alone And Built His Own Sky Machine

Larry Linville might appear to be a little flighty, keeping the fuselage and the wings for a giant sky glider in the living room of his Brentwood home, but there is lofty lucidity to his madness. See, he is building the prototype for a new "Sky Machine," which hopefully will bring him prestige and profit in the aeronautics world as much as the role of Major Frank Burns has brought him fame and fortune in the acting world via M*A*S*H.

"Why not turn a hobby into a profitable enterprise?" Linville asks me, or perhaps he is just asking himself as we sit down in May 1976, to talk about his career. "I'm a nut about soaring and love to get out there in the wide open spaces on the weekend. One day, up there in the blue, I was struck with the idea for a tailless glider. So I went to work with an aircraft engineer to design it."

M*A*S*H, which will enter its fifth season in a few months, has been one of CBS' few bulwarks in the current ratings war. "Our strength," says Linville, "lies in the fact we have time to rehearse, a luxury usually not afforded a filmed series. Oftentimes the writers are right there with us and can see first-hand whether a bit is working. If it isn't, instant rewrite. We rehearse our scripts like plays, really, then shoot with a single camera."

Unlike most series, which specialize in just a few recurring characters, M*A*S*H has a repertory company of seventeen players. Understandably, several of its original players have left to pursue more substantial roles (such as Wayne Rogers, who went on to star in the short-lived *City of Angels* as private eye Jake Axminster) or to bring an end to reported ego clashes with major star Alan Alda. (Remember how McLean Stevenson didn't want to put up with Alda getting the best material and left to star in a flop?)

Linville admits the many cast changes have had their downer effect. "You can't help but be affected by new actors; you're dealing with different personalities. It's a help in a way because you

Larry Linville as Major Frank Burns of M*A*S*H.

must re-examine what you're doing. I've kept from getting stale. As far as personal differences, I try not to get involved in the lives of others. God knows, I've had my own problems. If [McLean] Stevenson feels he's gotta go on to other things, so be it. They depart with my blessing and love and I wish them the best."

In connection with his aeronautics pursuits, Linville has written the screenplay for the Walt Disney film, *Grandpa's Fantastic Flying Ragwing Machine* [this film will not materialize] and is currently at work on a story about his grandfather, who experienced many great adventures as a wilderness doctor in Modoc County, CA. Writing, however, is only an avocation. It is, he admits, acting that remains his first love, with aviation zooming in second.

Next season Larry Gelbart, one of the head producers and writers on M*A*S*H, will be leaving to make movies. "I'm going to miss having him around," laments Linville. "He was surprising us every season with all those wildly ingenious ideas of his." Linville shrugs and, being the eternal optimist, adds, "On the other hand, new writers could breath new life and a whiff of fresh air into the series."

Linville, age thirty-four, is a third generation Californian (born in Oja, reared in Sacramento), who spent eight years learning aeronautical engineering at the University of Colorado before he decided to become an actor. That's when things got tough.

"I spent fifteen years in theater—some of those years were very, very lean. You could even say I starved. For me, theater was all trials and tribulations. High highs and down downs. I had some parts so small you couldn't find them in the scripts." His patience, however, paid off with a scholarship to London's Royal Academy of Dramatic Arts, where he studied for two years. There followed many years of repertory theater before he finally appeared with Ingrid Bergman in *More Stately Mansions*, which opened the Ahmanson Theater at the Los Angeles Music Center in 1967. "The main reason I got the role," he tells me, "is because I was the tallest actor they could find to stand beside Bergman." He stayed throughout the play's Broadway run. It was his part in another hit play, *In the Matter of J. Robert Oppenheimer*, that brought him to TV and years of character roles on *Mission: Impossible*. He also had a recurring role as a detective on *Mannix*.

"People have asked me the difference between film and theater acting, and to me there is no difference. Good acting is good acting. Each medium has its own demands. Each has its strengths and limitations. I'm aware of the stigmata some people have that actors are supposed to be freakish and bizarre. Actually, we're very responsible. We have to be to carry out the difficult roles and to survive in what is a fiercely competitive business. Especially in TV, where the pace can be exhausting."

Linville has made a handful of pictures (including *Kotch* and *Vanished*), but says he is now refusing new scripts he might have once accepted just for the money. "I'm accepting on the basis of merit alone. I'm having too much fun with my personal life to take on projects I don't appreciate. I went through a period when I thought money brought happiness. That's crap. Now I work for intrinsic satisfaction.

"There's nothing so rewarding as to stretch out flat on your back with a can of cold beer in the comfort of your own home and watch your program all cut together and know that it's working. That it's good! That's the ultimate moment for any actor."

As pleased as Linville sounded with things in 1976, he quit the series one year later, primarily because he felt he had done all he could in portraying Dr. Frank Burns. Rumors also flew that he had stopped seeing the daily rushes because he was tired of his character always having to bear the brunt of the jokes. He remained busy with TV work until 1998, when he underwent surgery and had a lung removed. Two years of ill-health followed. He died in 2000 at the age of sixty. That half-built airplane I saw in his front room? According to Gary Burghoff, who played Corporal O'Reilly on *M*A*S*H*, and who was a close friend, Linville eventually did fly that plane.

SALLY KELLERMAN
Torch Songs Flow From Hot Lips
–But Being a Singer Is Never Easy

Life isn't always chronological. Although I interviewed several stars of the TV version of M*A*S*H during the years it was in production, I wouldn't meet the film version's female star, Sally Kellerman, until July 1992, when she came to San Francisco for a one-night performance. Although an oddball form of comedy always seemed to perpetuate her image, and she rose up to become an oft-seen movie character, it was song and music that dominated her imagination and motivated her the strongest. Here's a glimpse into a part of her you might not have known about.

What a lousy day for Sally Kellerman. She's flown from Los Angeles to San Francisco with a sprained back that is killing her, and when she leans over to tell you about it, her silky, sexy voice—the one you should recognize from all those Clairol and Hidden Valley Ranch Salad TV commercials—is hoarse and lost to a case of laryngitis.

If there's pain and disappointment, she doesn't allow it to show on her angular face, which is tightly framed by blonde hair that has been clipped just above her eyebrows and clings to the sides of her head. Call it the Carol Channing pageboy look. Those wonderful come-hither eyes–watchful, sparkling and just a little sad, gaze out at the immensity of the Garden Court at the Sheraton Palace, where she had come for lunch in order to talk about her singing engagement later in the week at Bimbo's 365 Club.

Hold it a minute. Sally Kellerman, the gal who made a career for herself as a comedy star after she played Hot Lips Houlihan in the 1970 feature film version of M*A*S*H, has turned into a cabaret torch singer?

Kellerman plunks her lean, 5-foot 10-inch frame down at the table with a grimace and immediately stretches her legs out to relieve that pain in her backside. "Come closer," she whispers to me, as if we were alone in the Casbah, but we are in San Fran-

Sally Kellerman, in 1992, signed this publicity photo to me and the first line reads: "What a Pleasure . . . . " but I can't make out the second line.

cisco, surrounded by other diners. "It's the only way you're going to be able to hear me."

Snuggling up next to Kellerman, one quickly realizes—despite her low energy and weakened voice—that she is self-deprecating in a witty way, insightful about her own strengths and weaknesses, and willing to talk about her failures as much as her successes as actress and singer.

She gets off to a blazing start befitting a torch singer. "What a lot of people don't realize—because I've gone through my periods

*Sally Kellerman also signed this still from the movie version of M*A*S*H in which her character, "Hot Lips" Houlihan, is having a problem over by the women's shower stalls.*

of arrogance and self-centeredness and all those things that go with being a successful, well-paid actress—is that at heart I'm a singer. And singing has always been what I've wanted to do most. I was a cabaret singer before I was an actress. Being an actress was always just a stepping stone to becoming a bigger, better singer."

Until recently, she never quite hit the right chord. America still accepts Kellerman first as a movie actress. Not many recall those early days when she debuted in 1957's *Girls' Reform School* as a delinquent and then didn't get another role for three years. Only die-hard science-fiction fans remember she was in some episodes of TV's *The Outer Limits*, the beginning of a decade of playing glamorous women on tv in "Chanel suits and Veronica Lake hairstyles." Who remembers that she played a woman that was throttled to death in 1968 by Tony Curtis in *The Boston Strangler*?

Her real success started with the Hot Lips Houlihan role, and proceeded through numerous other Robert Altman-directed films in which she portrayed eccentric, fascinating, and sometimes kooky characters. These included *The Last of the Red Hot Lovers*, *A Little Romance*, and *Foxes*. Her biggest moneymaker in recent years was *Back to School* as Rodney Dangerfield's love interest.

So, an actress she remained. The songstress within her was still waiting in the wings, taking bows nobody saw. It didn't matter how many songs she sang in *Rafferty and the Gold Dust Twins*, *You Can't Hurry Love*, and other easy-to-forget pictures. Nor did she make the great dent in Broadway's musical version of *Breakfast at Tiffany's* opposite Richard Chamberlain and Mary Tyler Moore. That, she reminds me, "was a complete disaster!"

In an up-and-down career of good and bad films, her most recent efforts have been the USA-TV movie *Drop Dead Gorgeous*, the Showtime feature *Boris and Natasha*, a live-action Bullwinkle spin off in which she gets to sing five soul songs, and two cameo appearances as herself in Altman's *The Player*.

Her image already is undergoing change. In recent months in Los Angeles, critics have raved about her Rose Cabaret act, *The Voice Over America*, a title that alludes to the vast amount of voice-over work she does in national commercials.

"I've been on a search," she admits. "After years of trying to be a singing star, I realized I needed to learn how to be myself, because that's what it takes to be successful. Two years ago, I opened an act at the Cinegrill in Hollywood, but I wasn't satisfied."

About six months ago, without any advertising, she sang in a West Hollywood nightclub "in sweatshirt and Reeboks, because I feel at home dressed as a bum. Nothing was at stake. Nobody's come just to see me sing. It was a great training ground. Sometimes I was singing to as few as three people. I didn't care. For the first time I was developing an intimate feeling for an audience. I was getting past by own inhibitions."

Kellerman's undying love for song goes back to her childhood. Her mother was a piano teacher and her image lingers in memory: "She was warm and so beautiful. She wore this satin housecoat of dark turquoise. We lived in a warm house. I wasn't quite as intimate with my father, who was a vice president for a small crude oil company. There was a stern edge to him."

She went to Hollywood High and then to college to please her parents, but failed "pretty miserably. I was a child of the '50s, and I ended up taking an acting class with Jack Nicholson. At eighteen, I was signed to a Verve recording contract, but nothing came of it."

Kellerman goes into flashback mode to describe her renewed efforts in 1970, after the success of M*A*S*H, to become a singer, and the career ordeal that ensued. "I was all revved up with success, including being nominated for an Oscar, but an executive told me I'd never make it as a singer. I was an actress, period."

That, she says, "fired me up. I set out to prove otherwise, going on the road with seven guys and spending all my money and turning down good movie offers. The mistakes I made, they were incredible. I sang on Johnny Carson's show very badly, not knowing what was appropriate to sing. I was motivated by what I felt, without ever thinking things through to logical conclusions. A lot of obstacles in my life . . . I made myself."

Her blues-rock album, Roll With the Feeling, was no great hit, and the 1973 Burt Bacharach songs she sang in the film musical, Lost Horizon—expected to be big sellers—were utter flops like the film when packaged into an album. Someone labeled her "The Rock and Roll Marlene Dietrich," but nobody bought that bill of goods.

"I did such arrogant things in those days. I took so many giant missteps. I realized I was no diva. I'm from the Valley. I was getting more laughs in group therapy than I did on stage. I wasn't coming on as myself. That's when I realized I had to start all over."

Kellerman, who turned fifty-five only a month ago, could be on a comeback trail. In the fall, she's set to make another film with Altman, Pret a Porte (Ready to Wear). "I play this sexually depraved woman, the head of Vogue magazine."

Even if it all fails tomorrow, "I still have my [adopted] three-year-old twins, Jack and Hannah. Family, to me, is everything." Her husband of twelve and a half years, Jonathan Krane, is the producer of the Look Who's Talking films. "My first obligation is to myself. After that, it's show business gravy."

Sally Kellerman's show at Bimbo's 365 Club was a single performance, and she retrieved her voice just in time before the curtain went up. It was an enjoyable evening of blues and jazz favorites, and I sensed her heart was genuinely in it. Emotionally, she had what it takes.

As the years went by, Sally kept making films and stage appearances, and didn't get around to her *Something Kool* album—made up of songs from the 1950s—until 1995. She has continued to work a mixed bag of tricks, but music and song have never dominated. In 2014-2015, she portrayed a recurring character on *The Young and the Restless*. That very title reminds me of who she imagines herself to be, and it will probably remain so.

On the night of her show at Bimbo's, Sally Kellerman signed this publicity photo from her film, Foxes (1980), to my son Russ. I think it reads, "Russ, Sure Like You. [Something] Love, Sally Kellerman."

Funny Moments Visually Saved!

During my career as a journalist and TV horror host, there were some funny moments that were captured on camera. So here are a few visual memories to give you a few final tickles.

In November, 1993, in Las Vegas, I had the opportunity to interview Kenny Rogers about his ongoing TV miniseries, The Gambler. I had taken a deck of cards with me, and proposed to Rogers (not romantically) that he hold five cards in his hand visible to the cameraman behind him. Five cards being five aces. We both had a good laugh afterward. Unfortunately, when I returned to the San Francisco Chronicle two weeks later, I discovered I had been "promoted" to editor and would no longer write personality profiles for the paper. I left soon after. So, my intended story about Rogers was never published. At least I got that tongue-in-cheek photo, and you readers are among the first ever to see it.

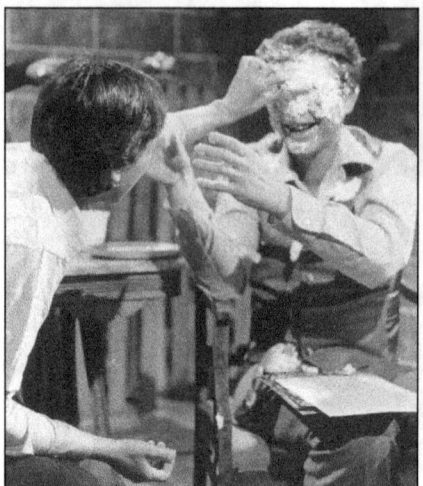

For one of my early Creature Features shows, I invited a lady reporter from the San Francisco Chronicle's rival newspaper, the San Francisco Examiner, to be my guest to talk about an upcoming food show in the city. Unknown to me, the pie she brought to use as a visual during our interview had been designed as a missile, one to be thrown into my face, not unlike the way Moe Howard might have done it had he been my guest. It was the newspaperwoman's way of symbolizing the "war" between the papers that we represented. Oh well, you can't win them all. And sometimes you have to eat it!

I first met Professor Taru Tanaka, a professional wrestler and boxer, when he was in the Bay Area in 1981 costarring with Chuck Norris in An Eye for an Eye. He returned in the summer of 1984 to be a guest on Creature Features to promote his new film, Chattanooga Choo Choo. He said to me, "So you think you're a tough guy-tougher than me!" My reply was simple: "Who, me?"

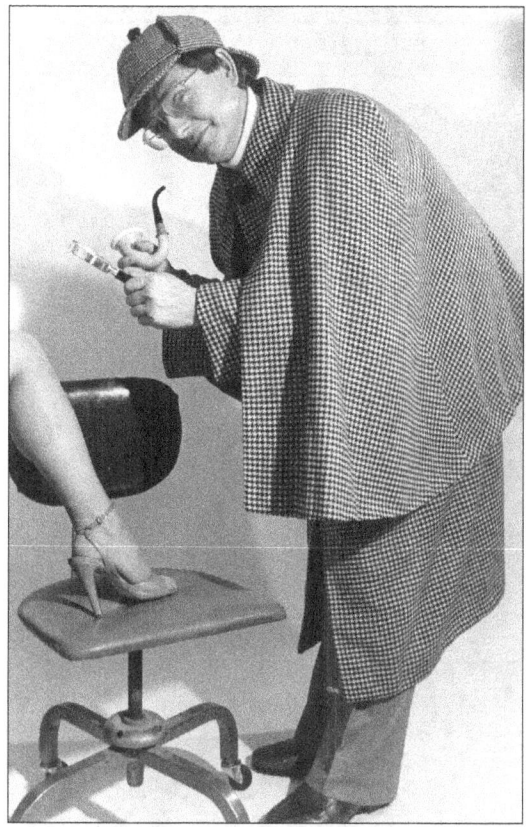

In 1979 I was able to do a parody of Sherlock Holmes entitled "The Adventure of the Persian Slipper," for which I used a San Francisco hotel's Sherlock Holmes Room. This is one of the production stills we used to promote that special moment. The leg you see belongs to my wife Erica, who often made sacrifices to keep the ratings up.

In 1979 I had the opportunity to visit the set of the syndicated music-comedy series, Heehaw, in Nashville, Tennessee. I had been granted permission to cut short promotions for my Creature Features show, using members of the cast in a cornfield set. Here I am with Lisa Todd, using the same magnifying glass (see above) I had used in my Sherlock Holmes comedy sketch so that I could "carry out a close-up examination of a popular TV star."

I cannot remember who created this publicity blurb for Creature Features, *but it had widespread exposure at the time of my program. The photo in the center of me thriving on popcorn was my very first publicity photo at KTVU, taken around March 1979.*

In 1986 I visited Robert Bloch, author of Psycho, *in his Hollywood Hills home and proposed I publish a collection of his famous short stories, to be entitled* Lost in Time and Space With Lefty Feep. *The stories had originally appeared in* Fantastic Adventures *pulp magazines of the 1940s. In his backyard, I asked Bob to hold one of his old pulps and appear to be shocked by his own story about a racetrack tout caught up in a fantasy plot. This was the result.*

The backyard photo is what gave me the idea to ask Bob to sit down in his home library and look shocked while reading a foreign edition of Psycho, one of many (domestic and foreign) housed in that library behind him. Bob had a wonderful sense of humor, a personality trait always reflected in his personal comments and often in his short stories.

Bob's collection of stories, in print for the first time in forty-five years, was published a year later and featured the first of eight Lefty Feep tales, plus an introduction by fantasy authoress Chelsea Quinn Yarboro, and a lengthy interview I conducted with Bob, which was sprinkled throughout the book along with numerous photographs. My collaborator, Kenn Davis, did the cover, as well as eleven original sketches of Feep, one of which is above. Two more editions were planned but never came to fruition, for Bob died soon after of cancer at the age of seventy-seven.

In one of my comedy segments on Creature Features, in which I made a monkey of myself, I found myself accidentally locked in one of the gorilla cages at the San Francisco Zoo after I had gone there to meet Carol Kane and Lee Grant, who were then starring in a new film, The Mafu Cage, about two sisters who live in an a decaying mansion with a monkey in a cage, and how Carol deteriorates into madness. Carol and Lee, who might have felt they were entering a new kind of madness that day in late 1979, each went in search of the key to my cage as I interviewed the other about the movie. Ultimately, neither could find a key and so off they went to further their careers while I remained locked away, screaming for help.

In 1979 members of the Maltese Falcon Society came to Creature Features to perform a condensed version of Dashiell Hammett's novel, with me (third from left) portraying private eye Sam Spade. To my right is Don Herron, famed for his Hammett Walking Tours of San Francisco. At far right, holding "The Bird," stands science-fiction author Ray Faraday Nelson, additionally famed for inventing the propeller beanie. Is there no end to the wonderment, intellectualism, and sophistication I brought to my viewers?

Index

—A—

Abbott & Costello, 291
Abbott and Costello Show, The (radio), 148
Ache in Every Stroke, An (comedy short), 246
Admiral Broadway Revue, The (TV), 12, 15
"Adventure of the Persian Slipper, The" (TV sketch), 327
Adventures of Hiram Holliday, The (TV), 256-257
Adventures of Ozzie and Harriet, The (TV), 161
*After M*A*S*H* (TV), 313
"After You're Gone" (song), 200
Ahmanson Theater, 316
Ah, Wilderness (play), 83
Aladdin (character), 87
Alcoholics Anonymous, 144
Alda, Alan, 300-303, 311, 314
Alice's Restaurant (film), 83
Alice Through the Looking Glass (film), 217
Allen, Fred, 122, 129
Allen, Grace (Gracie) Ethel Cecile, 59-61, 67, 125
Allen, Rex,
Allen, Woody aka Allan Stewart Konigsberg, 15, 113. 168, 174-180
"Alley Cat" (tune), 222
Altman, Robert, 293-296, 298, 320-322
Always Leave Them Laughing (film), 111
Ambassador Theater (Pasadena), 32
Ameche, Don, 199
American Conservatory Theater, 254
Anatomy of a Murder (film), 51
Anderson, Eddie, 123, 147
Andrews, Julie, 229
Ann Brebner Casting Agency, 255
Ann-Margret, 47

Anything Goes (film), 184
Arabesque (film), 237
Arbuckle, Fatty, 26
Arkin, Alan, 307
Armstrong, Louis, xiv, 42-43, 288
Arnaz, Desi, 57, 70, 72
Arnaz, Lucie, 26
Arnold, Buddy, 108
Astaire, Fred, 62-63
Auerbach, Artie, 152
August Moon (character), 148
Auntie Mame (character), 69
Auntie Mame (film), 71
Autry, Gene, 66
Avon Comedy Four, The, 42
Axminster, Jake (character), 314

—B—

Bacall, Lauren, 304, 332
Bacharach, Burt, 322
Back to School (film), 321
Backus, Jim, 178
Babbitt, Fenwick (character), 91
Bailey, Mildred, 42
Baker, Kenny, 134
Ball, Lucille Desiree, xi, 68-83, 100, 107, 112
Bailey, Pearl, 32
Baker, Joe, 288
Ball, Dr. August (character), 230
Balzer, George, 153
Barnaby and Me (movie), 7
Barney Rubble (character), 142
Batman (TV), 114, 269, 273-274, 277, 288
Bay Area Classic Learning, xiii-xiv
Baytide Films, 280
Beatles, The, 42, 223
Beau Geste (film), 187
Befera, Vic, ix
Being There (film), 231-232
Belle of the Nineties (film), 205

Belushi, John, 113
Bells of St. Mary's, The (film), 126,
Bendix, William, 87
Beneke, Tex, 235-236
Benny, Jack, xi, xiv, 58-59, 63, 65, 113, 117-138, 142, 146, 148, 150-155, 157, 161, 286
Benny, Joan, 154
Bensonhurst (district), 95
Bergen, Edgar, 199
Bergerac, Cyrano de, 210
Bergman, Ingrid, 316
Berle, Bill, 108
Berle, Milton, xiv, 102-116, 265
Berlin, Irving, 121
Berlinger, Sarah, 109
Berman, Shelley, xiv-xv,
Bernstein, Elmer, 237-238
Bertha the Elephant, 131, 134
Besser, Joe, 240, 245, 247
Best of Berle, The (TV), 112
Between Heaven and Hell (film), 272, 279, 281
Bevacqua, Anthony, 163
Beverly Hills Hotel, 68
Bicycle Thief, The (film), 15
Big Broadcast of 1938, The (film), 36
Big C, The (TV), 303
Big Eddie (TV), 136-137, 140
Billy the Kid (outlaw), 248
Biltmore Hotel, 187
Bimbo's 365 Club, ix, 318, 322-323
Bing and Other Things (book), 55
Biograph (Studio), 110
Birds Anonymous (cartoon), 144
Birnbaum, Louis Philip, 59
Birnbaum, Nathan aka George Burns, 59
Bishop, Joey, 260
"Black Bottom" (dance), 186
Blanc Communications, 143
Blanc, Estelle, 144, 148
Blanc, Mel, 120, 122, 126, 142-149

Blanc, Noel, 143, 149
Blazing Saddles (film), 89
Bloch, Robert, xii, 328-329, 332
Bluth, Dorothy, 59
Blyth, Ann, 189
Bob and Ray Show, The (TV), 94, 296
Bob Hope Memorial Garden, 38
Bob Hope: The First 90 Years (TV), 23, 26
Bogart, Humphrey, xi, 63
Bonanza (TV), 265
Bonnie and Clyde (film), 83
Bonzo Goes to College (film), 236
Boone, Pat, 83
Booth, John (nie) Wilkes, 121
Borie, Marcia, 150-151, 154
Boris and Natasha (TV), 321
Borsch Belt, The, 10
Bostock, Barbara, 286
Boston Strangler, The (film), 320
Botsford Twink (character), 148
Boyer, Charles, 145
Bradbury, Ray, xii, 332
Brady Bunch, The (TV), 78
Brando, Marlon, 259
Breakfast at Tiffany's (film), 233
Breakfast at Tiffany's (play), 321
Bridges, Lloyd, 288
Brinegar, Paul, 332
Broadhurst Theater, 89
Brooks, Mel, 6-7, 15, 129
Brown, Governor Pat, 288
Bruce, Lenny, 161
Bruhaha (play), 231
Buck Benny Rides Again (film), 127
Buckley, William F., 254
Buffano, Jules, 212
Bugs Bunny (character), 120, 142, 144-146, 148, 298
Burghoff, Gary, 317
Burnett, Carol, 43, 100
Burnette, Smiley, 66

Burns and Allen Show, The (radio/TV), 14, 56, 147
Burns, Major Frank (character), 314-315, 317
Burns, George, 56-67, 115, 130, 150, 284, 286, 288
Burns, Michael, 295
Buster Keaton Story, The (film), 189
Butler, David, 31
Buttons, Red, 83

—C—

Caan, James, 295, 307
Caburi, George, 231
Caddyshack (film), 156
Caesar, Florence, 6, 11
Caesar, Ida, 9
Caesar's Hour (TV), 7, 12
Caesar (Ziser), Max, 9, 11
Caesar, Sid, xiv-xv, 1-21, 65, 83, 100, 265
Caesar's Palace, 220
Cagney, James, 279, 288
Callas, Charlie, 288
Candelabra: My Life With Liberace (book) 224; (TV) 224
Cannon, Dyan, 225, 231
Cantor, Eddie, 42, 65, 107
Capitol Theater (NYC), 29
Carlin, George, 168
Carney, Art, 65, 72, 74-82, 90, 92, 96-97, 100
Carr, Teri, 74
Carrady, Mike (character), 282
Carson, Johnny, 154, 162, 168, 263, 288, 322
Casa di Baffi (San Diego), 86, 89
Casino Royale (film), 229
Cassandra (columnist), 224
Castle, William, 332
Cavalcade of Stars, The (TV), 87
Cavett, Dick, 200
Chamberlain, Richard, 321
Channing, Carol, 318
Chaplin, Charlie, 109-110, 245
Charade (film), 237
Charley's Aunt (film), 127

Chase, Richard, 280-282
Chase and Sanborn Hour, The (radio), 199
Chasin's (Restaurant), 65
"Chattanooga Choo Choo" (song) 236; (film), 326
Chief Ogone (character), 141
Cinegrill, 321
Cinemobile, 139
Circus Room (showroom), 131, 134, 213, 217, 220
City of Angels (TV), 314
"Clancy Lowered the Boom" (song), 132
Cleopatra, 104, 181
Cleveland Indians, The (team), 43-44
Clinton, Bill, 26
Clooney, Rosemary, 53
Clouseau, Jacques (character), 225-227, 229-230, 234
Club Durante, 212
Clyde, Andy, 177
Cobb, Lee J., 276
Coca, Imogene, 1, 12, 14-20, 265
Cohan, George C., 48
Colbert, Claudette, 26
Colgate Comedy Hour, The (TV), 184
College Holiday (film), 62
Collins, Joan, 45
Colman, Ronald, 125-127, 134
Colonna, Jerry, 34
Comedians' Round Table, 65
Comedy Star (club), 223
Come Fill the Cup (film), 136
Coney Island, 210, 215
Confidental (magazine), 224
Congregation B'Nai Emunah, 105, 116
Connery, Sean, 288
Continental Airlines, 97, 100
Conway, Tim, 100
Copacabana (night club), 12
Coppola, Francis Ford, 56
Cord, Alex, 47
Corey, Irwin, 83

Cosby, Bill, 139
Countdown (film), 295
Country Girl, The (film), 48
Cox, Wally, 252-259
Crawfod, Broderick, 272, 281-284, 312
Creature Features (TV), xii, 53, 268-274, 276, 326-328, 330-331
Creature Features Movie Guide (book series), xii
Creature Features Movie Guide Strikes Again, The (book), 332
Creature from the Black Lagoon, The (film), 236
Crosby, Bing, xiv, 26, 28-32, 35-37, 39-55, 59, 107, 126, 187
Crosby, Bob, 152
Crosby, Harry, 49
Crosby, Kathryn Grant, 32, 39, 49-55
Crosby, Mary, 49
Crosby, Nathaniel, 49
Crystal, Billy, 21
Culp, Robert, 139
Curtis, Tony, 320
Crystal, Billy, 21

—D—

Daffy Duck's Quackmasters (cartoon), 149
Dallas (TV), 98
Damon, Matt, 224
Damsel in Distress, A (film), 62-63
Dangerfield, Rodney aka Jacob Rodney Cohen, xiv, 156-163, 321
Dangerfield's (comedy club), 161, 163
Daniels, Billy, 115
Darcy, Steve (character), 136
Dashiell Hammett Walking Tours, 331
Davidson, Bill, 3
Davis, Kenn, 329
Davis Jr., Sammy, 260
Day, Daniel, 131
Day, Dennis aka Owen Patrick Eugene McNulty, 123, 131-135, 154
Day in the Life of Dennis Day, A (radio), 131

Day, Lucrezia (character), 131
Day, Peggy, 131, 135
Days of Wine and Roses (film), 233
Dean Martin Show, The (TV), 260-267
Dean Martin Celebrity Roast, The (TV), 266
"Dear Hearts and Gentle People" (song), 132
Dear Phoebe (TV), viii
De Camp, Rosemary, 87
De Carlo, Yvonne, 87
Decca Records, 41, 45
December Bride (TV), 312
De Cordova, Freddie, 62
Decoy (film), 136
Defenders, The (TV), 277
Dennis Day Show, The (TV), 133
Da Pron, Louis, 181
DeLuise, Dom, 264
Dennis, Sandy, 295
Derek, Bo, 167
DeRita, Joe aka Joseph Wardell aka Curly Joe, 240, 243, 247, 249-251
Desert Hawk, The (film), 87
Desilu Studios, 73-74, 82
Deutsch, Larry, 222
Devine, Andy, 177
Diamond Lil (play), 203, 205
Diamond Queen, The (film), 136
Dick Cavett's Backlot U.S.A. (TV), 200
Dick Van Dyke Show, The (TV), 139
Diller, Phyllis, 32-34
Dillon, Marshal Matt (character), 181
Dirty Ernie (character), 137
Disneyland (park), 56
Disney, Walt, xiv, 56
Dominic's (Restaurant), 65
Doc Boone (character), 47
Dodge City, 181
Donen, Stanley, 237
Donovan, King, 14
Double Life, A (film), 125

Douglas, Kirk, 181, 275-276, 286
Douglas, Michael, 224
Dozier, Bill, 273
Drag, The (play), 203
Dragnet (TV), 310-311
Dreyfus, Inspector Charles (character), 225
Drop Dead Gorgeous (film), 321
Dr. Strangelove (film), 230
Drury Lane Theater, 279
Peter, Duel, 286
Duke, Vernon, 11
Duncan, Arthur, 115
Dundee, Jimmy, 32
Dunlap, Paul, 240-241
DuPont Show of the Week (TV), 272
Durango Kid, The, 66
Durante Girls, The (dancers), 213
Durante, Jeanne, 219
Durante, Jimmy, 107, 121, 190, 210-219
Duvall, Robert, 295
Dynasty (TV), 45, 98

—E—

Eastwood, Clint, 332
Easy Money (film), 156-158
Ebert, Roger, 26
Ebsen, Buddy, 263
Edge of Night (TV), 284
Ed Sullivan Show, The (TV), 105
Ed the Guard (character), 152
Edwards, Blake 225, 228-231, 233-234, 236-237
Egan, Richard, 273
Eisenhower, President Dwight D., 37
Eisenhower Medical Center, 35
Elderhostel, xiii-xv
Ellington, Duke, 45
Ellis Island, 9
Elmer Fudd (character), 142
Elvira (character), 332
Empire (TV), 273
ER (TV), 303

Evans and Evans (dancers), 62
"Everybody Loves Somebody Sometimes" (song), 260
"Exodus" (melody), 222
Eye for an Eye, An (film), 326

—F—

Fabray, Nanette, 12
Fairmont Hotel, ix, 2, 53, 268-269, 275-277, 280
Fantastic Adventures (pulp magazine), 328
Fargo, Panama (character(, 91
Farrell, Mike, 308-313
Father O'Malley (character), 46
Faye, Alice, 122
Feep, Lefty (character), 329, 332
Fein, Irving, 58, 62, 64, 66, 150
Felton, Verna, 123, 131
Fergoda's Motorcycle Shop, 253-255
Fields, W. C., 62, 204-295
Fiendish Plot of Dr. Fu Manchu, The (movie), 8
Fine, Larry aka Louis Feinberg, 240, 243-245, 248-251
Firing Line (TV), 254
First National Bank of Denver, 100
"Five-Dollar Date, The" (routine), 12
Fleming, Rhonda, 189
Flintstones, The (TV), 142
Floradora (play), 110
Floyd the Barber (character), 148
Flynn, Errol, 256
Fong, Cato (character), 225
Fontaine, Frank, 288
Ford, President Gerald, 37
Forman, Joey, 284
Four Colleens, The (singers), 60
Four Seasons' Clift Hotel (San Francisco), 97
Four-Star Playhouse (TV), 237
Fowler, Gene, 210
Foxes (film), 321, 323
Fox, Fred, 58

Fox, Foxwell T. (character), 83-84, 89, 92
Fox Theater (San Diego), 83
Foxx, Redd, 140
Francis aka Francis the Talking Mule (1950), 189, 191
Francis, Connie, 270
Francis in the Haunted House (film), 191
Francis the Talking Mule (character), 190-192
Francis, John, 114-115
Frank, Melvin, 28
"Frankie and Johnny" (song), 200
Frederick, Lynne, 227, 231
Freebie and the Bean (film), 306
French Connection, The (character), 227
French Surete, 225
Frenzy (film), 238
Friars Club (Beverly Hills), 107-108, 115
Friars Club (NYC), 58
Friz Freleng's Looney Looney Looney Bugs Bunny Movie (film), 142, 144
Fuller, Samuel, 241
Funny Thing Happened on the Way to the Forum, A (play), 83

—G—

Gambler, The (TV miniseries), 325
Gang That Shot Up Hollywood, The (book), 332
Gannon, Officer Bill (character), 310
Garden Court at the Sheraton Palace, 318
Garland, Judy, 113
Garrison, Greg, 260-267
Gatlin Brothers, 66
Gatsby's (Restaurant), 65
Gelbart, Larry, 15, 83, 89, 316
"General Flipped at Dawn, The" (TV episode), 310
General Hospital (TV), 112
George Burns in Nashville (album), 59
George Burns' One-Man Show (TV), 59
George Washington Slept Here (film) 127-128; (play) 128

Gershenson, Joseph, 236
Get Smart (TV), 254
Ginger (Lucy's poodle), 71, 74, 76-78, 80-81
Ginger, Johnny, 248
Girls' Reform School (film), 320
Gleason, Jackie (Herbert John), 43, 72, 76-80, 83-92, 95-96, 98, 263
Gleason, Marilyn, 92
Glenn Miller Orchestra, The, 110, 235
Glenn Miller Story, The (film), 236
"God Save the King" (song), 59
Goebbels, Josef, 245-246
Goering, Hermann, 245-246
Going in Style (film), 65
Going My Way (movie), 48, 126
Goldberg, Whoopy, 26
Golddiggers, The (singers), 262
Goldenberg, Billy, 238
"Golden Classics of the Silver Screen" (class),
Golden Gate Theater (San Francisco), 109
Goldman, Hal, 58, 153
Gomer Pyle, USMC (TV), 139
Goodman, Benny, 235
Goodness Had Nothing to Do With It (book), 202
Goon Show, The (radio), 231-232
Gordon, Al, 153
Gorshin, Christina, 279
Gorshin, Frank, 268-286, 288
Gorshin, Mitch, 279
Gould, Elliott, 280-281, 289-299, 309
Grable, Betty, 87
Grant, Cary, 58, 195, 205, 288
Grant, Lee, 330
Great Dictator, The (film), 245
Great Gildersleeve, The (radio), 148
Great Lakes Revues, 117
Great Mating Game, The (TV), 254
Great Waldo Pepper, The (film), 237
Greene, Danford, 298
Greene, Lorne, 265

Guilt of Janet Ames, The (film), 12
Gunsmoke (TV), 181
Guys and Dolls (film) 136; (play) 109, 263

—H—

Hackett, Buddy, 108
Hammett, Dashiell, 331
Hammond, Julie, 286
Hanno's Bar, 176
Happy Postman, The (character), 147
Hargitay, Mickey, 207
Harmond, Manny, 115
Harrah's Tahoe, 120. 181
Harris, Phil, 122-123, 137, 151
Harry and Tonto (film), 78, 82
Harryhausen, Ray, 51, 332
Harry the Horse (character), 136, 140
Hart, Dolores, 272
Hart, Moss, 128
Hartline, Mary, 265
Has Anybody Seen My Gal? (film) 236
Hatari (film), 237
Have Rocket, Will Travel (film), 248
Hawks, Howard, 237
Hays Office, The, 205, 290
Healy, Ted, 244
Heathcliff (TV cartoon), 142
Heathcliff the Cat (character), 142
Hec Ramsey (TV), 312
Heehaw (TV), 327
Hefner, Hugh, 119
Helen Hayes Theater, 15
Heller, Seymour, 222
Hello, Dolly! (play), 222
Helm, Matt (character) 264-265
Helms, Mercer, 115
Here Comes Donald (TV), 187
Here's Lucy (TV), 71
Herrmann, Bernard, 238
Herron, Don, 331
High Chaparral, The (TV), 272
High Society (film), 42-43

Highway Patrol (TV), 272, 283
Hill, George Roy, 237
Hillcrest Country Club, 65
Hines, Gregory, 26
Hippodrome (theater), 215
Hitchcock, Alfred, 238
Hitler, Adolf, 129, 245
Hit the Surf (TV), 254
Hoffman, Dustin, 161, 277
Holden, William, 279
Hollywood Brown Derby, xi
Hollywood Forever Cemetery, 149
Hollywood Palace, The (TV), 43
Hollywood Reporter (newspaper), 150
Hollywood Squares, The (TV), 259
Holmes, Sherlock (character), 80, 327
Holt, Tim, 66
"Honeymooners, The" (TV sketches), 74, 88, 90, 95-96, 98; (TV series) 79, 88-89, 97-100
Honeymooners, The (specials), 91, 97
Hooker, Richard, 293
Hope, Avis, 24
Hope, Bob aka Leslie Townes Hope, xi, xiv, 22-38, 43-46, 58. 105, 130, 137, 154, 157, 288
Hope, Linda, 25, 35
Hope, William Henry, 24
Horn Blows at Midnight, The (film), 127-129, 152
Hotel (TV), 238
Hot Rod Girls (film), 271
Houlihan, Margaret aka Hot Lips Houlihan, 298, 300-307, 318-320
House I Live In, The (film), 126
Howard, Curly aka Jerome Lester Horwitz, 240, 244-248
Howard, Moe aka Moses Henry Horwitz, 240-251, 326
Howard, Shemp aka Samuel Horwitz, 240, 244-245, 247, 249
How Are You, Catherine Carter? (TV), 71
Hudson, Rock, 87

Hughes, Ken, 208
Hume, Benita, 125-127
Humpty Dumpty (character), 217
"Hundred Lives of Harry Simmons, The" (TV episode), 277
Hunnicutt, Captain B. J. (character), 310
hungry i (night club), 174-177
Hustler, The (film), 77, 86

—I—

"I'll Be Seeing You" (song), 222
I'll Never Heil Again (comedy short), 246
I Love Lucy (TV), 57, 70-72, 81
I'm No Angel (film), 195, 205
Imogene Coca Show, The (TV), 12
International House (film), 62
I Never Knew Heaven Could Speak (album), 134
"Inka Dinka Doo" (song), 210, 217
Interns, The (TV), 312
In the Matter of J. Robert Oppenheimer (play), 316
In the Sweet Pie and Pie (comedy short), 246
Invasion of the Body Snatchers (film), 14
Invasion of the Saucer Men (film), 272
Iroquis Trail, The (film), 141
I Spy (TV), 139
I Stooged to Conquer (book), 250
It Ain't No Sin aka *Belle of the Nineties* (film), 205
It Happened in Brooklyn (film), 211, 213
It's a Wonderful Life (film), 136
It's in the Bag (film), 129
I Was a TV Horror Host (book), xii, 332
I Wish I Was 18 Again (album), 59
Izzy and Moe (film), 92

—J—

Jack Benny (book), 150-155
Jack Benny: An Intimate Biography (book), 150
Jack Benny Program, The (radio/TV), 132, 146, 148, 150-155

Jack Benny Show, The (book), 150
Jackie Gleason Show, The (TV), 87, 92, 94-95, 288
Jack London Square (Oakland), xii, 268
Jackson, Eddie, 212-214
Jacobs, Seaman, 58
Jacobson, Arthur, 187
Jessel, George, 107, 121
Jetsons, The (TV), 142
Jewish Alps, The, 10
Jewish Contribution to Comedy, The (class), xiv
Jillian, Ann, 35
Jimmy Durante Show, The (TV), 212
Jinx Money (film), 140
Joe Palooka (film), 211
Joe Penner Show, The (radio), 146
Joe Palooka (movie series), 244
Joe the Bartender (character), 77-78. 88, 91
John Ascuaga's Nugget (casino), 131, 134, 213, 220-221
John Scott Trotter's Orchestra, 44
Johnson, President Lyndon B., 37
Jolson, Al, 42, 65, 107, 279
Jonson, Ben, 83
Jordan, Will, 286
Josefsberg, Milt, 150
Josie and the Pussycats, 42
Judy Canova Show, The (radio), 147
Judy Garland Show, The (TV), 288
Juilliard School of Music, The, 235
Julie Andrews Show, The (TV), 288
Jumbo (film), 215
Jumbo Schneider (character), 140
Justice, Buford T. (character), 91
Just You and Me, Kid (film), 65

—K—

Kane, Carol, 330
Kapp, Jack, 45
Karloff, Boris, 279
Kaufman, George S., 128
Kaye, Danny, 11

Kearns, Joseph, 152
Keaton, Buster, 215
"Keep Your Sunny Side Up" (song), 186
Kellerman, Sally, 298, 318-323
Kelly, Gene, 192, 194
Kelly, Grace, 48
Ken Darby Singers, The, 44
Kennedy, Elizabeth, 109
Kennedy, President John F., 37, 181
Kentucky Jones (TV), 312
King, Sonny, 213-214
Kinzell, Florence, 203
Kirby, George, 288
Kiss Me, Stupid (film), 227
Kiss of Death (film), 270
Kleinberg, David, xiii-xiv, 4, 177
Kleinberg, Pat, xiii
King Arthur, 144
Kirby, George, 288
Knight, Ted, 100
Knighty Night Bugs (cartoon), 144
Kopy Kats, The (TV), 272, 278, 288
Kotch (film), 316
Kottan (character), 280
Kovacs, Ernie, 108
Kramden, Alice (character), 77, 80, 93-101
Kramden, Ralph (character), 77-78, 88-89, 95-101
Krane, Hannah, 322
Krane, Jack, 322
Krane, Jonathan, 322
Kubelsky, Benjamin (Jack Benny), 117
Kubrick, Stanley, 230
Kuilimia Hotel, 225, 234
Kwouk, Burt, 225

—L—

Lady Diane, 59
Lady Godiva, 102
"Lady in the Tutti Fruitti Hat, The" (song) 104
Lady Killers, The (film), 229
Laine, Frankie, 332
Lamour, Dorothy, 30-31, 36
Lancaster, Burt, 274-276
Lane, Ken, 263
Langford, Francis, 34
Lardner, Ring Jr., 293, 298
Larry Clinton's Orchestra, 133
Larry the Lip (character), 137
Last of the Red Hot Lovers (film), 321
Laugh Stop (club), 113
Laughter on the 23st Floor [TV], 6
Laurel & Hardy, 225, 291
Lawford, Peter, 260
Lawrence, Dr. Gabriel (character), 303
Lawrence, Steve, 307
Lawrence Welk Plaza, 68
LeBlanc, Professor (character),
Lee, Christopher, xii, 332
Lefty Feep (character), 136
Leigh, Carolyn, 56
Leigh, Janet, 181
Leisure Village, 140
Lemmon, Jack, 286
Lenny (film), 161
Leno, Jay, 26
Leonard, Sheldon, 136-141
"Let That Be Your Last Battlefield" (TV episode), 274
Lewis, Jerry, 260-261
Liberace aka Wladziu Valentino Liberace, 220-224
Liebman, Max, 11-12
Lieutenant Dish, Maggie (character), 300
Life (magazine), 59
Life Begins at 8:40 (play), 110
Life of Riley, The (TV), 87
Linville, Larry, 314-317
Lippy Harris (character), 140
Little Big Man (film), 83
Little Romance, A (film), 321
Liszt, Franz, 222

Little, Cleavon, 83, 89
Little, Rich, 277, 286-289
Livingstone, Mary (Mrs. Jack Benny), 123-124, 127, 134, 150-155
Lloyds of London, 203
Lom, Herbert, 225
Lombard, Carole, 129
London Daily Mirror, The 224
Look Who's Talking (film series), 322
Loren, Sophia, 15
Lorre, Peter, xi, 279
Lost Horizon (film), 322
Lost in Time and Space With Lefty Feep (book), 328, 332
Louie the Lilac (character), 114
Louie the Louse (character), 137-138
Louis Armstrong and His All-Stars, 43
Love in Bloom (film), 62
Love on a Rooftop (TV), 286, 288
Love Thy Neighbor (film), 239
Lubitsch, Ernst, 129
Lubritsky, Fanny, 254, 258-259
Lucky Jordan (film), 136
Lucy: A Tribute (museum), 81
Lucy Show, The (TV), 71

—M—

Ma and Pa Kettle at the Fair (film), 236
MacDonald's (restaurant), 65
MacMurray, Fred, 286
Mafu Cage, The (film), 330
Magic in the Moonlight (film), 179
Magic of the Stars (TV), 112
Magnum Force (film), 332
"Make 'Em Laugh" (song), 184-185
Make Mine Manhattan (revue), 12
Make Room for Daddy (TV), 139
Malden, Karl, 92, 332
Maltese Falcon Society, 331
Mame (film), 71
Man and the City, The (TV), 312
Mancini, Henry, 120, 225, 233-239

Manhattan College, 133
Man in the Cocked Hat, The (film), 229
Mannix (TV), 316
Man's Favorite Sport? (film), 235
Mansfield, Jayne, 207
Man With the Golden Arm, The (film), 237
Man With the Plastic Sandwich, The (play), 278
Marines' Memorial Theater, 15
Marks, Hilliard, 150-155
Marks, Sadie (Mrs. Jack Benny), 123-124
Martin, Dean, 43, 260-264
Martin, Mrs. Iris (character), 100
Martin, Tony, 104
Marvin the Moose (character), 137-138
Marx, Groucho, 65, 296
Marx, Harpo, 65
Marx, Zeppo, 65
*M*A*S*H* (film), 140, 289-299-300-303, 322; (TV) 83, 280, 299, 300-323
*M*A*S*H: A Novel About Three Army Doctors* (book), 293
Mason, James, 288
Masonic Auditorium (San Francisco), 106, 114-115
Mathews, Kerwin, 51
Matthau, Walter, 63, 65, 112
Maurer, Norman, 248
May Company (store), 123, 154
McCarthy, Charlie (puppet), 199, 201
McIntyre, Captain John Francis Xavier aka Trapper John, 290, 311
McLean Stevenson Show, The (TV), 311
Meadows, Audrey, 77, 90, 93-101
Meadows, Jayne, 97, 101
Meet Me at the Fair (film), 236
"Melancholy Serenade" (music), 89
Mel Blanc Show, The (radio), 148
Melody for Two (film), 187
Men in Black (comedy short), 244
Merry Monahans, The (film), 188
Midler, Bette, 168

Miller, Glenn, 86, 110
Miller, Sidney, 181
Milligan, Spike, 231
Mills, Juliet, 7
Milton Berle Show, The (TV), 102
Milton Berle's Mad Mad World of Comedy (TV), 112
Miniskirt Rebellion, The 254
Minnesota Fats (character), 77, 86
Miranda, Carmen, 104
Mirren, Helen, 8
Mission: Impossible (TV), 316
Miss Jet Lag (character), 15
Mister Ed (TV), 205
Mitchum, Robert, 332
Mitty, Walter (character), 113
Moe Howard and The Three Stooges (book), 251
"Mona Lisa" (song), 132
Money From Home (film), 140
Monroe, Marilyn, 190
"Moon River" (tune), 233
Moore, Mary Tyler, 321
"More" (tune), 222
More Stately Mansions (play), 316
Morgan, Harry, 308-313
Morris, Hal, 6
Morton, Gary, 68, 70, 73, 80, 82
Moscone Convention Center, 22-23, 106
Motion Picture Production Code, The, 290
"Move 'Em Out" (song), 235
MPI Home Video, 92
Mr. Kitzel (character), 152
Mr. Magoo (cartoon character), 178
Mr. Peepers (TV), 252-253, 255-259
"Mr. Television," 102, 105
Muppets, The (TV), 223
Murray, Jan, 108
Musso & Frank's Grill, xi
My Fair Lady (play), 222
My Father, Uncle Miltie (book), 108

My Life With Bing (book), 55
My Little Chickadee (film), 204-205
Myra Breckinridge (film), 206

—N—

Nabors, Jim, 139
Napa High School, viii
Napa Junior College, viii
National General (studio), 56-57
National Enquirer, The 167
Nelson, Frank, 152
Nelson, Gary, 254, 258-259
Nelson, Lori, 271
Nelson, Ray Faraday, 331
Nelson, Ricky, 161
New Faces of 1937 (film), 110
Newhart (TV), 238
Newman, Alfred (composer), xiv, 238
Newman, Alfred E. (character), 177
New Three Stooges, The (TV), 243
Newton, Wayne, 154
Nicholson, Jack, 276-277, 322
Night After Night (film), 195, 197, 202, 205
Nightwing (film), 238
Nimoy, Leonard, xii, 74, 82, 332
Nixon, President Richard, 37, 288
No No, Nanette (play), 100
Norris, Chuck, 326, 332
North, Alex, 237
Norton, Ed (character), 96-98
Norton, Trixie (character), 97
Novak, Paul, 197, 199, 208

—O—

O'Connor, Arlene, 187
O'Connor, Donald, 26, 81-94
O'Flaherty, Terrence, 286, 300
Oh, God! (film), 64-65
Oh, God! II (film), 65
Odd Couple, The (play),
Oil Can Harry (character), 290
One Flew Over the Cuckoo's Nest (film), 277
One From the Heart (film), 56

Orchestra Wives (film), 86
Orpheum Theater (San Francisco), 84, 92
Our Lady of Mercy Catholic Cemetery (Miami), 92
Outer Limits, The (TV), 320
Outlaws Is Coming, The (film), 248
"Over the Rainbow" (song), 113

—P—

Pa (character), 147
Palace Theater (Broadway), 215
Palmer House (hotel), 7
Panama Fargo (TV),
Panama, Norman, 28, 45
Pan Pacific Hotel, 17
Paramount Studios, 82
Paramount Theater (Oakland), 184, 193-194
Pardon My Backfire (comedy short), 247
Parr, Jack, 286
Pat Novak for Hire (radio), 197
Patrick the Great (film), 181
Patzak, Peter, 280, 282
Pavuvu (island), 33-34
Peck, Gregory, 109, 286
Pedro the Mexican (character), 147
Peewee Quartet, The, 60
Penn, Arthur, 83-86, 89
Pennies From Heaven (film), 46
Pepe Le Pew (character), 145
Peepers, Robinson J. (character), 256
Pepsodent Show With Bob Hope (radio), 28
Perils of Pauline (film serial), 110
Pernicano, George, 89
Perrin, Sam, 153
Pete and Gladys (TV), 312
Peter Gunn (TV), 233, 237
Peterson, Axel, 68, 70, 79, 82
Peterson, Cassandra, 332
Phoenix Video, 187
Pierce, Captain Benjamin Franklin aka Hawkeye, 293, 300-303, 311
Pink Panther, The (film) 229, 234, 238; (TV) 233

Pink Panther, The (diamond), 227
Pink Panther Series, 225-235
Pittsburgh Pirates, The (team), 43-44
Plastic Man (character), 185
Playboy Mansion, 119
Player, The (film), 321
Pocketful of Miracles (film), 136
Point Sublime (radio), 148
Polly the Parrot (character), 146
Polo Lounge, 140
Popeye (character), 290
Poor Soul, The (character), 77, 88, 91
Porky Pig (character), 142, 145, 148
Porter, Cole, 183
Portland Express (film), 271-272
Portugal, Joe (character), 136
Postrio Restaurant, 183
Potter, Colonel Sherman (character), 310-313
Powell, Dick, 236-237
Powell, General Colin, 26
Preminger, Ingo, 140, 295
Preminger, Otto, 140, 295
Prentiss, Ann, 254, 258
Prentiss, Paula, 258
Presley, Elvis, 42, 223
Pretty Willy (character), 140
Price, Vincent, xii, 332
Prince Charles, 59
Prisoner of Zenda, The (film), 231
Professor LeBlanc (character), 122, 146
Projectionist, The (film), 156
Proud and the Profane, The (film), 279
Prowess, Juliet, 265
Pryor, Richard, 168
Psycho (film), 181; (book, 328-329, 332

—Q—

Queen Elizabeth, 24, 86
"Queen of Trash" (Mae West), 206
Quinn, Anthony, 312

—R—

Rabbit Test (film), 169
Rafferty and the Gold Dust Twins (film), 321
Raft, George, 195, 197, 268-269
Randall, Tony, 26
Randolph, Joyce, 97, 100
Rat Pack, The, 260
Ravenswood Apartments, 197, 208
Rawhide (TV), 332
Ready for Wear aka Pret a Porte (film), 322
Reagan, Ronald, 288
Real McCoys, The (TV), 139
Regina General Hospital, 8
Reiner, Carl, 4, 6, 65
Remington Steele (TV), 238
Remley, Frank (character), 152
Remus (Bing Crosby's dog), 39-40, 44, 48
Revenge of the Creature (film), 236
Revenge of the Pink Panther (film), 225-228
Reynolds, Debbie, 192, 194
Rhythm on the Range (film), 46
Richard Diamond, Private Detective (radio), 236-237
Richards, Johnny, 56
Riddler, The (character), 268, 272-274, 277-279
Riley, Chester A. (character), 87
Ringling Bros. Barnum & Bailey Circus, 186
Rin Tin Tin (dog), 74
Rising Star (club), 113
Ritter, Tex, 66
Rivers, Joan, xiv, 162-173
Road Pictures (series), 22, 30-32, 36, 45-46
Roadrunner, The (character(, 145
Road Scholar, xiii
Robin (character), 288
Road to Hong Kong, The (film), 44
Road to Morocco, The (film), 30, 46
Road to Singapore, The (film), 46
Road to the Fountain of Youth, The (film), 32
Robbins, Gordon, 222

Robinson, Edward G., 270, 276, 279
Rochester (character), 123, 126, 147, 152
Roddenberry, Gene, 74, 82, 332
Rogers, Roy, 26
Rogers, Kenny, 325
Rogers, Wayne, 311, 314
Roll With the Feeling (album), 322
Roman, Ruth, 111
Romano, Tony, 34
Romanoff's Restaurant, xi
Rooney, Mickey, 191
Roosevelt, President Franklin D., 37
Rosenberg, Edgar, 164-165
Rose, Billy, 215
Ross, Diana, 279
Ross, Shirley, 36
Roth, Jack, 212
Roy, Jack aka Rodney Dangerfield, 159
Roy, Phil, 160
Royal Academy of Dramatic Arts, 316
Rozsa, Miklos, xiv
Ruddy the Repairman (character), 88
Rumdum (character), 91
Runyan, Damon, 140
Russell, Jane, 26, 332
Russell, Rosalind, 71
Ryan, Peggy, 188
Rybinski, Chester. See Novak, Paul

—S—

San Diego Chargers, 89
San Fernando Mission Cemetery, 38
San Francisco Chronicle, The viii, ix-xiii, 4, 49, 53, 105-106, 150, 163, 174, 176-177, 218, 276, 286, 289, 300, 325-326
San Francisco Examiner, The 218, 326
San Francisco State College, ix
San Quentin Prison, 179
Savalas, Telly, 277
Savoy and Brennan (act), 42
Saxons, The (jugglers), 115
Say Goodnight, Gracie (play), 284

Schlesinger, Leon, 144
Schnozzle, The (book), 210
Schubert Theater, 83
Schwarzenegger, Arnold, 332
Science Fiction Theater (TV), 272
Scott, George C., 89
Scott, Geoff, 287
Scott, Randolph, 66
Secombe, Harry, 231
"Second Hungarian Rhapsody" (tune), 222
Selleck, Tom, 26
Sellers, Peter, 8, 225-233
Selzer, Ed, 144
Seventh Voyage of Sinbad, The (film), 51
Sex (play), 202
"Sex" (painting), 203
Sextette (play), 201
Sextette (film), 208-209
Shatner, William, xii, 74, 82, 332
Shavelson, Melville, 28
Shaw, Artie, 42
She Done Him Wrong (film), 195, 205
Sheridan, Ann, 128
Shields, Brooke, 65
Shire, David, 238
Shot in the Dark, A (film), 230
Shriner, Herb, 177
Sid (Mexican character), 122, 146
Silent Movie (film),
Silent Service (TV), 271
"Silent Night" (song), 48
Silvers, Phil, 97
Simmons, Harry (character), 277
Simon, Danny, 6
Simon, Neil, 6, 15, 59
Sinatra, Frank, xiv, 66, 107, 113, 126, 130, 200, 211, 213, 223, 260, 263
Sinbad the Sailor (film), 136
Singin' in the Rain (film), 184-185, 192, 194
Sing You Sinners (film), 187
Siskel, Gene, 26

Six, Robert, 97
Six On, Twelve Off (revue), 11
Skelton, Red, 88
Slip Moran (character), 136
Sly Fox (play), 83-84, 89-90, 92
Smithsonian Institute, 210
Smokey and the Bandit (film), 91
Smokey and the Bandit (sequels), 92
Socher Hotel (Vienna), 280, 283
Someone Is Killing the Great Chefs of Europe (film), 238
Something Kool (album), 323
Somewhere in the Night (film), 136
South Shore Room (Lake Tahoe), 181
Spacely (cartoon character), 142
Spade, Sam (character), 331
Spartacus (film), 181
Speak Easily (film), 216
Spearchucker (character), 300
Spooks (comedy short), 247
Springtime in the Rockies (film), 87
Stagecoach (1966 remake), 47-48
Stand at Apache River (film), 236
Stanford Court (hotel), 4
Stanley, Erica, iv-v, 40, 53, 68, 79, 82, 134, 182, 197, 208, 308-309, 327
Stanley, Jordyn, iv-v
Stanley, Russ, iv-v, 37-38, 193, 273, 287, 323
Stanley, Shelby, iv-v
Stanley, Trista, 273
Stanwyck, Barbara, 332
Star Is Born, A (film), 288
Star Trek (TV), 74, 82, 274
State Fair (play), 55
St. Clair Luncheonette, 9
Steele, Major General Bartford Hamilton (character), 310
Steiger, Rod, 276
Steiner, Max, xiv, 238
Stevenson, McLean, 311, 314-315
Stewart, James, 68, 134, 136-137, 236, 264, 288, 332

Sting II, The (film), 92
Stone, Sharon, 66
Stop, You're Killing Me (film), 136
St. Patrick Choir, The, 133
Strand Theater (Broadway), 11
Straw Hat Revue, The 11
Streetcar Named Desire, A (film), 237
Streets of San Francisco, The (TV), 332
Streisand, Barbra, 113, 290
Sullivan, Maurice W., 55
Sunday Datebook, The ix, xiii, 4, 280
Sunday Nights at Seven (book), 154
Sunshine Boys, The (film), 59, 63-64
Sun Valley Serenade (film), 110
Super Circus (TV), 265
Superman (character), 296
Sutherland, Donald, 289-299, 301, 309
"Swinging on a Star" (song), 48
Switt, Loretta, 304-307
Sylvester the Cat (character), 142, 146

—T—

Take Me Along (play), 83
Take the Money and Run (film), 179
Tall, Dark and Handsome (film), 110, 140
Tamiment Playhouse, 11
Tanaka, Professor Taru, 326
Tars and Spars (revue), 11
Tars and Spars (film), 11
Tasmanian Devil, The (character), 146
Taylor, Elizabeth, 167, 181
Taylor, June, 92
Taylor, Robert, 107
Ted Healy and the Stooges (comedy team), 244
Television Academy Hall of Fame, 116
Texaco Star Theater, The (TV), 102, 109, 111
"Thanks for the Memories" (song), 36
That Cold Day in the Park (film), 295
"That's Jazz" (song), 42-43
"There's No Business Like Show Business" (song), 121

There's No Business Like Show Business (film), 190
This Island Earth (film), 236
This Time for Keeps (film), 211
Thomas, Danny, 139
Thomas, Patty, 34
Thorson, Scott, 224
Three Country Gentlemen, The (comedy team), 244
Three Stooges, The (comedy team), 240-251
Three Stooges Meet Hercules, The (film), 241
Three for Two (TV), 72
Tillie's Punctured Romance (film), 110
Tina the Elephant, 131
Tiomkin, Dimitri, 238
To Be or Not to Be (film), 129, 152
Todd, Lisa, 327
Together Again (revue), 15
Tolkin, Mel, 6
Touch of Evil (film), 236
Toulouse-Lautrec, Henri de, 226
Tom Sawyer—Detective (film), 187
Tomlin, Lily, 168
Tonight Show, The (TV), 164, 168, 288
Too Close for Comfort (TV), 100
Too Much Harmony (film), 43
Toots Shor's, 6, 79, 86
Top Banana (play), 97
Tout, The (character), 136, 138-140
Trader Dick's (restaurant), 213-214
Trapper John (character), 290, 300
Trigger (horse), 26
Truman, President Harry S., 37
Tufts, Sonny, 177
TV Guide 59, 265
Tweety Bird (character), 56, 142, 146

—U—

Udo, Tommy (character), 270
"Uncle Miltie," 102, 105, 107, 109
Underground Aces (film), 278
Universal Studios Theme Park, 81

Universal Studios Tour Plaza, 123
Uppercrust, The (film), 280-284

—V—

Vacationland Hotel, 10
Van Gleason III, Reggie (character), 77, 88, 91
Vanished (film), 316
Venetian Room (Fairmont Hotel), ix, 2, 4, 53, 268, 277
Victor-Victoria (play), 238
Viner, Mort, 262
Vinick, Senator Arnold (character), 303
Vogue Magazine 322
Voice Over America, The (cabaret act), 321
Volpone (play), 83
Von Bismarck, Otto, 178
Von Hauffe, Walter, 192, 194
Von Knowitall, Ludwig (character), 3

—W—

Wagner, Robert, 272
Waikiki Wedding (film), 46
Waldorf Hotel, 32
Walsh, Knobby (character), 211
War Arrow (film), 236
Ward, Burt, 273
Warfield Theater (San Francisco), 166, 208
Warner, Jack L., 153
Wayne, John, 200, 237, 277, 286
Webb, Jack, 197, 310-311
Welch, Raquel, 206
Welk, Lawrence, 115, 134
Welles, Orson, 263-264
Werner, Harry (character), 282
Wessler, Karen, 222
West, Adam, 114,
West, Mae, 195-209
West Wing, The (TV), 303
What Gap? or What's It All About, Wally? (TV), 254
"When Irish Eyes Are Smiling" (song), 60
When Johnny Comes Marching Home (film), 187

Where Have I Been? (book), 3, 13
Where the Boys Are (film), 270-272, 279
"White Christmas" (song), 41, 44
White Dawn, The (film), 237
White, Jesse, 108
Widmark, Richard, 270
Wile E. Coyote (character), 146
Wilkins, Bob, xii, 332
Williams, Esther, 211
Williams, Pat, 238
Wills, Chill, 189, 191
Wilson, Don, 147, 152
Windsor Castle, 24
Windsor, Marie, 332
"Wings Over Boomerschnitzel" (comedy routine), 11
Winner, Michael, 74
Winters, Jonathan, 24
Wooley, Sheb, 332
Won Ton Ton: The Dog That Saved Hollywood (film), 74, 76-77
Woodbury Soap Hour, The (radio), 28
Woody Woodpecker (character), 145

—Y—

Yarboro, Chelsea Quinn, 329
Yarnell, David, 254-256, 258-259
Yankee Pasha (film), 236
Yosemite Sam (character), 142, 146
"You Can Bounce Right Back" (song), 184
You Can't Hurry Love (film), 321
"You Made Me Love You" (song), 113
You Nazty Spy! (comedy short), 245
"Young at Heart" (song), 56, 59
Young, Victor, 238
Young and the Restless, The (TV), 323
Youngman, Henny, 115, 166
Your Show of Shows (TV), 2-3, 7, 12, 15, 265

—Z—

Zanuck, Darryl F., 295
Zelig (film), 180
Ziegfeld, Florenz Jr., 216

Ziegfeld Follies, The (revue), 102, 110
Ziser, Max aka Caesar, Max, 9, 11
Zoetrope Studios (L.A.), 56
Zookie (character), 148

OTHER BOOKS BY JOHN STANLEY

Available at His Website: www.stanleybooks.com
E-mail: creature@netwiz.net

THE GANG THAT SHOT UP HOLLYWOOD - Exclusive Interviews with Clint Eastwood on the set of *Magnum Force* (and four other encounters), Robert Mitchum, Chuck Norris, Paul Brinegar and Sheb Wooley of *Rawhide*, singer Frankie Laine, Karl Malden of *Streets of San Francisco*,
 James Stewart, Lauren Bacall, Jane Russell, Barbara Stanwyck, Marie Windsor ... Exclusive History on the Marine Flag-Raisers on Iwo Jima. (Personally signed to the buyer)

I WAS A TV HORROR HOST - Exclusive Interviews with such sci-fi and horror icons as Ray Bradbury, Christopher Lee, Robert Bloch, Vincent Price, William Shatner, Leonard Nimoy, Gene Roddenberry, Elvira (Cassandra Peterson), Arnold Schwarzenegger, Bob Wilkins, Ray Harryhausen, William Castle, plus profiles of famous radio horror hosts. (Personally signed to the buyer)

LOST IN TIME AND SPACE WITH LEFTY FEEP - A lengthy exclusive interview with *Psycho* author Robert Bloch, with new photos taken by John Stanley, woven around nine Bloch short stories about Feep, a racetrack tout who is always falling into a world of fantasy. (Personally signed to the buyer)

THE CREATURE FEATURES MOVIE GUIDE STRIKES AGAIN. The fourth edition in what became a six-edition series. Featuring reviews of 5,614 genre movies of science-fiction, fantasy, and horror, with 232 photographs of popular monsters, actors, and historic scenes, 24 new sketches, and 1,709 cross references to secondary titles.

www.ingramcontent.com/pod-product-compliance
Lightning Source LLC
Chambersburg PA
CBHW071953220426
43662CB00009B/1109